PASSION

PASSION

P A S S I ✝ O N

RETURNING PASSION, PURPOSE AND PRIORITY TO THE CHURCH

TONY ANTHONY

WITH ANGELA LITTLE

16 15 14 13 12 11 10 7 6 5 4 3 2 1

First published 2010 by Authentic Media Limited
Milton Keynes
www.authenticmedia.co.uk

British Library Cataloguing in Publication Data
A catalogue record for this book is available from the British Library

ISBN 978-1-86024-804-7

Cover design by Paul McDermid and Matt Crew (www.insightdesign.co.uk) and Paul Airy (www.designleft.co.uk)
Photo of Angela by Andrew Griffiths, Creating Smiles Photography
Printed in Great Britain by Bell and Bain, Glasgow

Contents

I dedicate this book with love, hopes and prayers to my two wonderful sons Ethan and Jacob. My prayer is that the ceiling of my faith and ministry would just be your floor.

Acknowledgements

My deepest thanks and appreciation go first and foremost to my co-writer, Angela Little, who framed the entire narrative and told it in the simplest but most reflective terms. She worked so hard to make this book a reality.

I want to thank my friend and publisher Malcolm Down and the rest of the team at Authentic for doing such an excellent job with the production and publication of this book. Special thanks must also be extended to the many friends and supporters who advised on the manuscript, with particular acknowledgement to Michael Wright, Revd Stephen Hembery, Revd Nigel Little, John Sephton, Beryl Spikings, Graham Matthews and Dorothy Little.

I owe a deep debt of gratitude to the Avanti Board of Directors, of which I am privileged to belong, including Phil Smith, David Duell, Martin Eady, Sara Anthony, Heather Crosskey, Richard Newton and Mark Griggs. Thanks always to my immediate support team, Faye Anderson, Naomi Spurgeon, Sarah Griggs, Jamie Kidd, George Osborn, John Lawson, Sonya Newton and Stephen Silverson, whose service, patience and diligence are exemplary, even under the strains and pressures of ministry.

My greatest appreciation goes to my wife, Sara, our two sons, Ethan and Jacob, and my mother-in-law, Barbara Coleman, who sacrificially support my work, keeping our precious family together in my many absences. These are the real workers and the unsung heroes that enable this ministry to take place.

Finally, thanks and glory to God for the gift of His Word and for the privilege of preaching it. I trust that multitudes worldwide will experience a greater joy by knowing God and His ways more fully.

With a grateful heart

Tony Anthony

Introduction

The Artist

There's not much to do in prison, especially a prison like Nicosia Central in Cyprus. In the late eighties and early nineties I was incarcerated in what was then one of the world's most notorious detention centres. Films such as *Bangkok Hilton* or *Midnight Express* portray something of the horror of the institution. This was no place for reform or even considered penance; it was a place where men were literally left to rot. My sentence was shorter than most (in truth, far less than I deserved), though three years in a place like that is enough to drive even the toughest of men to tortured distraction. There were days when I feared I would descend into the same corpse-like state of many of the other inmates. On better days I could bribe a guard for some brushes, paint and paper and I'd create pictures. As a child I had spent many hours with paint and easel so it wasn't long before the other prisoners and some of the guards noticed my work. In prison everything has a price and my artwork kept me in cigarettes as I painted portraits of loved ones copied from photographs. Other times I'd paint for myself; paint for my life. It helped stop me going crazy. I imagine that a psychologist, examining my scenes, would expound on my anger, depression, misplaced childhood, suicidal tendencies . . . I'd surely be labelled a 'dysfunctional character, a tortured soul'.

It's probably fair to say that my pictures were inevitably inspired by my upbringing. In the eyes of my parents, I was a mistake. At four years old I was sent from my London home to Canton in China. There I was raised into the harsh regime of my grandfather, Cheung Ling Soo, a renowned grandmaster in the way of Kung Fu. My childhood was brutal by Western standards but it instilled in me absolute drive and discipline. In the hands of my master I developed extraordinary physical ability and came to excel in the ancient arts of my ancestors. The story of my rise – to a highly applauded, powerful, by some enviable, lifestyle – and demise – through grief, into crime and personal breakdown – has been documented in the book, *Taming the Tiger* and its follow-up youth edition, *Cry of the Tiger* (published by Authentic Media, 2004, 2006 respectively). Since the publication of my story I have had the privilege of speaking to millions of people around the world who have responded to its message. Personally, I hate the story, and I don't say that lightly. I am deeply ashamed of my life and of many of the terrible things I have done. Indeed, if not for one or two single key chapters, I would rather have it banished to the depths of Hell than see it appear on a best-sellers list. And yet it remains. Why? Because beyond me, beyond my story, beyond the horror of my dirty, grey, blackened painting, it is a testimony to Almighty God, the Master Artist and Creator Himself, who met me in absolute depravity of sin and shame and gave me a new, spotless, blank canvas.

It was 3 May 1990 when I first responded to the Gospel message; when I acknowledged and embraced the 'good news' about the truth of Jesus Christ. At that time God used one man, Michael Wright, a missionary from Belfast, to tell me this marvellous Gospel. For the entirety of my prison sentence Michael faithfully came to visit me in that Cypriot hell-hole. Obedient to the call of the Great Commission (Matthew 28:19), Michael set himself aside and, undeterred by my abhorrent rudeness and arrogance, he persevered, in love, to make certain that I got the message. Why did he do that? I was a complete stranger to him – just another newspaper headline, another serial number in Nicosia's melting pot of depravity.

When, after six months of visiting, I allowed Michael to spell it out to me, God worked one of his mightiest miracles. He forgave me. He picked me up, washed me clean and gave me a new life. That very same day I became a passionate and determined evangelist. I *had* to share the Gospel. I had no theology and no training. I barely knew anything about the Bible and certainly nothing about church life or what it meant to live as a Christian. But I knew first-hand what it meant to be forgiven, accepted and loved by Jesus Christ. That was news that I simply had to shout about. I had no choice. I had found life and I wanted every man in that prison, every scumbag dope dealer, murderer, thief, rapist, child abuser, drug addict, prison officer . . . to know that they too could be forgiven, start a new life and secure their eternity because of Jesus' death on the cross and His miraculous resurrection.

My passion and zeal only grew stronger as I saw other men like me radically transformed as they too encountered the living Christ. As my prison sentence came to an end I couldn't wait to get to England where I could join a church. I believed there I would find people just as passionate as I was about the Gospel. But I was to be dealt a bitter blow. My early church experience was good in so many ways, but I had naively imagined that all Christians were like Michael Wright, that all were concerned to share the Gospel and see other souls saved above all else. Reality hit in a big way and today I am no less pained to see well-meaning, God-loving Christians who fail to embrace one of Jesus' most fundamental instructions. Sad to say, however, that only a few short years after my release from Nicosia I became that which I most despised – a 'comfortable Christian'. I, too, slipped into 'respectable' church life. I led youth camps, preached on

Sundays, dedicated myself and my family to church life, even became a youth worker, but somehow along the way my passion for sharing the message of the Gospel became just one among a long list of things in my crowded and complicated life.

In 2001 I made a huge mistake. Driving home on a rainy wet night I knocked a lady from her bike. At the time I believed I had hit an animal and thought little more of it. Days later local news screamed of the so-called 'hit and run' that had left a woman dead. In sickening realisation about the truth of that night I panicked and made a mistake that I will regret for the rest of my life. Terrified of the consequences, I delayed an instant confession and waited until the police finally caught up with me. It was a stupid decision that also implicated my wife, then pregnant with our first son, in the deception. I was sentenced to fifteen months in prison, although no earthly punishment could come close to my shame, guilt, despair and utter regret.

HMP Bullingdon in Oxfordshire was a far cry from Nicosia but I was more of a broken man then than at any other time in my life. This wasn't the first person whose life I had taken, but this time it was an innocent woman, not one of the gangsters or charlatans that were part of my seedy world when I was a very different man. Now I was living as a 'new creation', I had new life as an adopted son of the living God, but I believed I had failed Him so badly. I believed I had let God down in such a big way that I could never presume to publicly utter His name again. My faith in Him couldn't be shaken – He was too real to me – but I reasoned that I was such a terrible advertisement that I couldn't allow anyone to know I was a follower of Christ. I vowed to become a 'quiet' and inactive Christian.

That was one of my biggest mistakes. God had plans. God always has plans. He was to use me, and my big mouth, in a staggeringly huge, very public way. It started very gently, but within days of me making my vow of silence, I discovered that the last thing He wanted was for me to be 'quiet' about Him! No, God was with me in that prison and He wanted to use me to reach the wicked, the hurting and the broken by standing alongside them, even – especially – in the midst of my own disgrace.

My decision to be quiet was quickly overturned and today I am not ashamed to say that I actively seek the biggest crowds possible so that I can preach the Gospel to anyone willing to listen. Today I am a full-time evangelist. It is my job. It is also my absolute passion and *raison d'être*. I stand with the apostle Paul when I say I would rather die than not preach the Gospel of Jesus Christ. Paul described himself as the chief of sinners (1 Tim. 1:15, KJV). All I can say is, 'He hadn't met me!'

If Jesus can use me, He can use you. In fact He wants to use you, He yearns for your company, longs for you to join Him in His work of saving those He loves. All you need is recognition of that calling and a willing heart. If you already have fire in your belly to go out and share the Gospel, then this book is for you. I hope it will challenge you and give you some fresh ideas and even more impetus to engage in the big picture, to paint lavishly and creatively with joy and great gusto. But if you have doubts, misgivings, fears, reservations, this book is also – and probably more so – for you.

No matter where you are on the journey of faith, or how experienced you are at sharing it, I hope that you'll be inspired by the words and ideas that follow. I am no theologian, just a man saved by the grace of the Lord Jesus Christ and desperate to share His story and His love with others. In the last few years I have taken this simple teaching around the globe and thousands have been motivated, inspired and challenged to get involved in Jesus' Great Commission. In the following pages I hope you'll enjoy exploring what that might mean. I want to break down some of the myths about evangelism – what evangelism is and is not, who it's for, why we do it and why we don't, how to do it and why we absolutely have to. So please, stay a while. Join me on the journey . . .

Preface

Picking Up the Paintbrushes

It's late October and I find myself in a beautiful house in Scotland, surrounded by twenty or so friends. They are a wide mix of people, all ages, from many walks of life. We have come together as 'Avanti Ministries', the ministry established to enable me, and others, to embrace and practically live out Jesus' Great Commission.

Our host initiates a 'team-building' exercise and I am intrigued to find myself with a paintbrush in hand. The group is divided into six small teams and our host hands each team a small, unrecognisable section of what is obviously a much bigger picture. There are splashes of colour, lots of yellow, and seemingly random shapes which we are to duplicate onto large square pieces of canvas. We are given only a faint pencil outline on our canvas. Now it's up to us to mix our colours and recreate the very abstract pattern we see on the small piece of card. I am quickly absorbed in the work, only vaguely aware of the conversations around me and of Thom, a gifted artist and one of the team, going from group to group offering help and encouragement.

When our canvas squares are complete there's still an air of confusion and expectation among us. Chris, our host, carefully gathers our abstract pictures and starts piecing them together.

There are smiles all round as the bigger picture begins to emerge. It's Van Gogh's famous painting, *The Sower*. We all stand back to admire the wonder of the complete picture and marvel over the fact that our six individual pieces of canvas all match up, almost perfectly. Everyone learned a great deal from the experience and, as we thought more deeply about the painting and its process, we realised that it was so much more than just a team-building project.

We had begun the journey with only a line sketch. Many of our group had not painted since their school days and set out very tentatively dipping their brushes into the vibrant colours. With encouragement they put the first splashes of paint on the canvas and set about following the guidelines. The sketch gave them the confidence to step out, to begin the journey, to 'go'. So it strikes me: isn't this just the way with God? He has given many things to be our guide, to be our blueprint. Consider creation, the Bible, Jesus' crucifixion and resurrection, prayer, our own conscience, the Holy Spirit, other people, the Church. All these things are given so that we might seek and come to find God's will. He gives us a blank canvas, and we can do with it whatever we like. But engrained in the canvas is a sketch line, His sketch line. The canvas has an edge, a boundary to safely hem us in. Imagine if our painters had been faced with a huge piece of canvas stretching further than the eye could see and no sketch line to follow. The work would have been so terribly daunting; we couldn't possibly have faced it.

And so we painted. Some with confidence, some not so sure, but we began imitating the great master, Van Gogh. Here's another obvious parallel. At first we didn't know what the complete picture would be, nor did we know the original artist, but by carefully following the guidelines we began to imitate the great master and finally all was revealed to us in full glory. So, too, we are called to persevere in our walk, to 'seek' and discover by imitating our Master.

During the process we also had an 'encourager' in Thom. He went from team to team urging us to be bold with the paint and brushes. Sometimes we slipped over the edge of our sketch line, or got the mix of the paint wrong. When that happened he was there to scrape off the paint and redirect, gently encouraging each person in the right way. He was careful not to be too invasive. He must have been tempted at times to take over and do sections himself, but instead he simply coached us so that the work remained our own. Most found his help invaluable. Some leaned on him more than others. On the other hand, Sara, a primary school teacher by profession, wasn't so encouraged by Thom. She struggled to believe and trust his positive comments, all too aware that she offers similar praise to the children she teaches, even when their work is not so good. This continued to bother her, especially when we reflected that Thom was behaving as God does, constantly encouraging and urging us to keep going. What did this mean for Sara?

It was something to puzzle over. How many of us are like this in our relationship with God? Perhaps we don't fully trust that He can shine through us. We don't recognise that we are at our best when He is fully working in us, even – especially – in our weaknesses. We still try to go our own way, to work in our own strength. Yet He offers nothing but encouragement. He has nothing but love and adoration for us, His children. Of course, in Sara's case the truth of her skill was only revealed in the final unveiling of the bigger picture. She didn't think she was doing her job very well. She didn't fully trust Thom, but when she stood back and looked at the finished result she struggled to identify her, supposedly inferior, work amongst the rest. In the end it had become part of the perfect picture.

Sara might also remember that her kitchen is festooned with pictures painted by her young children. The rest of the world might never acclaim them, but to Sara, these paintings are the precious results of her children's fun-time creativity and her heart swells with pride each time another is pinned to the wall. Doesn't God delight in every colourful effort made by each of His children, no matter how much paper is screwed up and thrown in the bin, or how much paint is spilled along the way?

No one square of canvas was better, more beautiful or more important than all the rest. Some people had seen my artistic efforts before and during the session I was aware that they were particularly watching my handiwork, anticipating that mine might be better than others. I'm sure some felt slightly intimidated or inadequate. So, too, in the Church, many of us look to other people – leaders of huge churches, well-known evangelists, authors of inspirational books, acclaimed worship leaders, 'personalities' – as though they are so much better than us. Worse still, we can find ourselves turning to such people as though they can almost live our faith for us because we don't feel gifted enough ourselves. It's easy to feel like the useless child not picked for the team when our gifts might not be as visible as those of others. But the Kingdom of God is not like that, and the Bible, time and again, is quite clear on that teaching. Take the shepherd boy David – just a small boy of no notoriety or acclaim, yet in his weakness he defeated Goliath and went on to become God's chosen king. Throughout the Scriptures we find it is the lowly, the weak, the inadequate, the unpopular, the poor in spirit who are favoured in the eyes of God. Could he make his point any clearer than to send His own precious Son into the world by means of a humble young girl in stable squalor?

General Eisenhower once rebuked one of his generals for referring to a soldier as 'just a private'. Eisenhower reminded him that the army could function better without its generals than it could without its foot soldiers. 'If this war is to be won,' he said, 'it's more likely to be won by privates.' In the same way, if the Gospel is to be taken to the lost, it is 'ordinary' Christians who are needed to do it.

Sara and her partner Wendy, in the context of the painting, might have felt like the foot soldiers. Of all the areas of the picture, their top left section was perhaps the most artistically tedious. It was composed wholly of yellows and browns, with little apparent form or contrasting areas of interest. The two women may well have felt rather insignificant as they painted their piece of canvas. Only when the piece was fitted neatly into context did the true glory of their work shine through. Indeed, it is this section – the sun – that is perhaps the most prominent aspect of the finished picture. Without it, the painting wouldn't have such tremendous impact. It was quite sobering to recognise that the area once seen as the most boring and inconsequential was actually the most crucial of all. The picture without the sun would be almost no picture at all. The meaning and essence of the painting is lost. Take the 'Son' out of Leonardo da Vinci's *The Last Supper* and we're left with a picture of only backstabbers and traitors!

One of the most remarkable aspects of the finished painting was the way the small details came together. The branches of the tree all met up, even though different people painted them on separate pieces of canvas. This speaks to me of the importance of good communication and team-work in our Christian walk. We rely on others, and we, too, are relied upon. One of the greatest strengths among the 'resistance' in the Second World War was their network of message carriers. In order to get vital information to allies across borders they relied on the precision and dedication of individual people. Messages could be carried over thousands of miles, passed from person to person. Imagine, then, the potential impact of the Gospel when we tell even just one person. Who knows what branches might spring from that one conversation or how far-reaching they might become.

Finally, as I stand back and gaze in awe at our painting and at the many stories and messages it embraces in its creation, I am reminded of another tale. In the Highlands of Scotland some fishermen went back to an inn for tea. As the waitress was serving them, one of the men began describing the day's catch, using typically large, sweeping gestures. In an instant his right arm collided with a teacup. The tea splashed all over the whitewashed wall causing an ugly brown stain to appear. 'I'm so terribly sorry,' the distraught fisherman apologised, repeatedly. 'Never mind,' said a man, jumping up from the next table. Pulling a pencil out from his pocket he began to sketch around the tea stain. The others watched in amazement as there emerged a magnificent royal stag with antlers spread. The artist was Sir Edwin Henry Landseer, England's foremost painter of animals.

If an artist can do that with an ugly brown stain, what can God do with my mistakes – my sins – if I only turn them over to Him? Perhaps then we should flip the imagery drawn from the painting on its head. Maybe it is not that God does the sketching and we fill in the gaps, but the other way round. Maybe we do the sketching and God takes our faltering efforts and fills them in with colour, making our picture into a thing of beauty, something worthwhile, a creation of Father and child that gives glory back to Him.

One more point to remember, before we begin our journey into the great commission. Van Gogh was largely unrecognised as an artist during his lifetime. (Interestingly enough, he was a passionate evangelist who dedicated much time to working amongst the poor.) It was only after his death that people started to appreciate his work and celebrate him as one of the great masters. Little could he have imagined that his legacy would be among the most distinguishable and expensive in the world. In a similar way, our remit on evangelism is to sow seeds into people's lives. Very often we don't get to see the fruit of our labour. We can only look forward to finding out what God has done with the seeds we have sown as we enter the gates of Heaven!

1

Passion

The drive of the athlete, the enthusiasm of the volunteer, the tenderness of the nurse, the dedication of the scientist, the endurance of the body-builder, the gusto of the musician, the resolve of the soldier . . . In just about every walk of life, every vocation, every institution, every field of endeavour you will find people with great passion.

Nothing great is accomplished in life without passion. Nothing great is sustained in life without passion. Passion is what energises life. Passion makes the impossible possible. Passion gives you a reason to get up in the morning with the conviction that 'Today I am going to do something with my life.' Without passion life becomes boring. It becomes monotonous. It becomes routine. It becomes dull. When God gave us life, He gave us more than just breath in our bodies, more than just blood in our veins, more than just muscle and sinew and bone. 'Life' is Christ's gift (John 10:28) and He, Himself, is *'the life'* (John 14:6). When Christ gave us life it was so that we *'may have life, and have it to the full'* (John 10:10). To that end He gives us emotion from which can spring fervour, ardour, zeal, excitement. He gives us expression and individuality; the ability to love and be loved, to make choices, to interact with others, to feel, to celebrate, to be something special, someone unique, someone significant. God created us to have passion in our lives and He wants us to live a passionate life.

In fact God wants us to be passionate about Him, and He has warned us about being indifferent towards Him. In the book of Revelation we read a letter to the church in Laodicea, a church that, it seems, had little passion for God. To these people Christ said, *'I know your deeds, that you are neither cold nor hot. I wish you were either one or the other! So because you are lukewarm – neither hot nor cold – I am about to spit you out of my mouth'* (Revelation 3:15).

I meet many passionate people in my work of sharing the Gospel. All around the globe I encounter individuals whose passion for Christ is played out in their zeal to spread the Gospel or to reach out through His indwelling compassion to lost and hurting people.

Catalin Baciu is a passionate man. Our campaign to Romania was very fruitful. I had spoken to packed auditoriums and shared the Gospel in prisons in each city. I met Catalin at the end of the tour. There was great joy in my heart over the hundreds of people who had committed their lives to Christ but after three weeks away I was physically tired and weary for home. Catalin took me to the inner city of Bucharest where he had helped organise an event that would be attended by many of the homeless people in the area. God worked powerfully and the evening saw a tremendous number of men, women and children step forward in the altar call. As the last stragglers left the auditorium my thoughts began to turn to a decent meal, a warm bed and the flight home to my family, but Catalin had another plan. Instead we took to the streets.

Catalin is well known. He meets and greets, with a hug, many of the crumpled rags that huddle in doorways. There was no room for phobias or inhibitions and I had to set aside my disgust at the smells and the horror of the degradation in what we were about to do. Catalin knew just where to go. With relative ease he lifted a heavy iron lid in the ground and I silently prayed as we climbed down into the depths of the city's steaming, stinking sewers. The pipes down there are devilish hot but as I peered into the darkness I made out a mass of little bodies lying as close as they dared without getting burned. Down here in filth and squalor hundreds of children risk their lives to keep warm from the bitter cold. As my eyes grew accustomed to the dark, I saw that many tightly clutched small carrier bags that they repeatedly breathed in and out of to inhale fumes of various toxic substances. Such is their desperate attempt to numb themselves from the bitterness of an uncaring world that walks on by.

Catalin and Teen Challenge work daily with the homeless to identify children at risk before they are irreparably damaged by street culture, and to aid those wanting to break away from addiction. They have set up a live-in centre where they run a discipleship programme to help people from the streets to make that change. This is passion. This is a man (and there are many others like him on his team) who, living in the fullness of life in Christ, is reaching out to others, reaching out with food, with warmth, with practical help and friendship, but also reaching out with the message of Jesus Christ, reaching out with life, reaching out in passion.

The word 'passion' has many meanings including 'strong emotion' such as love, joy, hatred or anger; 'ardent love' such as strong sexual desire or lust; 'boundless enthusiasm' and 'abandoned display of emotion'. The dictionary also refers to the 'suffering of Jesus', specifically the period following the Last Supper and including the Crucifixion, as related in the gospels. Some dictionaries

---

The Passion is the Christian theological term used for the events and suffering – physical, spiritual, and mental – of Jesus in the hours before and including his trial and execution by crucifixion. (Wikipedia)

---

also list more ancient definitions of passion relating to 'martyrdom' and 'passivity'. Interestingly the word 'passion' stems from the Latin word pati, meaning 'to suffer'. The stem 'pass' comes from the word 'passive' meaning 'capable of suffering'.

The writers of the gospels tell us a lot about the passion of Jesus. Whilst the narratives each have their own different approach to the story, all are careful to illustrate that Jesus knew what was going to happen. He knew His destiny and recognised that immense suffering lay in Him fulfilling His purpose for mankind:

> *And he said, 'The Son of Man must suffer many things and be rejected by the elders, chief priests and teachers of the law, and he must be killed and on the third day be raised to life.'* (Luke 9:22)

Christ suffered for us physically, but He also suffered in worse ways. He was scorned and hated by those He came to save. Can you imagine that pain? Having His unconditional love not only denied, but thrown back at Him with such hatred. Such rejection must have cut deeper than the horrendous physical wounds He endured. Luke points out that both Herod and Pilate could find nothing wrong with Jesus. They would have Him punished but neither wanted to put Him to death. Pilate appealed to the crowd a number of times but Jesus had to hear the united brutal cries of His own people screaming, *'Crucify him! Crucify him!'* (Luke 23:20):

> *'With one voice they cried out, "away with this man!"'* *(Luke 23:18)*

> *With one voice they cried out, 'Away with this man! Release Barabbas to us!'* (Luke 23:18)

How great the sin of man at that moment, that with 'one voice' (some translations speak of a mighty roar rising up from the crowd) they should demand the death of God's own Son. What suffering did He endure and what love sustained Him? We can never imagine:

> *For God so loved the world that he gave his one and only Son, that whoever believes in him shall not perish but have eternal life.* (John 3:16)

What greater love is there than this? I adore this verse because it makes me feel more loved than I could ever believe possible. Some of the synonyms for passion are fervour, ardour, enthusiasm and zeal. I feel these emotions when I think of what Jesus went through for me. How could Jesus willingly experience this torture and pain for us? What human being could do what Jesus did? Luke talks about the pain Jesus went through in the Garden of Gethsemane:

> *And being in anguish, he prayed more earnestly, and his sweat was like drops of blood falling to the ground.* (Luke 22:44)

Only Jesus (with God as His Father) could follow through like He did, knowing the pain and torture He would experience. But the outcome was the goal: our forgiveness, Salvation for mankind. Jesus knew the plans of His Father. He knew the outcome. That is the fantastic part of the passion of Jesus; that He died for our sins. It makes the word passion all the more 'passionate'. When we read the account of the Passion in the gospels it should fill us with emotion, with strong feelings of passion. To get a glimpse of understanding of who Jesus is to us, and truly feel what His death on the cross means, is an experience of passion itself. Jesus died on the cross for our sins, so we don't have to suffer the way He did. God doesn't want us to suffer like Jesus did, but He does want us to live with Jesus as our example, loving one another and sharing our love with those who don't know the 'Passion of Jesus'.

My wife Sara and I have two sons and I'll never forget the day each of them was born. The feeling was like nothing else on earth. I was so excited, so thrilled, so bursting with joy that I wanted to shout the news from the rooftops. It makes me grin now just thinking about the journey home from the hospital. Sara had to stay in overnight but once I left her I couldn't wait to get home and set about telling all our friends, 'We've got a boy.' I most clearly remember the taxi driver, after the birth of our second son, Jacob. He was so good to me. I burst into his car with the news that I'd just become a dad again and he listened so patiently to me before gently interrupting to find out where I wanted to be taken. All the way home he listened, nodded and smiled as I enthused about my beautiful son and the wonders of the birth. All the time I was talking I was simultaneously text messaging friends and family.

Pulling up outside the house I left the driver a big tip and dashed straight to my neighbours' door, 'Great news, we've got a boy!' Then into the house where I didn't even take off my coat before sending an email out across the globe. Sara and I had been looking forward to sharing the good news and we'd prepared a birth announcement already. Within the hour I'd filled in all the details – the baby was a boy, his weight, the time he was born, etc. – and got the pre-addressed envelopes in the post. Call me crazy, but this was news worth sharing!

No-one had to persuade me to tell the good news about the birth of my children. I didn't need a course or a book or a manual on how to do it. I doubt it was articulate, or balanced or well thought through, but when I was filled with the joy of becoming a dad I was consumed with passion to tell everyone and anyone and I used all resources in my power to get the message far and wide.

No-one had to persuade me to tell the good news about the birth of my children. I didn't need a course or a book or a manual on how to do it.

It's normal to want to share the things we are passionate about, isn't it? Despite the majority of newspaper headlines, people do love good news. We're quick to make announcements about births, marriages, new homes, exam results, parties, holidays and many other beautiful things in life. Good, life-changing things happen to both wealthy and poor people, to privileged and deprived, academic and uneducated, intellectual and illiterate . . . Wherever we are in the spectrum of life we all love to share and celebrate news of good things. We don't keep the news to ourselves because we're not clever enough, or because we haven't been on a course or read a book on how to do it. We just do it because it's a big deal to us. It means something to me. It's the best thing that's happened to me, the greatest thing I know. I share it, naturally. So why do so many of us who profess belief, faith and even 'relationship' with God our Maker and Christ our Saviour, struggle to share the Gospel?

The words in Mark 16:15 are simple: *'Go into all the world and preach the good news to all creation'. 'Go into the world. Go everywhere and announce the Message of God's good news to one and all'* (The Message).

It doesn't sound too complicated, does it?

I believe that the problem here is more than not knowing how to share the good news about Jesus Christ. We talk about 'evangelism' and get all tied up about what that means and who should do it, but when we look at Jesus' words here we surely have to realise the simplicity of the task. Do we need a book or training course or a special manual to teach us what it means to reach lost people? Do we even need a special word to describe the practice? The disciples were not learned people. They didn't go to college or study the Scriptures, but they did spend time with the Master. So with us. We need to spend time with Him, we need an encounter with Jesus, so that the Holy Spirit might convict us towards love and compassion for the lost. As I travel I meet many Christians who share this same realisation, those who are truly living the joy of their own Salvation and are desperate to share it with others. They might stumble and struggle to find ways of expressing it, but their heart is right. They're always looking for the next opportunity and for different ways of telling the good news. They're hungry for resources that might help or new ideas and anecdotes on how to communicate the message. Such people are obediently, joyfully and naturally living out their purpose.

But many more Christians, it appears, are simply not that way. Many take part in church every week, they might sit on dozens of committees and dedicate themselves to many good works, but for some reason sharing the Gospel and reaching out to the lost with God's message of love and life is not even on their radar. For such people it's not an issue of knowing *how* to do it, but of whether they should do it at all. 'Leave all that to the evangelists and the preachers, it's really not for me.' I'm amazed at how many Christians sincerely believe that they are exempt from sharing good news and believe that only a certain gifted few are called to the task of evangelism. The tragedy is that this lie is perpetuated in many of our churches. There's a good analogy here in medicine. Only a small number of people are trained to be pharmacists and doctors, yet we all have a duty of care. Most of us can buy and use basic medicine to help others. The truth is that God's requirement is universal. He calls on the whole Body of Christ to participate in the act of sharing the good news of Salvation. It is an obligation for *all* who have this gift to share it. The idea that evangelism is just for the chosen few – it may be done, or not done, as we choose – is a lie and perhaps one of the greatest diseases the Church is suffering from in this current age. Such wrong thinking is unbiblical and also illogical as it means that multitudes of people around the globe do not hear the Gospel.

God's requirement is universal. He calls on the whole Body of Christ to participate in the act of sharing the good news of Salvation.

Salvation is a gift. It is *my* gift from *my* Father and it ensures *my* eternity so surely with that personal gift comes *personal responsibility*. If I have been transformed by the Gospel and understand what I have been saved from, then surely I am determined, even in my weakness and inadequacy, to communicate this news to others who are lost in this world and heading for terrible punishment after death. Charles Spurgeon had a wonderful description of evangelism as one beggar telling another beggar where to find bread.

With the material in this book I hope to inspire, to challenge and to offer solid practical help on how all Christians can share the Good News of Jesus Christ. But, to be honest, I don't believe any book or training course is necessary or adequate to teach a Christian how to reach lost people. Rather this is something we need to simply wake up to. If, as Christians, this is not our passion we need to ask, 'Why isn't it?' We need to go back to the truth of our own Salvation. Furthermore we need to allow God and the Holy Spirit to convict us and to

One beggar telling another beggar where to find bread.

instil in us love and compassion for the destiny of our fellow human beings. Like the early apostles, we need little more than to spend time with the Master.

Anyone working in marketing knows that to sell something to the best of their ability they have to really know and believe in the worth of that product. It's like visiting a travel agent for advice on a holiday. You're much more likely to choose a destination that the agent can sell you through personal experience. Their personal testimony to the quality, the fun, the ease and the living up to expectation speaks far more than anything they can show you in a brochure. So it's important to understand that if we are to get anywhere with this discussion on evangelism – on sharing the good news of Salvation, on releasing the handbrake on the Great Commission – we must set our foundation. We must be sure of our own destiny. We must discover (or rediscover) what it means to have 'eternity' stamped on our eyeballs, as well as our hearts (Ecclesiastes 3:11), so it is that which we see every day in all we do and with everyone we encounter.

Perhaps what I'm saying here is ringing a little too true. Let me assure you, you are not alone, but if reading this does nothing more than jolt you back to the reality of your Salvation, then I consider its writing worthwhile. General William Booth, founder of the Salvation Army is quoted:

> Most Christian ministries would like to send their recruits to Bible college for five years. I would like to send our recruits to Hell for five minutes. That would do more than anything else to prepare them for a lifetime of compassionate ministry.[1]

The famous evangelist Charles Finney advised Christians:

> Look, as though through a telescope and see the misery of the lost and hear their groans; and then look to Heaven and see the

> joys and hear the songs of the redeemed. Then each believer should ask, 'Is it possible that I should so prevail with God as to be the means of elevating the lost sinner to that glorious place?'[2]

So please, put this book down for a few moments and consider your own destiny. Are you sure of your Salvation? Are you spending enough time with the Master? Is the Gospel transforming you and do you understand what you have been saved into and saved from? Only then will you begin to grasp that this is truly and desperately good news, worth sharing.

Father God, I pray that you will stir our hearts, that you will turn our passion to the Passion of Christ.

- What benefits are there to non-Christians seeing evidence of passion in the Christian life?

- Do you struggle to feel passionate in your daily relationship with God? Why do you think this might be? What can you do to re-ignite your passion for God?

- Consider the things you are passionate about. Are there any ways you can use these things in your application of Mark 16:15? (For example, Stephen is passionate about football and he seeks every opportunity to share his faith using this field of interest).

2

War and Romance

When I first met Sara it's probably fair to say I fell head over heels in love with her. I know it's a bit of a cliché but after only a couple of hours in her company I could think of no-one else. I was totally enthralled by her and wanted to make the very best of myself to ensure she noticed me. I had very little to offer. I was not long out of prison in Cyprus and had been reduced to something of a social wreck. My days as a self-assured, gutsy young man were long gone. My prison encounter with Jesus had put to death my overwhelmingly arrogant nature and was teaching me a new humility by breaking me down to nothing. I recognised that, and accepted it gratefully, but I didn't enjoy the fear of normal things, my stammering speech, my panic at meeting 'nice' people. I had nothing, I was nothing, and here was this wonderful girl who I dared to dream might come to care for me.

At the time Sara was training to be a teacher and living in a shared house in south London. I have never been so nervous as I was the evening I decided to visit her. I had no money and walked a considerable distance to her house. She deserved flowers. A little way down her street there was a house with a well-kept garden embellished by a glorious rose bush stretching out onto the pavement. I looked around. No-one was in sight. In an instant, I picked the most beautiful long-stemmed red rose I could find.

Guilt came over me. I shouldn't have stolen the rose, but when I thought of Sara, I knew it was a risk worth taking.

This behaviour continued as our courtship blossomed. I'm ashamed to say I stole every rose until the bush was bare! Perhaps it's the fact that I'm half Italian, but I've always believed in big romantic gestures. All through the early years of our marriage I have bought Sara the biggest bouquet of flowers I could find. 'If it's worth doing, it's worth doing on a big scale' has been my motto. In recent years, however, times have changed. Since I became a full-time evangelist through Avanti Ministries, our family has lived 'by faith'. I take no salary, nor do I charge for what I do. So much of our activity runs at a financial loss, but the Lord provides for all our needs and we are very blessed. Naturally, every penny we have has to be very wisely considered.

A little while ago I found myself walking past a flower stall and a beautiful bouquet, marked at £20, caught my eye. I found myself fingering the twenty-pound note in my pocket and thinking how much I'd love to buy the flowers for my wife. 'Don't be ridiculous,' I told myself, 'this money has to last all week.' I knew I had some travel to pay for. In fact I needed the bus fare to get home! I walked on, but somehow it was as though God was prompting me, 'Go back. Get the flowers for Sara.' I turned in surprising giddiness and went back to the stall. Even then, the flower lady had to virtually pull the note out of my hand as I offered it to her. It was a long walk home but I was excited at the thought of seeing Sara's face when I walked in with the flowers. I imagined her beaming smile and knew I'd done the right thing, even if I'd pay for the sacrifice for the rest of the week.

When I gave Sara the flowers, however, I didn't get the reception I anticipated. Normally she would give me a mocking telling-off but we'd have a cuddle and kiss and the rest I wouldn't dare to write about! This time it was different. She didn't say anything, but instead began to cry. I was dumbfounded. Sara is a strong woman who has fully dedicated herself to our ministry. It occurred to me that she was upset that I had recklessly spent the money when we had more pressing needs. I was wrong. Tears began streaming down her face and I held her as she sobbed. 'I'm sorry,' she said, 'it's just that it's been so long since you brought me flowers.'

I was so ashamed. I realised that in nobly dedicating myself to ministry I had done the very thing that God would hate. I had neglected my first love. In all the striving and believing I was doing the right thing, I had actually lost sight of what matters most and I'm sure Sara will testify that it came down to much more than flowers. There's an important lesson here.

The church in Ephesus was a strong gathering of committed people, doing many things right, but as we read, there is a fundamental problem at heart:

> *To the angel of the church in Ephesus write: These are the words of him who holds the seven stars in his right hand and walks among the seven golden lampstands: I know your deeds, your hard work and your perseverance. I know that you cannot tolerate wicked men, that you have tested those who claim to be apostles but are not, and have found them false. You have persevered and have endured hardships for my name, and have not grown weary. Yet I hold this against you: You have forsaken your first love. Remember the height from which you have fallen! Repent and do the things you did at first. If you do not repent, I will come to you and remove your lampstand from its place.* (Rev. 2:1–5)

I hate to think I would treat Sara like that again, though I fear I probably have and will, many times over. I love her, but it's shameful how we can so often take those who mean the most to us for granted. Relationships grow stale and predictable and too comfortable until we drift into co-existing rather than truly *living* with one another. If we treat those we love in this way how easy is it then to do the same with God, to let our communication and our loving Him grow tired and weary? All too soon we stop buying roses for God – we grow tired and bored of going to church, we find prayer and Bible reading nothing more than a chore. We stop talking about our beloved One. Our relationship settles into the realm of an occasional cup of tea as our dancing shoes are well and truly put away, the thrill of the courtship fading into distant memory. And yet, when the romance is gone, Jesus calls us back. He tells us clearly to repent and go back to how it was when we first met, when we first encountered Jesus as living and real, as our Love.

In Matthew 5:15–16 Jesus talks about the lampstand shining out to everyone:

> *Neither do people light a lamp and put it under a bowl. Instead they put it on its stand, and it gives light to everyone in the house. In the same way let your light shine before men, that they may see your good deeds and praise your Father in heaven.*

This is a wonderful analogy for the Church and yet, as we've seen, Revelation heeds a chilling warning that God can, and will, take away our lamp if we neglect our first love and fail to remember the joy of our first courtship, our Salvation.

> *'In the same way let your light shine before men, that they may see your good deeds and praise your Father in heaven.' (Matt. 5:16)*

The last chapter concluded with a challenging enquiry: what is your passion? But the crux of my message focuses as much on the corporate Church as the individual. As we have already seen, we have a big problem concerning not just our ability, but primarily our motivation and desire to partake in the Great Commission. It is a problem of sin, a problem of disobedience and, overwhelmingly, a problem of blindness. It's a problem that cuts the very heart of the contemporary Church.

The Church has become blinded to its priority in this world.

I believe that the Church has become blinded to its priority in this world. We need to understand that we are in a war. The first fiery arrows were shot the moment sin entered this world and the battles have been raging ever since. You only have to look at Scripture to see how God Himself speaks of this war. In Exodus 15:3, depending on the translation you look at, God is described as 'a man of war', or 'a warrior', or 'a fighter'. Calvary is also described in the language of the battle scene, *'And having disarmed the powers and authorities, he made a public spectacle of them, triumphing over them by the cross'* (Col. 2:15). The second book of Timothy 2:3 speaks of Christians as soldiers and, of course, there's the powerful image of the Christian graces illustrated as pieces of armour in Ephesians 6:14–17:

The helmet of Salvation
The breastplate of righteousness
The belt of truth
Feet fitted with readiness from the gospel of peace
The sword of the Spirit
The shield of faith

The Bible isn't shy when it comes to stating who the enemy is, either. 'Resist the devil,' we are instructed in James 4:7. *'Put on the full armour of God so that you can fight against the devil's evil tricks. Our fight is not against people on earth but against the rulers and authorities and the powers of this world's darkness, against the spiritual powers of evil in the heavenly world'* (Eph. 6:11–12, NCV).

'Put on the full armour of God so that you can fight against the devil's evil tricks. Our fight is not against people on earth but against the rulers and authorities and the powers of this world's darkness, against the spiritual powers of evil in the heavenly world'.
(Eph. 6:11–12, NCV)

This kind of language and imagery might be hard to reconcile with our daily lives. Maybe it's more the stuff of Tolkien or C.S. Lewis, the stuff of wild, outlandish, cinematic fantasy; little to do with the housework, the office, the school run, the social club, the old lady for whom you held the door open, the homeless man you passed by on the way to the supermarket . . . Yet from what we know of these great authors, there is biblical incitement behind their portrayals of the battle of good and evil. OK, so it's not every day we come face to face with some Tolkienesque demon but, as we see in just a handful of scriptures, we – God's people – are inevitably and inextricably right in the centre of one almighty cosmic war. The battle might be in the heavenly realms, but as 'soldiers', adorned in the armour of God, our earthly battles are no less bloody.

What are we warring over? How about injustice, poverty, starvation, physical abuse, sickness, disease, prostitution, pornography, every kind of abuse from tobacco and alcohol to sex, drugs, materialism, to name but a few; from the very obvious to the subtle and hidden conditions of the mind, depression, desperation, loneliness . . . and who are we fighting for? Well, that hasn't changed since the time Jesus walked the earth. We're fighting for the outcast, the homeless, the disabled, the disadvantaged, the hurting, the starving, the abused, all who suffer affliction. Many compassionate men and women are instinctively compelled to go some way to relieve the suffering of fellow human beings. As Christians we are called to walk as Jesus walked, to care for the widows and orphans, seek justice for the imprisoned, feed and clothe the impoverished, heal the hurting (Jam. 1:27; Ps. 146:7). All these battles, and many more, are critical and vital aspects of our Christian witness in the world. We must fight vigorously and relentlessly, but ultimately what is our focus? What is the purpose of the battle? What are we truly warring for?

Our true fight is for the souls of men and women for the glory of God. Think again about the point of church. Why do we have church services? Well the answer is clear. Ephesians 5:19 exhorts us to *'speak to one another with psalms, hymns and spiritual songs'*. Throughout the New Testament we see believers meeting together, breaking bread, making music, giving thanks to God. The Church on earth is primarily a sign to all around that God is great and Jesus is alive and, if our motivation is pure, there is no greater reason to attend church week after week than this. The Church is a witness to Christ. It is our testimony to Him, so again we must consider the big picture of God's divine plan. The reason we have church services, Bible studies, conferences, summer camps, Christian books and numerous other resources is surely because God is trying to reach the whole world to have a relationship with Him. So we're reading about it, we're studying, talking and praying about it . . . when are we actually going to get out there and *do* it? The average university course is three years, then a graduate will go out into the world and hopefully use and apply their training. Indeed, this was the way with the early disciples. They had three years in the presence of the Master, learning from Him, before being sent out into the world. Is there not a parallel here with our learning in church, house groups, and personal study? Do we expect to sit in school for fifty years, without ever actually using what we've learned?

It's great to spend time with other believers singing and talking about the joy of Salvation and the wonder of our relationship with God, but I believe that when we're getting out there, sharing Jesus' message with others, that's when we're demonstrating genuine gratitude to Him.

Jesus said that His mission was to seek and save the lost (Luke 19:10). The apostle Paul emphasises Jesus' mission in 1 Timothy 1:15, *'Christ Jesus came into the world to save sinners.'* Time and again, the Bible makes it clear that the very purpose of our time here on earth is to choose to turn away from the wrong things in our life and to invite Jesus to be our Saviour. *'What good is it for a man to gain the whole world, yet forfeit his soul?'* (Mark 8:36). In the report leading up to this much-quoted verse we again see Jesus clearly at war with Satan: *'"Get behind me, Satan!" he said. "You do not have in mind the things of God, but the things of men"'* (Mark 8:33).

William Booth, founder of the Salvation Army was clearly signed up for battle in his declaration to King Edward VIII:

> Some men's ambition is art,
> Some men's ambition is fame,
> Some men's ambition is gold,
> My ambition is the souls of men.[1]

What Booth and many others like him[2] recognised was that the priority of God's people had to be the same as that of Jesus Himself – to seek and save souls. Here is one of my favourite quotes from nineteenth-century preacher Charles Finney:

> If the leading feature of your character is not the absorbing thought and effort to reconcile men to God, you have not the root of the matter in you. Whatever appearance of religion you may have, you lack the leading and fundamental characteristic of true piety – the character and aims of Jesus and His disciples. Look at them and see how this feature stands out, in strong and eternal relief, as the leading characteristic, the prominent design, and the objective of their lives.[3]

So if our battle is to win souls, to join with Jesus' followers down the ages in the Great Commission, why are we failing so badly? It's easy to confine ourselves in the security of church, but Jesus also said *'Go . . .'* (Matt. 28:19; Mark 16:15). He told us to get out there and proclaim the Gospel to everyone on earth. When he said that, he wasn't just talking to the likes of amazing evangelists like Billy Graham or other 'Ephesians 4:11–12' type evangelists (*'it was he who gave some to be apostles, some to be prophets, some to be evangelists, and some to be pastors and teachers, to prepare God's people for works of service . . .'*), he was talking to everyone and anyone who has received the gift of Salvation for themselves. He was talking to everyone in every church, in every town or village or suburb. He was talking to me, and to you.

> Men are mirrors, or 'carriers' of Christ to other men . . . Usually it is those who know Him that bring Him to others. That is why the Church, the whole body of Christians showing Him to one another, is so important. (C.S. Lewis)[4]

Some wish to live within the sound
of Church or Chapel Bell.
I want to run a rescue shop
within a yard of Hell. (C.T. Studd)[5]

When I stole that first rose for Sara I wasn't thinking of the consequences. The moment I met her I engaged in a battle – a battle to win her for myself. I was prepared to go to almost any length, to really put myself out on a limb, to take any imaginable risk if it meant that she could be mine. When you first fall in love you do crazy things – go way out of your way to see each other, stay up until the early morning together, have phone conversations that last for hours. It's fresh, exciting and passionate. I don't endorse stealing roses, but the point I'm making is how naturally willing we are to take risks and set all other things aside when we're first in love. After years of marriage it's easy to drift into routine, to stop doing crazy things that shout of our love. Our relationship becomes sensible and sanitised by all the other demands on our time. In the same way, if church becomes nothing more than a bit of liturgy, a prayer, a song and a cup of coffee with familiar friends, it soon grows stale and boring and we neglect the very thing, the very One, that brought us there. Yet it's not too late. When we get out into the world and share the Gospel – yes, facing possible ridicule and rejection – we put ourselves on the line again, and in doing so we taste afresh the exuberance of taking risks for the One we rightly adore.

Sara's reaction to that bunch of flowers was a wake-up call for me. It showed me how dangerously clouded I can become when it comes to life and love. How easily I let other things get in the way, things that vie for my attention and swallow up the precious moments that make a love affair. I will always make sure from now on that Sara gets flowers! It's so easy to become distracted by things that appear to be important. This is exactly what I perceive is happening in our churches. We have lost sight of our priority. The gladness, the romance, the excitement of our walk with Jesus has faded and we have become less attentive, less passionate and more busy with other things. Jesus used the parable of the wedding guests, reported in Matthew 22, to emphasise

God's desire to see His people – His precious and chosen guests of Heaven – give their very best in gratitude for His gift. First there were those who completely ignored the king's invitation to the special wedding feast for his son. So the king cast the net wider and generously invited many others in from the streets. But what did he find when he came to meet the guests? He noticed there was a man who was not wearing wedding clothes. How could this man be so disrespectful? How could he expect to partake of the great feast and share the generosity of the king when he wasn't prepared to make any effort himself? Jesus says that the king told the attendants to throw him out . . . *'into the darkness, where there will be weeping and gnashing of teeth'.*

We can talk about wedding clothes, or we can talk about battle dress. Whichever analogy appeals, the question is the same. Where is our first love? Where is our attention? Do we recognise the war, or are we too distracted with other things? Are we on the front line or has the watchman fallen asleep in the tower? When will we wake up and realise the fortress of the Church is opened wide and whilst we slumber in ignorance we lay exposed and vulnerable to the slings and arrows of the enemy?

- Spend some time thinking about and thanking God for the ways He has blessed you:

  In your life
  This week
  Today

- Why do people so easily appear to 'sideline' the greatness of God as they go about everyday living? What are some of the contributing factors and distractions in your own life?

- Think about the ways you take God for granted. Spend some time saying sorry to God and think of ways you can buy flowers for Him today.

- In Ephesians 6:14–17 the Christian graces are illustrated as pieces of armour. In practical terms, what does it mean to put on the pieces of armour?

3
All in the Balance

Jesus' mission was to seek and save the lost (Luke 19:10). And what greater mandate could He leave His followers than to continue His legacy? The scriptures that speak most clearly of this are undoubtedly those we have come to know as 'The Great Commission', yet elsewhere the gospels sing out of Jesus' intention for His people. Meditate on Jesus' prayer in John 17:20–26 and embrace just a glimpse of Christ's love for us and His longing for unity among believers. *'I have given them the glory that you gave me, that they may be one as we are one,'* He declares and I find it so easy to imagine the face of God beaming down at His Son at this point. Such tenderness, such passion! What honour is ours!

> *Righteous Father, though the world does not know you, I know you, and they know that you have sent me. I have made you known to them, and will continue to make you known in order that the love you have for me may be in them and that I myself may be in them.* (John 17:25–26)

So if this is our clear mandate it seems to me that we urgently need to examine first our own priorities, and then especially those of the wider body of the Church. In many of our churches every ministry has been given equal priority. Whilst it is true that every ministry in a local church ought to have *equal* value, biblically speaking not every ministry ought to have equal *priority*. Imagine you are called to the bedside of a dying person. You know they only have a very short time left on this earth. You have also discovered they have never fully heard the Gospel and are not saved. What do you do? Do you sit with them and keep them company, perhaps helping them remember the good years? Do you plump their pillows, help them drink and try to make their last hours as physically comfortable as possible? Do you just go off and pray for them? Take a look at Jesus' prayer, as reported in John 17. This is a tremendously tender passage where Jesus places His friends before His Father. First He prays for His disciples, then for all believers but note His words in verse 20:

> *My prayer is not for them [the disciples] alone. I pray also for those who will believe in me through their message, that all of them may be one, Father, just as you are in me and I am in you.*

Back in verse 18 Jesus had spoken of the mission of His followers to go out into the world. He was confident that they would spread the Gospel, so He prays here for those who would believe as a result of their work. It seems that all future believers are included in this prayer.

So, back with my dying friend, I have to highlight again verse 20 and pray that he or she might 'believe' through the 'message'. Surely then this message must be 'given'? My priority must be to pray, of course. What could have more value than speaking directly to our Creator God on behalf of this person? But in doing so I must share the Gospel with them so that they have the opportunity to respond, hopefully under the conviction of the Holy Spirit by the power of prayer. Yes, I must pray, pray at all times and in all things, without ceasing (1 Thess. 5:17) but I must also proclaim the Gospel. For my dying friend it might be the only time he or she would ever have heard the good news of eternity. With what urgency, what desperation, what love must I share it!

The priority of Jesus was to spread, or proclaim, the Gospel. The priority of the Church should be the same.

The priority of Jesus was to spread, or proclaim, the Gospel. The priority of the Church should be the same. And it's not just me, an over excited evangelist, who makes this claim. Respected theologians[1] from across denominations of the Christian church make this same assertion. Dr John Stott compares the priorities of evangelism and social action, asserting, 'Our first duty is to communicate the Gospel.'[2] He writes:

> The church's mission of sacrificial service includes both evangelistic and social action, so that normally the church does not have to choose between the two. But if the choice has to be made, then evangelism is primary.[3]

Many others agree with Stott. Distinguished Professor of Theology, Millard Erickson, notes that the one topic emphasised in both accounts of Jesus' last words to his disciples is evangelism.[4] Erickson expounds more on these passages[5] and concludes that Jesus appeared to regard evangelism as the very reason for the disciples' being.[6] Dr Derek Prince goes so far as speaking of the 'supreme purpose', the 'chief duty', the 'main responsibility', and the 'supreme task' of presenting the Gospel, claiming that every other duty and activity of the Church must be secondary and subsidiary.[7] Missionary statesman Oswald J. Smith commented on Mark 13:10, 'And the Gospel must first be preached in all the nations. Why did Jesus use the word "first"? He stated

'And the Gospel must first be preached in all the nations. Why did Jesus use the word "first"?' (Oswald J. Smith)

that the Gospel must first be proclaimed among the nations. He wanted to say that before we did anything else, we were to evangelise the world.'[8]

As I travel from church to conference, seminar to workshop, I often perceive a certain reaction in this point of my teaching. Sometimes it's as though there's an awakening, as if the truth and consequence of Jesus' words is just beginning to dawn. Others I see begin to bristle, and perhaps understandably so. After all, surely there is much preparation, much legwork to be done before we can stand before a person and proclaim the Gospel? Look at Jesus Himself. He met people at their point of need. He healed, He showed them love, friendship, acceptance. Surely this is the role of the Church?

All such assertions are valid, but again I turn to William Booth for a perspective on the balance between social action and saving souls. Booth questioned the worth in taking a man out of the slums, healing his body, giving him decent clothes, providing him a home in the country, then letting him die and go to Hell! No-one can argue that William Booth did not value social action. The legacy of the Salvation Army speaks for itself. However, Booth recognised the sheer folly of putting all one's zeal into comforting the body, whilst ignoring the eternal soul.

Dr K.P. Yohannan, Indian missionary to Asia, made similar observations regarding the Church's error in putting social programmes before Gospel proclamation. 'I am not trying to minimise the social and material needs of the Asian nations, but it is important to re-emphasise that Asia's basic problem is a spiritual one.'[9] Yohannan is definite in his insight into the war in the heavenlies (Eph. 6:12) and the way it is manifested here on earth.

He points out that when Western media focuses entirely on problems of hunger, showing pictures of starving children on television, it is difficult for people in the West not to get the false impression that hunger is the biggest problem. 'But what causes the hunger?' Yohannan asks.

> Asian Christians know the horrible conditions are only symptoms of the real problem – spiritual bondage. The single most important social reform that can be brought to Asia is the Gospel of Jesus Christ. The trouble with the social Gospel, even when it is clothed with religious garb and operating within Christian institutions, is that it seeks to fight what is basically spiritual warfare with weapons of the flesh. A spiritual battle fought with spiritual weapons will produce eternal victories. This is why we insist upon restoring a right balance to Gospel outreach. The accent must first and always be on evangelism and discipleship.[10]

Cynics might struggle with his emphasis on the spiritual realm. Surely it's common sense that the problem of hunger and poverty in this world is due to mismanagement of the earth's resources and exploitation of the poor and vulnerable? Where's the spiritual battle in that? Well surely the answer is obvious? Firstly, we only have to consider who and what is behind greed and drive for power in this world. But there are also far more obvious manifestations of the spiritual realm at work. Let's consider why one of India's own statesmen declared, 'India's problems will never cease until her religion changes.'

According to those who believe in reincarnation, the rat must be protected as a likely recipient for a reincarnated soul on its way up the ladder of spiritual evolution to Nirvana. The result of this is that 20 per cent of India's food grain every year is eaten or spoilt by rats. One survey in the wheat-growing district of Harpur in northern India revealed an average of ten rats per household. Large-scale efforts of extermination have been thwarted by religious outcry. Of the 1982 harvest of cereals in India (one of the smallest harvests in the last three decades), the 20 per cent loss from rats amounted to 26.8 million tons. Can you picture that amount of grain? Imagine a train of container cars, each car holding about 82 metric tons. The train would need to contain 327,000 cars and stretch 3,097 miles – that's longer than the distance between New York, on the east coast, and Los Angeles on the west coast of the USA! 3,097 miles of railway wagons full of wheat are lost every year while people are starving. Why? Because of a false religious idea. Atheists often throw out the question, 'How can a loving God allow disease and starvation?' Well, look at this case. It's not *God* allowing anything, it's people who are allowing fellow human beings to suffer in this way. There *is* food in the world, it's in that train. How many other spiritual runaway trains are there that we don't even know about?[11]

Similarly, India's so-called 'sacred cows' are allowed to roam free eating tons of grain, while nearby people go hungry. In 2007 the Hindu community around the world was in uproar when the UK health authority in South Wales wanted to kill Shambo the sacred bull because it was a carrier of tuberculosis. Hindus threatened to pour into the area to make a human chain to protect the cow. TB is a disease that is known to kill human beings, and yet there was a campaign to save this animal because of a religious belief. 'How can a loving God allow disease?' they ask. Not in this case. Yet again, this is an example where massive social problems – disease and starvation – can occur because religion is sustaining that situation.

No wonder, then, that Dr Yohannan speaks so strongly about the folly of putting social programmes before Gospel proclamation. Yohannan recognises that poverty, hunger, injustice and the like are symptoms. Their cause is wrong thinking and the root of wrong thinking is false religion. False religion is a spiritual problem and to fight a spiritual problem we must use spiritual weapons. The greatest and most powerful spiritual weapon Jesus has given us is the one true Gospel. Now I'm not saying that if we find a starving person, we proclaim the Gospel first and feed them later. Of course we should meet their bodily need first, just as Jesus did. In all circumstances we should be the 'Good Samaritan', no matter what the personal cost, but at some stage we must also be aware of that person's greater need. When the body is stable we must then progress to the state of the soul. The issue, though, is always how we see people. C.S. Lewis is extensively quoted as claiming: You don't *have* a soul. You *are* a Soul. You have a body. When we look through these lenses we begin to recognise why many scholars assert that the spreading of the Gospel should be our supreme priority and prime weapon. Let's not be mistaken here. The *purpose* of the Church is clear. Jesus said, '*"Love the Lord your God with all your heart and with all your soul and with all your mind and with all your strength." The second is this: "Love your neighbour as yourself." There is no commandment greater than these*' (Mark12:30–31). Yes, this is our purpose, both as individual human beings and as corporate Church. But if this is our *purpose* then our *priority* has to be to fully live out this 'love'.

> *You don't have a soul.*
> *You are a Soul.*
> *You have a body.*
> *(C.S. Lewis)*

> *As the Father has loved me, so have I loved you. Now remain in my love. If you obey my commands, you will remain in my love, just as I have obeyed my Father's commands and remain in his love. I have told you this so that my joy may be in you and that*

> *your joy may be complete. My command is this: Love each other as I have loved you. Greater love has no-one than this, that he lay down his life for his friends.* (John 15:9–13)

This then means firstly showing our love for God by obeying Jesus' command to 'Go . . . spread the good news' and secondly loving our neighbour by making as many attempts as possible to open up the way of eternal Salvation for them. Think of it this way: when we work for a company we prioritise our actions. At one time Coca Cola's mission statement was to put a bottle of Coca Cola on the table of every household in the Western world. If you work for the company your *purpose* is Coca Cola. But within your daily work life you have different priorities. For example, depending on your job, you might put dealing with customers before dealing with your junk email. When we look at the Christian life I would suggest that a biblical model dictates our purpose as 'to love God'. This will be done and demonstrated in many ways and have many different facets, but according to Scripture, and a whole host of authorities from across denominations, it quite clearly seems that our *priority* should be to preach the Gospel.

Dr Billy Graham summarises, 'I am convinced that if the Church went back to its main task of preaching the Gospel and getting people converted to Christ, it would have a far greater impact on the social, moral and psychological needs of men than any other thing it could possibly do.'[12]

If we want to change a nation, we must change the people who make up that nation. If we want to change the people who make up a nation, we must change their hearts. And if we want to change their hearts, we must plant the incorruptible seed of the Gospel in every individual. If our *purpose* is to love, then our *priority* must be to preach.

- In church and among the Christian community:

    What priority is given to evangelism?
    What else has become the priority?
    Why have other things gained priority above evangelism?

- What changes need to be made to establish evangelism as top priority:

    In your church?
    In your life?
    How do we keep these changes in place?

- Why do you think the Lord Jesus put such a strong emphasis on proclaiming the Gospel?

- Why have Christians put a stronger emphasis on other aspects of spiritual life such as social programmes, worship, etc.?

4

Words, Works and Effects

So how is our picture coming along? It's still very early in our discussion but I hope the previous few chapters have convinced you of our essential role as Christians in the world. We sit with a blank canvas before us, but hopefully now we're ready, willing and enthusiastic about picking up the brushes and getting stuck in.

I've talked a lot so far about 'The Gospel', 'Salvation' and I've even dropped in the word 'evangelism' every now and then. In doing so I may have fallen into the trap of assuming a lot about our understanding of such words and this in itself is where the Body of Christ can fall at the first hurdle. We need to be clear in our own minds what we mean by the 'Gospel', or the good news about Jesus Christ. Many of us can easily reel off the Lord's Prayer or other pieces of Christian liturgy, but when it comes to clearly explaining the Gospel – defining for another its truth, meaning and consequence – we begin to stumble and falter. When it comes to this Gospel I perceive many of us have become confused about the difference between three key concepts: 'works', 'effects' and 'words'.

We need to be clear in our own minds what we mean by the 'Gospel', or the good news about Jesus Christ.

When I gave my life to Christ on 3 May 1990 it was largely because God had used the willing spirit of Irish missionary Michael Wright to visit me in prison. Michael behaved as Jesus did. Just as Jesus dined with the tax collectors, passed time with the prostitutes and sought out the company of society's despised and rejected, so too Michael came into the stinking melting pot of depravity that was Nicosia Central Prison, just to offer the hand of friendship. I was a complete stranger to him. I was a violent, threatening and extremely rude individual who deserved nobody's compassion. Instead Michael showed me kindness and interest, going to significant lengths to ensure he was able to visit me every single week. Michael was committed to the 'works' of the Gospel. His actions couldn't help but soften my hardened spirit. Michael had always promised not to preach at me but the love of God so clearly shone through him that it was inevitable I would question his motivation. What made him tick? What was behind such compassion? Why did he believe a scumbag like me was worth the sacrificial giving of his time? When I eventually invited him to explain himself, Michael was able to speak to me about his relationship with God and tell me the truth of the Gospel. Using stories and anecdotes he was able to clearly lead me through the biblical truth of God's gift of Salvation. Michael opened up the 'words' of the Gospel and I was in no doubt as to how I must respond.

When I surrendered to God, my life changed in an instant. It was like the difference between night and day. I was delivered from all kinds of bondages and addictions. My despair, self-loathing and hatred of the world turned to hope, vision, passion and a longing to see my fellow cellmates released into the same new-found freedom. Though physically still in prison, I felt freer than I had ever been in my entire life. Everything about me changed – my character, my motivation, the way I looked at and responded to others . . . such was the 'effect' of the Gospel. Very soon I, too, was operating in the 'works' of the Gospel. I was trying to help others. The effect of the Gospel meant my eyes were opened to the dreadful suffering of my fellow inmates and I could act towards them in kindness. I could pray for them, support them and soon I could also offer some of them the 'words' of the Gospel, even in my limited understanding.

Perhaps you'll agree that it's easy to define the 'works' of the Gospel as the 'actions of Christians'. They might include visiting people in prison, feeding the hungry, giving money, time and expertise to support charities and missions; there might be teaching, discipling, running children's groups, visiting the elderly and those in need, praying, fasting, ministering to all kinds of needs . . .

Inevitably all these 'actions' have wonderful 'effects'. Many kinds of changes take place because of the Gospel: from darkness to light, from corruption to justice, bondage to liberty, blindness to sight, prison to freedom, hopelessness to hope . . .

But whilst the 'works' and the 'effects' of the Gospel are easy to identify and define, we have more of a struggle with the 'words'. Just what is the Gospel of Jesus Christ? What is this 'good news'? It doesn't help us that – unlike the Lord's Prayer – we can't pick out a particular passage in the Bible that encompasses the entirety of the message. When Jesus walked the earth He didn't need to explain, step-by-step, to the people He met 'how to become a Christian'. He was the living embodiment of the Living God (John 1) and just to be in His presence was to encounter the Christ revealed (although, of course, there were still those who chose to reject Him). To Peter, Andrew, James and John He simply said 'follow me' (Matt. 4). Nicodemus He told, 'You must be born again' (John 3). With the Samaritan woman at the well He spoke of living water and of worshipping God in spirit and in truth (John 4). The blind man at the pool He told to stop sinning (John 5:14) . . .

In everything Jesus said and taught, the Gospel was there – living, vibrant, dynamic and compelling – because He *was, is, became* and *delivered* the Gospel. Yet two thousand years on we are in the same position as the apostle Paul and Silas' jailer in Acts 16. Clearly moved by the Spirit of God and trembling at the revelation of His power through the earthquake, the jailer cries out to Paul and Silas, *'Sirs, what must I do to be saved?'* So here's the crux of our discussion. Ultimately, we need to be able to give the answer to that question, 'What must I do to be saved?' Return to Acts and we see Paul and Silas' answer couldn't be clearer. *'Believe in the Lord Jesus and you will be saved'* (Acts 16:31). Yet this passage goes on to tell us, *'Then they spoke the word of the Lord to him and to all the others in his house.'* After this we are told that the jailer and his household came to a point of baptism. So we might ask, 'What is that word?' What was the extended message they went on to hear, the one that brought them into understanding and embrace of their Salvation through Jesus Christ?

'What must I do to be saved?' (Acts 16:31)

This idea that there is a particular message that constitutes the good news of Jesus Christ becomes even clearer when we look at how the Bible refers to '*the* Gospel'. In Mark 16:15 (KJV) Jesus tells us to 'preach *the* Gospel'. In Galatians 1:6–9 Paul warns us to jealously guard *the* Gospel. In Romans 1:16 he reminds us that *the* Gospel is *'the power of God for Salvation'*. In all these areas Jesus and the apostle Paul are very clearly referring to the 'words' of

The Gospel is 'the power of God for Salvation'. (Rom. 1:16)

the Gospel, not the works or the effects. Of course, these three things are intrinsically linked. The words of the Gospel *have* effects. Mark makes this clear in chapter 16:20 when he records that, as a result of the disciples' preaching (i.e. speaking out the Gospel) *'the Lord worked with them and confirmed his word by the signs that accompanied it'.*

May we conclude, then, that when we're talking about '*the* Gospel' we're looking at something that communicates the *message*, the *words*, of Salvation?

How was that message communicated to you? Across denominations, Christians seem to agree that there are several key verses in Scripture that are helpful in explaining the message of Salvation. Paul's letter to the Romans especially focuses on this question of 'What must I do to be saved?' and the Gospel presentation known as *The Roman Road* incisively covers all the key points:

The Bad News

- The *Problem*: We have all sinned and fall short of the glory of God (we've all done things wrong) – Romans 3:23.
- The *Predicament*: We can't earn our way into Heaven. The Bible says no-one is good enough as the standard of Heaven is perfection and we all fall short – Romans 4:4–5.
- The *Penalty*: Sin leads to spiritual death and separation from God – Romans 5:12.

The Good News

- The *Provision*: God loves us so much that He sent Jesus to die to pay the 'penalty' that was rightfully ours – Romans 5:8.
- The *Pardon*: The free gift of God is eternal life through Jesus Christ our Lord – Romans 6:23.

- The *Process*: The way to receive the free gift is by confessing with your mouth that 'Jesus is Lord' and believing in your heart that God has raised Him from the dead – Romans 10:9–10.

Perhaps this kind of illustration is familiar? There are many ways of explaining the message of Salvation, or delivering the *words* of the Gospel. The heart of this book lies in being *able* to proclaim this wonderful Gospel, so we'll go on further to explore what constitutes its 'words' and how they might be delivered later. The crux of this chapter, however, is to emphasise the importance of recognising the difference between the works, the effects and the words of the Gospel. All three are vital in Christian witness, but alone they are of extremely diminished wealth. James' epistle is well known for its emphasis on the essentiality of backing up our words with 'works'. As he famously claims *'faith without deeds is dead'* (Jam. 2:26). This whole epistle is a call to action – if you believe, then *do*, wake up, act on it!

> *Do not merely listen to the word, and so deceive yourselves. Do what it says. Anyone who listens to the word but does not do what it says is like a man who looks at his face in the mirror and, after looking at himself, goes away and immediately forgets what he looks like. But the man who looks intently into the perfect law that gives freedom, and continues to do this, not forgetting what he has heard, but doing it – he will be blessed in what he does.* (Jas. 1:22–25)

Notice here how the 'word' inspires the action (the 'work'). The result, or the 'effect', is blessing.

Similarly, if we get too caught up in the 'effects' of the Gospel and neglect the work or the words we diminish the power of the Gospel for the Salvation of the world. To seek to further our relationship with God is commendable, indeed vital, but how often do I come across Christians so caught up in their own 'spiritual experience' that they neglect the lonely neighbour, the hungry child, the suffering friend and don't even consider the terrifying destiny of those who have never heard the Gospel message. How many 'evangelists' like me come off stage having preached their heart out but go home not noticing the opportunity with the man at the petrol station or the girl at the coffee kiosk. We seem to be living in an era of 'thrill seeking' Christianity, always looking for the next big move of the Holy Spirit, the next amazing happening. Yet we forget that the church is far more about the servant on hand and knee. Jesus told a number of stories warning of the consequences of such neglect. Matthew's report of His salt and light analogy makes clear our purpose in this world:

How often do I come across Christians so caught up in their own 'spiritual experience' that they neglect the lonely neighbour, the hungry child, the suffering friend and don't even consider the terrifying destiny of those who have never heard the Gospel message.

> *You are the light of the world. A city on a hill cannot be hidden. Neither do people light a lamp and put it under a bowl. Instead they put it on its stand, and it gives light to everyone in the house. In the same way, let your light shine before men, that they may see your good deeds and praise your Father in heaven.* (Matt. 5:14–16)

Interestingly this same report in Luke's account emphasises the destiny of the Gospel truths to become known as the disciples begin universal proclamation:

> *For there is nothing hidden that will not be disclosed, and nothing concealed that will not be known or brought out into the open. Therefore consider carefully how you listen. Whoever has will be given more; whoever does not have, even what he thinks he has will be taken from him.* (Luke 8:17–18)

Furthermore this verse is also cross-referenced with Matthew 25:29 where, using the parable of the talents, Jesus again warns of the severity of not sharing and multiplying our precious gift.

The word of God is described as *'living and active. Sharper that any double-edged sword'* (Heb. 4:12). Ultimately it is the 'words' of the Gospel that deliver the message that, in turn, delivers the hearer into the Kingdom. But still, just as works and effects are futile on their own, so, too, the words of the Gospel are rarely given a listening ear unless embedded in ground work – the hand of friendship, concern, practical care, prayer – and the passion, vision, hope, love, etc. that is the effect, the motivation, of the transforming Gospel. Jesus Himself usually met a felt need before opening His mouth to preach or impart wisdom. It was full awareness of this that inspired Francis of Assisi to urge his followers: 'Preach the Gospel at all times and when necessary use words.' Sadly these famous words of Francis have often been misused. Indeed the travesty is that, taken out of context, this quote has been held by some to suggest that Francis of Assisi was asserting the spoken word was unnecessary or should only be used as a last resort in spreading the Gospel. The effect is that millions have been discouraged from spreading

'Preach the Gospel at all times and when necessary use words.' Sadly these famous words of Francis of Assisi have often been misused.

the Gospel on the basis of this false teaching. Yet when Francis' words are read in true context – as they appeared in chapter 17 of his book *Rule of 1221* – it is clear that they were meant as teaching to emphasise the importance of good deeds to back up words. Francis of Assisi was no heretic and would never contradict the commands of the Lord Jesus to proclaim the Gospel. St Francis and his followers were staunch evangelists, emphatic in speaking out the Gospel, as we read in Dr Lewis Drummond's account:

> In the early manhood Francis searched for thrills and essential pleasures but after the disillusionment of an illness and a subsequent crisis he came to vital faith in Jesus Christ. Immediately he preached Christ in purity. Disciples soon began to gather about Francis and an order was established. The disciples fanned out all over Italy and into other parts of the Roman Empire to preach. The spirit of evangelism so gripped the disciples of the Franciscan order that they learned the languages of the nations and travelled throughout the empire sharing Christ.[1]

When Michael Wright visited me in prison he opened up what was literally going to be a 'life-saving' experience. Because of the 'effect' of the Gospel on his life, his 'work' brought me to a point of interest. What was his motivation and purpose? Why was he so bothered to visit someone like me? Just being Michael and doing what he did softened my spirit. It took time, it took patience and, no doubt, a great deal of prayer. But, when the time came, Michael was able to explain the 'words', the message of the Gospel in a way that cut straight to my heart. Michael

On hearing this message, delivered with passion, with love, with urgency, it became my greatest desire to turn and surrender my life to God.

simply shared his own story, but through it he was careful to explain exactly what God had done to forgive me, to save me, to bring me into a relationship with Him, to love me with such furious, relentless, sacrificial love that only a Father can know for His beloved Son. On hearing this message, delivered with passion, with love, with urgency, it became my greatest desire to turn and surrender my life to God.

- The Works of the Gospel = The Actions of Christians

  Might include:

    Feeding the hungry
    Clothing the naked
    Ministering to people's needs
    Visiting those in prison
    Giving money and time to support missions, churches, ministries and charities
    Praying, fasting and intercession
    Acts of kindness and charity
    Counselling, listening, caring, serving and loving
    Teaching and discipling

- The Effects of the Gospel = The results of the actions of Christians as God works through them

  Might include:

  - Evidence of the fruits of the spirit:
    - Love
    - Joy
    - Peace
    - Patience
    - Kindness
    - Goodness
    - Faithfulness
    - Gentleness
    - Self-control
  - Deliverance from bondages and addictions
  - Changed character and motivation
  - Change from corruption to justice
  - Change from unbelief to belief and faith
  - Healing of body and mind
  - Change from hopelessness to hope, passion and vision

- The Words of the Gospel = A carefully-crafted Salvation message

5 The Whole Truth

People love stories, especially those packed with action, intrigue, romance, mystery, the extraordinary. It seems we're naturally programmed to be interested in other people's stories, be they fact or fiction. No-one knew this more than Jesus, which is why time and again He used parables to deliver His message. He used stories of human interest and common ground. When He spoke of sowing seeds and the importance of the right conditions for nurturing crops, the majority of His hearers would immediately switch on. This is what they were about. It was the 'hot topic', it was what mattered to them. Jesus knew how to attract people and speak right into their hearts. His message was simple, colourful and engaging but never compromised.

I'm very aware that one of the reasons large crowds are drawn to my speaking events is because – apparently – I have a very interesting story. People flock in looking for action, for spectacle, for heroism and tragedy. Publicity usually focuses on my being sent alone at the age of four to China to be raised in the harsh tradition of martial science; on becoming a Kung Fu World Champion and an elite bodyguard, and on my prison experience. I wonder, would I draw as many people if the posters simply invited them to come and hear the story of Jesus Christ? I think we all know the answer. Sad though it might be, sometimes the best way to introduce the Gospel is presenting it through another story. I use my story as a vehicle to draw people in, to make that human connection, to capture the imagination. It's like a warm-up act to then present the most important message of all time, the best true story ever told – the Gospel.

When I present the Gospel in a public meeting I usually use a 'packaged' presentation of the kind we will examine in a later chapter. However, I recognise that it is actually the Gospel shared through my own story that people seem most naturally to assimilate. The Gospel message is not a packaged and set formula (though we will soon see the benefits of using a blueprint model). Whilst its truths remain unchanged, its presentation must always be fluid, according to who we are talking to. A pastor friend of mine explained, 'When I lived in London I mixed with City bankers, stockbrokers and business people. My communication with them was always couched in my own experience of secular business that my previous career afforded me. Because of this I was able to relate on their level and understand their concerns, struggles and debates. Since moving to a parish in an area of the country where people have very different aspirations and life experience, I now find that my approach has to completely change. Now I draw on my experience of saving up to buy my first old banger or my life as a dad struggling with the delights of young children and managing the school run. My message hasn't altered, but these days it's communicated in a very different way.'

Sharing personal experience is always a powerful way to present the Gospel, but we must also be very careful. I wonder how many times you've heard a testimony something like this:

> My life was a terrible mess, I'd really hit rock bottom. I had no-one to turn to and nowhere to go. One evening I found myself thinking about God. I didn't know anything about prayer, but I

> just said, 'God if you are there, please help me.' Suddenly I felt a warm glow all over. It was as though I was being loved for the first time. The next day was Sunday and I went to the church on the corner. The vicar there was preaching about the love of God and it was as though he was talking directly to me. After the sermon the old lady sitting next to me asked if she could pray for me. Again, as she prayed, I felt that wonderful warmth. I've been going to church every week since then and I've met some really great new friends.

This is a fabulous story and its emphasis on God's tangible love is powerful. It's very important that Christians testify in this way, continually talking about the way God moves in our lives. However, when it comes to communicating the important truths of the Gospel, this testimony is terribly incomplete. The story might be a great witness, but its telling should not be mistaken for 'evangelism'. Certainly it might move someone towards interest in God and church, but the hearer is only getting a small glimpse of the big picture – a picture that is vital to capture if one is to make a true decision to follow Christ. Again we come back to that same question: 'What is the Gospel? What is its message?' What are the 'words' of the Gospel? It seems to me that when we're talking about defining the Gospel we must make sure that our definition is as complete as possible. We must tell the whole story, paint the whole picture, otherwise our hearer is left piecing together fragments of truth and the message of Salvation is diluted or compromised (and that's assuming they are interested enough and inclined to do it!).

What is the Gospel? What is its message?

Through my work with Avanti Ministries I find myself spending a lot of time in airports. Have you ever thought about the process of making an aeroplane journey? Whether we're a frequent flyer or a first-timer there's always a certain protocol, a set of rules and procedures that we need to adhere to in order to get on the plane and arrive at our destination. We can take a number of different approaches – book online or through an agent, speed through to the first class lounge (if you're lucky enough) or stand in line with the rest of the economy passengers – but ultimately we all have to buy a ticket, pack our bags according to weight and other rules, arrive at the airport at a required time, check in with the correct airline, go through passport control and security, arrive on time at the departure lounge, more security, find the correct allotted seat on the plane, turn off the mobile phone, fasten the seatbelt, go through the pre-flight instructions . . . all before take-off.

What happens if I arrive at the airport without my passport? What happens if I get to the check-in desk only five minutes before departure time? What happens if I don't know I have to leave the duty-free shops and go to a departure lounge, or if for some reason I don't have an allotted seat on the plane? Well it's obvious, isn't it? The chances are I'm unlikely to get to my destination. Like with most things in life, there are things we need to know and understand, procedures we need to follow, rules we need to accept if we are to get to where we want to be. If our knowledge is incomplete, because we haven't been given the full picture, our journey may be seriously hampered.

When it comes to defining the Gospel message I believe there are at least four essential areas of content. If we are to communicate the very purpose of God sending His Son to the earth 2,000 years ago then we need look at:

- *Why* we must be saved
- *How* Jesus can save us
- *What* we must do to be saved
- The *cost* of discipleship.

These are all essential details of the Gospel message that we cannot afford to miss out.

Let's go back to the aeroplane scenario for a moment. Evangelist Ray Comfort uses a powerful analogy to communicate the importance of telling the whole story about why we must be saved:

> A stewardess goes up to a passenger on a plane and gives him a parachute. 'Here you are, sir,' she says with a smile, 'please put this on because it will improve your flight.' He looks at her a little bewildered. 'How will this improve my flight?' he asks politely. The stewardess just smiles and offers to help him put it on. Not wanting to cause offence the man accepts the parachute and straps it onto his back. After a little while he begins to feel very uncomfortable and squashed in his economy seat with the big package on his back. He also notices that people around him are looking and sniggering. He begins to regret ever putting the parachute on. Eventually he gets so fed up that he takes it off. 'I'll never put that on again,' he says feeling foolish and resentful.
>
> Another stewardess meanwhile goes to another passenger and gives him a parachute. 'Please put this on,' she says, 'because you're going to have to jump 25,000 ft.' The man puts the parachute on without any question. He, too, sits in his economy seat feeling hot and growing more uncomfortable. But that's not what's troubling him most. What's concerning him is the thought of jumping 25,000 ft. When he looks around he wonders why people are laughing at him. 'Why aren't they, too, wearing parachutes? Why are they laughing at me when they're going to have to jump without a parachute?' he asks himself in amazement.[1]

The difference between the two men is that one was told the whole truth and the other one wasn't. We're told in the New

Testament to *'clothe yourselves with the Lord Jesus Christ'* (Rom. 13:14). If we're not told the whole truth of why we are to 'put Christ on', then what is going to stop us taking Him off when we come across difficulties, when people mock us or when we grow too uncomfortable and wonder if it's all worthwhile?

How often when we talk to people about Christianity are we like the first stewardess? 'Come along to church, it will improve your life.' 'Come along to church, you'll make some great friends.' 'Come along to church, the music is fantastic.' But what is the truth? The truth is that everyone needs to be saved. Saved from what?

The Gospel of John reports Jesus giving a clear indication here of why we need to be saved:

> *The thief comes only to steal and kill and destroy; I have come that they may have life, and have it to the full.* (John 10:10)

Perhaps we only grasp the slightest essence of what this 'life to the full' can mean for us. We'll look at this a little more later on, but surely we need go no further than this wonderful promise of the Lord to convince ourselves of the *worth* of being 'saved'. Yet Jesus does go further. John 10 keeps our focus on Christ and the benefits of partaking in His goodness, yet elsewhere in Scripture there are sinister and severe warnings. I find it interesting that it is primarily Jesus Himself who speaks of 'Hell'. It is described as a place of utter darkness (Jude 1:3–13), a lake of fire (Rev. 20:11–15), a place of weeping and gnashing of teeth (Matt. 8:11–12), a place of eternal separation from the blessings of God, a prison, a place of torment (Luke 16:9–23) where the worm doesn't turn or die (Mark 9:42–48). These graphic images of punishment provoke many questions regarding whether the descriptions should be taken literally or symbolically. Personally I find no relief in debates either way. No matter how we analyse the concept of Hell, it surely appears a terror and trauma to be avoided at all cost.

There's never going to be a comfortable way of explaining this fundamental aspect of the Gospel. The Gospel isn't comfortable, but if we believe it is real we must be compelled to tell people, even if it appears they don't want to listen. Let's be clear here, what kind of loving God would send anyone to Hell? The answer is, 'He doesn't!' This is the very last thing He wants for any of His creation yet it appears this is what our free will affords us. We know that God has made the ultimate sacrifice because He *wants* all to enter into a relationship with Him and to share eternity in Heaven. He has made the way open to all. If we can grasp even the smallest inkling of His grace we recognise the extreme lengths to which God goes to ensure our eternity with Him, even for those who the world judges far from worthy. He makes it easy for us, but it seems that ultimately the choice is ours.

In 1982 in Louisiana, USA, there was a trial that held the attention of the entire nation. A man was condemned to die for the murder of a family. As he sat on death row, his lawyers frantically tried to secure a pardon for their client. They used every means within their grasp, but as the hour approached, all hope seemed to fade. Then, unexpectedly, at 11.30 p.m., only half an hour before he was to be executed, the Governor of Louisiana extended a full pardon to the man. The lawyers were overjoyed as they brought the news to their client. As they told him of his freedom, however, something happened that brought the nation to a near standstill. He refused the pardon. At precisely midnight, the man was strapped to an electric chair and within a few moments he was dead. Everyone was in shock. The man had a full pardon, yet chose to die anyway.

A fierce legal battle soon erupted. Was the man pardoned because the Governor offered the pardon? Or, was he pardoned only when he accepted the pardon? The highest court in the State was the arena for the debate. Ultimately it was decided that the pardon couldn't take effect until it had been accepted.

Isn't this an illustration of what God has done for us? He has given the pardon, but until we accept it, we are condemned to death. The choice is ours and it is this that we need to communicate in our discussion of the Gospel.

Back on the aeroplane we're all getting comfortable in our seats. We've stowed our hand luggage in the locker above, arranged our belongings, switched off our mobile phones and are happily sucking our way through the barley sugars whilst scanning the pages of the in-flight magazine. The cabin crew take their places and so begins the very familiar safety talk. The passengers are reduced to a respectful hush, but looking around, there's hardly anyone giving the cabin crew their undivided attention. Most are reading the paper, some secretly tap away on mobile phones, others survey the movie schedule. Meanwhile the aircrew are explaining how to fit life-saving oxygen masks.

I spot a lady in the opposite aisle. She stands out because she's so avidly paying attention. She's hanging on every instruction, as though her life depends on it. And really it could. On her lap is the safety instruction leaflet. It was the first thing she picked out and meticulously studied. I smile, knowingly – obviously a first-time flyer. Meanwhile everyone else listens with only half an ear. 'Oxygen, floor lighting, emergency exits, life rafts, yeah, yeah, pass me the sports section.'

Life-saving instruction? Then why are so many ignoring it? Isn't this the way with the Gospel? People don't want to hear. They don't want to hear that they must be saved. They don't want to know what they need to be saved from.

It's not necessarily that people don't believe the information to be important. They're not altogether ignoring the airline's safety protocol. Rather, frequent flyers tend to assume that they already know what they're being told. I think this is often the case with Christianity too. People in the West feel they already know enough. They don't need to listen and they certainly don't want to be confronted with the full story. After all, 'If I don't hear about death and eternity I won't have to deal with it. I can just carry on comfortably with what I'm doing.' Meanwhile, on the aeroplane the safety crew are going to every length to get their message across. There's the leaflet to read when you get in your seat, there are exit plans and escape routes signposted all over the aeroplane, there are announcements over the speaker system, a video presentation and a full-blown demonstration by the crew of how to give yourself the best chance of survival. So, as Christians, what do we do then when people don't want to hear? Do we give up at the first attempt out of politeness? Or, like the airline, do we keep trying to get their attention, hoping and praying that eventually, by some means the message will be taken on board?

Sara takes our boys swimming most Saturday mornings. One day, as she set off from home in the car, the fuel gauge showed her the tank was nearly empty. She worked out that she had enough miles left to be able to get to the swimming pool before filling up nearby to make the journey home. Unfortunately her plan didn't work. Before she could get to the petrol station the car ground to a halt on the busy dual carriageway. When the phone rang at home I could tell she was quite distressed. I quickly called a taxi and we sped off to her rescue, picking up a can of petrol on the way. As we turned onto the highway the traffic was backing up. We crawled along and eventually, up ahead, I could see Sara's car, blocking the road. A police car had also stopped and was trying to direct the traffic around the stranded vehicle. I felt dreadful for Sara. I knew she'd be terribly embarrassed and suspected the boys' usual back-seat squabbles might be adding to the tension.

The taxi driver did his best to push through the traffic, but other drivers were quickly becoming irate. Some beeped their horns and made angry signs at us as we tried to break our way through. The irony, of course, was that I had the solution to their problem. If only they would let me through I could get the petrol to Sara and all the traffic could be on its way. I tried to show them the petrol can, to make signs about what I was doing, but the other drivers didn't want to see, or hear. They simply looked straight ahead, pulling in close to the car in front refusing to let my taxi driver through. They didn't want to know. They had no idea that I could save them from their trouble.

Isn't this the way with the Gospel? As Christians we have the answer. We have the promise of eternity with God. We know – though our earthly minds can barely comprehend – what we are being spared because of our acceptance of the Lord Jesus Christ as our Saviour. We have the solution to the problem of death. Yet people don't want to know. They'd rather battle on through the traffic, focusing only on the way ahead, not even seeing the reality and root of the problem. They don't pause to consider that the driver trying to push through might have the petrol to solve the problem of the roadblock. Despite the struggle they choose to ignore the good news that there is a Saviour and battle on in their own way.

For Christians this is a problem of epic proportion. It is one that often leaves us feeling hopelessly deflated, almost to the point of wanting to give up. Walking through London's Covent Garden on a fine Saturday afternoon recently, I watched as people gathered around the street entertainers. Children clambered up on parents' shoulders and tourists strained to see above the crowds as each round of applause or whoop of laughter drew more people in anticipation of the unfolding spectacle. Magicians, musicians, mime artists . . . all demanded attention. Yet in the middle of the busiest thoroughfare, as people came up out of the underground station, a small group were trying to speak to passers-by. They were Christians, faithful servants who had given their Saturday afternoon to try to speak the message of Salvation to anyone prepared to listen. Most people paused only a moment then, realising what they were about, hurried on by. Some, out of politeness, took a tract (a small booklet explaining the Gospel) but a few metres away the street was littered with the discarded literature. Hardly any were prepared to stop and listen.

Jesus knew there would be many lost this way. They are the seeds that fall on the path and are eaten up by birds, the ones who can see and hear but never do so. Yet did the sower in Jesus' parable give up sowing? No. He knew that though he would lose seeds to the path, to rocky ground, to shallow soil, to thorns and weeds, there would be some that fell on good soil and ultimately these seeds would sprout and grow into strong, mature crops. The faithful people of Covent Garden are to be applauded louder than any street entertainer. They might be labelled 'religious nutters' by some, but I am sure that in their hearts these people are living out the New Testament mandate, taking to the crowds winsomely, with joy and expectancy of harvest. Despite the continual rejection, despite being ignored, humiliated, even abused, they held their ground, usually with a smile. Occasionally there would be one person interested in their message – one lost person willing to at least hear the good news of Salvation, one who might see the other side of eternity because of a few moments in Covent Garden one Saturday afternoon.

Thinking about this I'm reminded of the story of the boy and the stranded starfish. A young boy discovers thousands of starfish washed up on the beach, all drying out on the sand. He looks around at the hopeless creatures but quickly gets to work trying to toss them back into the sea. Tears stream down his face as he works tirelessly, gathering as many creatures as he can.

When his father catches up with him he tries to comfort him, 'Come on, leave them. There's nothing you can do. You'll never save them all.' But the child continues, now with more determination. 'I can save this one,' he says, picking up another failing life and throwing it back to safety, 'and this one . . . and this one . . . and this one.'

What are we being saved from? Imagine being caught in the horror of a gas chamber. You're crammed in with hundreds of panic-stricken others, all expecting the next few moments to bring deadly poison rushing into your bodies. You're standing by a door and you know that you can open that door and walk out to life and freedom.

How can you not tell them? How can you not offer them a chance at life? Dramatic, I know, but isn't this the truth of the Gospel? Aren't we talking about life and death?

The Gospel isn't about, 'Come to church, you'll make lots of friends,' or 'Try Christianity, it'll make you feel better,' or 'Jesus will give you peace . . .' No, the Gospel is about God's love for His creation, about us being loved by a God who lays Himself down to demonstrate that love; it's about turning in surrender to Him, as He so rightly deserves and it's about where you will spend eternity. These have to be the first crucial points in presenting the Gospel message.

- Why is it important for Christians to be able to clearly define and articulate the Gospel message?

- What are the barriers that make it so difficult for us to discuss the issue of eternity and the reality of Hell?

- Ponder each of these points and consider why and how they are essential areas of discussion when delivering the Gospel message:

  Why we must be saved
  How Jesus can save us
  What we must do to be saved
  The *cost* of discipleship

- What else might you add?

6

The Price of Freedom

In the previous chapter I introduced my belief that there are at least four essential areas of content when it comes to presenting a genuine Gospel message. Back there we focused on the necessity of telling people why we must be saved and acknowledged that this is a massive stumbling block in a misguided world that is happily ignorant of that fact. Yet to the hearer who actually listens, the next crucial piece of information they need is centred in the person of Jesus Christ, on God's redemption plan, on the good news that there is a boy on the beach waiting to throw our lifeless bodies back into the reviving water.

The issue of 'how Jesus can save us' could be content for a whole book – indeed it is! When we look at the Bible with New Testament eyes we see that everything points to that one man, sent down from His throne in Heaven, born in squalor, crucified a criminal and raised to life as Saviour of the world for all eternity.

There are many discussions to be had concerning the person of Jesus – evidence of His historical existence, whether He was more than just a 'good man' or a prophet, how He could be both man and God, the influence of His teaching on society's moral code etc. – but for the purpose of communicating the *Gospel*, our focus must remain on Jesus as 'Saviour', Jesus as the solution to the problem of death, the Jesus of John 3:16, God's beloved Son, given up to death, so that we may not die but have eternal life.

'I am the way and the truth and the life. No-one comes to the Father except through me.' (John 14:6)

The reality of Jesus as Saviour is what carves out the difference between Christianity and all other religions. Let's face it, when we're communicating God's redemption plan for His people we *have* to speak about Jesus, otherwise what stops our hearer from looking for God in Buddhism, Islam, Hinduism or any other form of religion or spirituality? Remember, Jesus is the one who said, '*I am the way and the truth and the life. No-one comes to the Father except through me*' (John. 14:6). Have you ever stopped to consider the weight of that statement and the consequent weight of responsibility we now have to keep the name of Jesus on our lips? To some, such a statement appears unfashionably exclusive, arrogant even, but then we need only look at Jesus on the cross to witness sheer humility, ultimate sacrifice and love beyond comprehension. Unlike any other religion or philosophy or 'way', our God is the only One who '*demonstrates his own love for us in this: While we were still sinners, Christ died for us*' (Romans 5:8) and '*Having cancelled the written code, with its regulations, that was against us and that stood opposed to us; he took it away, nailing it to the cross*' (Col. 2:14).

What other god says, 'It doesn't matter who you are, come to me. It doesn't matter what you've done, I can forgive you. It doesn't matter how much baggage you're carrying, I'll take your load. It doesn't matter that you've so many questions you can barely believe – *I am* the answer?' What other god says come just as you are? What other god demonstrates such mercy, such love, such compassion, tenderness and desperate longing for his people? And how does He do it? Through the sacrifice of the One closest to His heart, the One who cost Him the most – His own Son.

There was once a man who worked in a small town as the operator of a drawbridge on a river. A train track ran across the bridge and the operator's job was to keep the bridge up when no train was coming so that the boats could pass underneath. When a train approached he would blow the whistle and let down the bridge. One sunny Saturday morning the man brought his young son along to work with him. The boy loved to play along the riverbank, skimming stones on the water and spotting fish.

Shortly before noon, a passenger train was due to come through the area. The man began to make preparations to let the bridge down so the train could pass safely across the river. As he examined the bridge he noticed that a small child had somehow climbed over the guardrail next to the bridge and was playing at the very spot where the bridge would come down. As he looked closer, he realised with horror that the child was his son. In desperation he yelled out his son's name, but the sound of the approaching train drowned out his screams. He knew he had to make a quick decision. If he lowered the bridge now his son would die. But if he didn't, all the people on the train would die as the train plunged into the river. He barely had time to think.

Screaming in agony, the man thrust forward the lever to lower the bridge just as the train arrived. His son died instantly. As the train passed by the people just smiled and waved at the man in the control booth, with his head bowed low.

For any parent this is a dreadful scenario to even contemplate. Jesus himself said, *'Greater love has no-one than this, that he lay down his life for his friends'* (John 15:13). The truth is that when God ordained His own Son to lay His life down, it was for all humankind, even those who, like the passengers on the train, remained completely oblivious to the sacrifice made for them. Yet think about those passengers for a moment. How would they feel if they heard what the bridge operator had done? When they were resting at home with their families, their life still stretching out before them, would they not want to thank the bridge operator from the bottom of their heart? Would they not want to prostrate themselves before him in thanks for the sacrifice made so they could live? Would they not want to give him anything he asked in expression of gratitude or serve him in any way that might ease his agony? And how would the bridge operator feel about those who never said thank you, who never even acknowledged his momentous decision? Or what about those who never heard about what had happened that day? Would he regret saving them?

Isn't this the wretchedness of the Gospel that our Father and the Lord Jesus had to bear? What about the millions of people still going about their lives – still making that same train journey – without knowing what has been done to save them? How can we not tell them? Some might not even believe when they are told. Could any be so hard-hearted that they don't care? Surely there are many who would want to know, those who when they hear and understand what sacrifice has been made in their name, would want to meet the bridge operator and pay every respect to his son.

So we come back to this vital piece of information that must be communicated when we are giving the message – the words – of the Gospel. It is *impossible* to speak the Gospel without talking about Jesus Christ. What He did and what He is and what He offers us *is* the Gospel. Yet how often when we're asked about our faith might we start talking perhaps about the merits of our church or the good things God has given us. Sometimes we hesitate and falter when it comes to speaking the name of Jesus, as though it might offend or embarrass. Yet both Mark and Luke

It is impossible to speak the Gospel without talking about Jesus Christ.

record Jesus' severe warning. *'If anyone is ashamed of me and my words, the Son of Man will be ashamed of him . . .'* (Luke 9:26). We can't expect people to somehow stumble across Jesus. Though God can certainly move in divine power and reveal Himself to anyone at any time, He asks that we embrace the Great Commission, that we get stuck in, get our hands dirty, that we speak the name of Jesus and the entire Gospel message. When it comes to giving the Gospel, it's up to us to be clear in telling people the truth of how Jesus can save them.

Earlier I spoke of four essential areas of content to cover in the Gospel message. We've looked at 'Why we must be saved' and 'How Jesus can save us.' The next issue we must surely look to communicate is 'What we must do to be saved.' There's something of a spiritual dynamic to consider here. If you've got someone's ear and their interest and you've spoken to them about the fact that they must be saved and gone on to talk about Jesus' sacrificial act on the cross to save us, they are likely to be coming to a point of wanting to embrace these things for themselves. Just stop now to imagine the wider cosmic battle going on here. All over the spiritual realm there are alarm bells ringing. God and His angels are preparing for a momentous party, a glorious homecoming, but the devil isn't giving up that easily. He's busy realigning his attack, pulling together his army in a mighty advance of burning arrows of distraction and destruction.

God and His angels are preparing for a momentous party, a glorious homecoming, but the devil isn't giving up that easily.

So far we've only touched the surface concerning the devil's part in our story, but as we move on you'll see how he is very much at work, muddying the waters, distracting us from the truth and going to any length to prevent someone turning to Christ. He is always looking for any kind of gap so he can get a foothold in the door. If we fail to progress our discussion from our first two points about the Gospel, I believe we are allowing just that. We are making space for the devil to creep in and turn our hearer's attention. It is therefore imperative that when we speak of the necessity of being saved and of how Jesus can save us, we follow on with instruction on *what we must do to be saved.*

Obvious? Well, maybe, but when we've invested time in the notion of God's grace and the fact that Jesus died for us whilst we were sinners, it's easy to leave people with the opinion that because He did all the work, we don't have to. To accept that God loves us is a massive step for some people. To accept that Christ died for us is even bigger. How dreadful it would be then if we were to leave it at that and not see a friend saved because we have not told them the whole picture.

When someone stops us at the roadside and asks for directions our natural instinct (usually) is to be as helpful as possible. We give them as much information as we can, pointing out helpful landmarks and giving as thorough direction as we know. It would be rather remiss if, although familiar with the route, we only bother to tell them, 'turn around, go back down this road and you'll find it down there,' when we know only too well they're about to encounter an unmarked crossroads, several roundabouts and a complicated intersection.

When I'm travelling to a new place my assistant Sarah Griggs is always very careful to ensure I have good directions and a comprehensive itinerary. This often involves numerous taxis and train journeys, flights and extensive details about pick-up points and people to meet. Without such good directions I would inevitably lose my way and probably not even make it to my destination. Sarah's good work managing my itinerary is motivated by her concern for me and for our ministry. It demonstrates her commitment to see me fulfil my purpose and her tender care in making my travel as comfortable and stress-free as possible. In exactly the same way, we are responsible for giving good direction when it comes to our hearer making a response to the first two points we have communicated. We do it out of love and care for them and out of our passion to see them turning and surrendering their life to Christ.

I sometimes get a little concerned when people talk about giving their testimony or explaining the Gospel in 'one minute'. OK, so I get the idea, but realistically what are we saying about the Gospel and its importance if we are to reduce its communication to something so concise? Doing 'street' or any kind of 'cold approach' evangelism is always difficult. Sometimes a passer-by will be happy to stop and listen to what you've got to say, but most will hurry on, irritated by your interference. Often, out of politeness, some might say, 'OK, but I've only got one minute.' This is fine, you've got their attention, but to imagine you can effectively present the Gospel in just one minute is folly. Charles Spurgeon when asked to summarise his Christian faith in just a few words said, 'Jesus died for me.'[1] Dr J.I. Packer writes, 'In short, the Good News is just this, that God has executed His eternal intention of glorifying His Son by exalting Him as a great Saviour for great sinners . . .'[2] These statements are full of truth but, realistically, are such quick phrases alone going to convince the passer-by in the street? Whenever we're presented with this situation I would much rather support my brief announcement with the offer of a tract or a book that they can read for themselves later and digest when they've got more time and space.

If we deliver the Gospel out of love and care for a peron's Salvation, then we must do it carefully, being sure to tell them the whole route.

The point I'm trying to emphasise here is that if we deliver the Gospel out of love and care for a person's Salvation, then we must do it carefully, being sure to tell them the whole route. They need to know that in response to Jesus dying on the cross for them they must be willing to come under the control of God's Holy Spirit and turn away from the 'sinful nature', renouncing their old ways and surrendering their life to God's laws of right-eousness (Rom. 8:9–17).

Centuries ago in China a teacher practised a ritual that struck fear and trepidation in the hearts of his young students. He would summon one of his students to the front of the class and hold out both of his clenched fists, 'Are you brave enough to choose the one hand to reveal the gold coin,' he asked sternly. The students knew that if the boy chose correctly he would be allowed to keep the prize coin. But, if he chose the empty hand, the teacher would strike the boy with his clenched fist. 'Only the bravest will take the challenge. If this is not you, return to your seat,' the teacher always said. Most students, fearful of the beat-ing, refused to go any further and opted out of the challenge.

The ritual was carried out each day in the teacher's classroom. Because the students knew of the teacher's strength and skill as a fighter, they were afraid to make a choice. They knew that to be hit by him would result in serious suffering. On the rare occa-sion that a student would choose a hand, the teacher would ask, 'Are you sure?' As the student looked more closely at the teacher's hard fist and even harder scowl, he would invariably change his mind and hurry back to his seat. One day a boy named Chin was called to the front of the classroom. Chin's father had died in the wars five years before and his family was having trouble putting food on the table. Chin really needed the gold coin. The instructor held out his fists and Chin's classmates held their breath as Chin stood boldly before him. He studied both his teacher's hands for a long time. Finally he pointed to the teacher's left fist. 'Are you sure?' the instructor asked. Chin nodded bravely. 'Would you like to forget about your choice and return to your seat?' the instructor offered. Chin shook his head.

The instructor's fist shot out and struck Chin squarely in the face, knocking him to the floor. The class gasped, then there was silence. Chin lay on the floor looking up at his teacher in a daze. The teacher turned both fists over and revealed that each of them held a gold coin. 'You cannot expect anything for free,' he told the class. 'There is a price that comes with everything.' The teacher helped Chin to his feet, smiled and placed both gold coins in his hands. He never repeated the exercise again.

When we speak of God's Salvation we often find ourselves focusing on the truth of God's gift *freely* given. Certainly, God offers this gift whilst we are still sinners and before we ask for it. The gift has already been presented to us. However, the universal notion of 'you get nothing for free, there's a cost to everything' is not negated here. There was a massive cost to Salvation – God sacrificed His Son and Jesus gave up His heavenly throne, sacrificed His life with His Father and then His physical life when He died on the cross in agony. What greater expense could we imagine? We are also told in the book of Romans that because of our relationship with God as His children, we are His heirs:

> *Now if we are children, then we are heirs – heirs of God and co-heirs with Christ, if indeed we share in his sufferings in order that we may also share in his glory.* (Rom. 8:17)

Scripture is clear. What are we to conclude then? There most certainly is a 'cost' to following Jesus. The cost is giving Him our lives and also rolling up our sleeves and getting involved in fulfilling His purposes in the world. Why then do we so often fail to speak about this when we're trying to communicate the

Gospel? Jesus didn't. He spoke very clearly about the small gate and the narrow road that leads to life (Matt. 7:14); about losing life to gain it (Matt. 10:39); willingness to love Him more than those we love the most (Matt. 10:37) . . . In these and several other illustrations He calls for absolute commitment. Can we ever imagine what is really required in taking up our cross, denying ourselves and following Him (Mark 8:34)?

Perhaps our hesitance to speak about 'choice' and 'cost' stems from our general resistance to make decisions and commitments. Our society increasingly tells us 'You don't need to make a choice, you can have both,' or 'Give it a try, if you don't like it you can bring it back.' Like the students in the classroom, we are afraid of failure, afraid of pain and afraid of commitment. We are always afraid that it might cost us something, that it might hurt. Yet everything *does* have a cost and most good things require commitment. It's interesting how we weigh up the costs, even in our church lives. The call to the 7 a.m. prayer meeting is a tough one and just too painful and costly for many of us. Yet the Saturday night social? Usually a different matter, isn't it? And what about the way we spend our money. It's so easy to spend on ourselves, yet somehow it seems to cost us dearly to give 'sacrificially' to missions that might lead to the eternal Salvation of others.

To be a world champion you have to work hard. You have to practise. To play good football on Saturday morning you can't have a heavy drinking and clubbing session on Friday night. You have to show up for training, you have to keep fit and you have to commit to being available to play when your team has a match. These are the costs of partaking in the 'beautiful game'.

The Gospel does cost and it is not pain-free. It requires commitment and it can be – and often is – tough. To give the impression that when we commit to Christ, our life suddenly becomes like a bed of roses is a massive misconception and a danger to the truth. God's 'free gift' cost Him everything and it requires everything of us too. Oswald Chambers coined a beautiful phrase, 'My utmost for his highest . . . all that I am for all that He is,'[3] and it is with this commitment that we embrace the Gospel. It is also with this commitment that we should approach the Great Commission – sacrificially and without embarrassment to speak out the truth of the Gospel; the message that we must be saved, that Jesus can save us, but also that there is a choice to be made and there will be many costs.

God's 'free gift' cost Him everything and it requires everything of us too.

- Meditate on God and Jesus' sacrifice. We hear much today about soldiers sacrificing their lives for our freedom and this is commemorated in many special ways through ceremonies and services. But unless we have lost a loved one to war, many of us go about our daily business with little thought to what has been given so that we can be happily ignorant. What of the sacrifice of Christ? Is it that His actions are enough steps removed from your daily consciousness that you forget the horror of the cross and what He has done in your name?

- What if Jesus came today and made the same sacrifice for you?

- Do you respond differently to Him just because His death and resurrection happened more than 2,000 years ago in a far-away country?

- Think about the cost of the Gospel for you. Does it really cost your everyday life, your career, your family, your leisure time . . . ?

7

The Words of the Gospel

A carefully-crafted Salvation message? You might remember this is where I began – exploring exactly what we mean by the 'words' of the Gospel so that we might appropriately distinguish them from the 'works' and the 'effects' of the Gospel. This next chapter includes the actual 'words' that I often use in my meetings and also in some of the tracts we have produced for Avanti Ministries. Just as Jesus used stories, anecdotes and parables, so, too, this is an illustration to help communicate Salvation. It is by no means the only, or the best, way of communicating the good news of Jesus Christ and at the back of this book you'll find several other similar illustrations. As you read through the story, look out for the four biblical elements that embody a full and genuine Gospel message. (In Chapter 19 we will revisit this blueprint looking at the scriptures that underpin the message.)

The Gospel

The Bible describes God and Heaven as 'Holy'. 'Holy' just means 'perfect'. Now it's really important to understand that God can't let anything imperfect in to Heaven, otherwise it just wouldn't be Heaven.

The Bible also says that all of us have a body and a soul. At death, our body is either buried or cremated, but our soul –

which is the real you – lives on forever, either in Heaven or Hell.

From beginning to end the Bible cries out with God's love for us. Right back in Genesis we are told how God made us in His own image and breathed His own breath of life into us. The Old Testament is full of stories of God giving chance after chance to His beloved people, despite their continual betrayal, because He longed for relationship with them. Then comes the New Testament and God makes the ultimate move to draw all people to Him.

> *For God so loved the world that he gave his one and only Son, that whoever believes in him shall not perish but have eternal life.* (John 3:16)

We are left in little doubt that God wants us with Him in Heaven. Unfortunately, we've got a bit of a problem, because the Bible says that if we've broken just one of God's laws – for example if we've lied once, cheated once, hated once, just once (like we all have, let's be honest!) – then our soul becomes imperfect and we cannot enter Heaven.

Do you know anyone who has never broken any of God's laws? The answer is obviously 'no'. So here's our problem. All people have broken God's laws; therefore all people have imperfect souls. So, if at death your soul could either go to Heaven or Hell – but to get to Heaven you must have a perfect record, and none of us have one – then sadly all of us must be headed for Hell!

That might seem harsh, and you might ask the question, 'How could a loving God create a place like Hell, let alone send someone there?'

Let's look at it this way: think of someone you love very much. Now imagine that person is brutally murdered. The police catch the murderer and the murderer pleads guilty in court. But to your horror, the judge says, 'This is a really bad thing you've done. But, because I'm a loving judge, I'm just going to let you off.' You would be very angry wouldn't you? Why? Because you know that when someone has broken the law, they must be punished, otherwise there is no 'justice'. So you see Hell is not a *love* issue, it's a *justice* issue.

Let's consider three questions to help us understand why there's got to be this place called Hell.

Have you ever told a lie in your life?
The answer is surely 'yes', even if only a so-called 'white lie'. If you've lied once, then you're *guilty* of being a liar.

Have you ever taken anything that's not yours?
For example, have you ever gone to work late or left early and got paid for it? Have you ever used the boss's telephone or photocopier without asking permission, or knowingly taken an office pencil home? This is stealing of course. Most people have taken something that's not theirs, which makes them *guilty* of being a thief.

Now, do you think that God is going to let a bunch of thieving liars like us into Heaven? Not likely, because if He did, He would be the same as the unjust judge who failed to punish the murderer of the one you love. We can't have it both ways!

But many people say, 'Wait a minute, I'm a "good person" and there's a big difference between lying and stealing and murder – I've never murdered anyone!' But, what's interesting is the way Jesus redefined murder. He said that if you've hated a person in your heart, you've murdered them in your heart. So here's the last question:

Have you ever hated anyone?
The truth is that most people have felt anger or hatred in their heart towards another, which in God's eyes makes us *guilty* of murder!

So you see this is the bad news. For the sake of justice there has to be a place called Hell. But there is good news. This is where Jesus Christ comes in.

The most significant thing that distinguishes Jesus from everyone else is that He is perfect. Unlike us, He has not broken any of God's laws so He has a perfect record, a 'perfect soul'.

Picture the scene before Jesus came to earth 2,000 years ago. Jesus looked forward in time and saw you here today. He turned to God the Father, and asked Him, 'Father, I love the people in the world, and I don't want them to go to Hell for breaking Your laws. Is there a way for them to be forgiven?'

God the Father looked at His Son and said, 'Jesus, there is one way. Go to earth and become a human being, but live a perfect life. Then die a cruel death on a cross to take the punishment that the people in the world justly deserve for breaking My laws. When you do this, I can make it possible for them to be forgiven the day when they ask You to exchange their imperfect record for Your perfect record.'

Jesus willingly agreed, and 2,000 years ago He came to lay down His life for us, to pay the price for all of God's laws that we have broken – and there is no greater love than when someone lays down their life for another. But there is still something that we must do to be forgiven.

There are three major events in everyone's life. There's birth and death – ultimately we have no control over these – but the third major event is the day when we can ask Jesus to forgive us; when we ask Jesus to give us His perfect record.

There are some popular misconceptions about this, but in the Bible God's gift of forgiveness is clear. We're not forgiven by being christened or baptised, or confirmed; not even by praying occasionally or going to church, or by believing in God, or by trying to be good. These are all good things, but none of them give us forgiveness. Jesus said that there are two things that we must do to be forgiven. The first is that we must be willing to turn away from anything we know is wrong in our life and say sorry to Jesus. Notice the word 'willing'. There may be some things in your life that you feel powerless to give up in your own strength, like addictions, habits or other complicated things. That's OK, because God will help us, as long as we are willing and want to turn away from those things and say sorry.

The second thing we must do is surrender to Jesus. Surrender means this: if God made you, and the entire universe that surrounds you, don't you think He deserves to be the central person in your life? Surrendering to Jesus is when we acknowledge Him as our Saviour, and humble our lives to Him in service.

When you were born it is as though God opened a book about your life. Now bear in mind that God sees everything you do. He knows every attitude, every thought, every motive and every action. Every time we break just one of God's laws it's written down in that book. You can imagine that by the end of our lives there's a whole library written against us.

But when you turn and surrender to Jesus something incredible happens. It's like Jesus takes your book and stands at the top of a cliff and tears out all the pages, the whole record of the things you have done wrong, and He throws them into the deepest sea. He promises never to remember those things again.

Jesus then takes a copy of His perfect record, which you've asked Him to give you, and He places it inside the cover of your book with your name on the spine. That book is then stored like a precious library book in Heaven.

The miracle is that your book is not touched again between the point that you ask Jesus to forgive you and death – even though in that time you may make mistakes and break God's laws again. Becoming a Christian doesn't instantly make you perfect, nor does it mean you can say a quick prayer and return to your old ways. Remember, God forgave you 'for ever' when you asked for Jesus' perfect record. All he asks is that you surrender everything to him and let him daily refine you from your wrongdoing.

When you die, you will go before God on judgment day, and God will command His angels to get your book. He will look inside that book and say, 'This person was perfect!' You will probably say to Him, 'No I wasn't, I broke your laws. Don't I justly deserve to go to Hell?' And Jesus will say to you, 'For the sake of justice, you do deserve to go to Hell. You did break My laws, and some you broke many times. But you, My beautiful child, have My perfect record, which I gave to you when you turned and surrendered to Me on earth and I forgave you. Welcome to Heaven!'

That is why Jesus is so amazing. He made it possible for everyone in the world, regardless of what mistakes we have made, to be forgiven and to one day enter Heaven.

But say you never turned and surrendered. Think about what would happen. When you die, you will go before God at judgment, and God will say to you, 'I'm sorry, I can't let you enter Heaven. I have to send you to Hell. You never asked Me to forgive you. I loved you so much that I tried six ways to get through to you. First, my Son Jesus died on the cross to take your punishment. Second, someone explained to you in a simple way that you could be forgiven. Third, there were churches throughout the world – some were good and some I was ashamed of. You could have found the good ones. Fourth, I gave you a conscience, so you could tell right from wrong. Fifth, I created a world around you that was so awesome, how could you not wonder about Me? And finally, My Son rose from the dead to prove that I was God and that everything I said was true – but you still did nothing. I'm sorry I can't let you enter Heaven. I have to send you to Hell.'

So how about you? If you die tonight, where will *you* go?

Remember, to get to Heaven you need a perfect record, which you could never have unless you ask Jesus to give you His. To receive this free gift you only have to do two things: first, be *willing* to turn away from the wrong in your life and, secondly, *surrender* to Jesus. Unless you do these two things it's impossible to be forgiven and at death it's impossible to get to Heaven – which is so sad because this is the very reason Jesus died for you!

The beauty of this illustration is that it starts by addressing the logic of the inevitability of Hell and why a loving and almighty God has to allow a person to go there. I meet many different kinds of people around the world – from the poorest communities of Eastern Europe to the affluent of Singapore, from primary schools to high-flying business communities, from the very 'churched' to the most sceptical of unbelievers . . . amongst all of them I perceive one same stumbling block. 'But, Tony, I'm not a *bad* person. I love my family, I give to charity, I even go to church sometimes. I have the respect of my community, I work hard . . . and I've never broken the law.'

You might think that having spent two periods of my life in prison, the very last place I would want to visit is any kind of detention centre. And yet this is where my heart so naturally connects, for it is only amongst this community of convicted criminals that I find easy and open acceptance of the issue of sin. OK, so there will always be the inmates who protest their innocence but, on the whole, a convicted criminal is more honest about his or her capacity for sin than the majority of the 'free'. Like the repentant thief, crucified next to Jesus, they acknowledge that they are receiving the just reward for their crimes. They have nothing to be proud of and stand before Jesus in broken honesty, free from the delusion of being a 'good person'.

Notice then how our presentation of the Gospel is careful to focus on the biblical truth that *all* have sinned and fall short of the glory of God (Rom. 3:23). Your 'wrong-doing' might not be punishable by your country's justice system, but according to God's definition of sin, you break His laws many times over and are therefore subject to judgment. By approaching the issue of our separation from God in this way we can also address one of the most common debates about our 'all loving Father God'. The issue is simple – it is one of justice, not love, and by getting our hearer to understand for themselves the logic, necessity and, indeed, their own desire for justice, we are then free to move on towards Jesus' role in taking the punishment we deserve.

The presentation always makes good effort to blow away any misconceptions about what we must do to accept God's gift of Salvation. Down the centuries there have been many un-truths propagated by the Church that have people believing that being a Christian is to do with how good you are; whether or not you go to church; whether or not you've been christened or baptised, confirmed, been to confession or gone through any other church-based ceremony; whether you believe in God . . . of course there are elements of truth in all these things, but as they stand alone they are abominations against the truth. They are misguided notions that serve only to distract people from the reality of the whole Gospel. Our presentation here is clear that none of these things make us a Christian; that it is only when we surrender to Christ as our Lord and are willing – with His help – to turn away from our old sinful selves, that we are made righteous before God. These things should not be considered lightly.

Again, through my work in prisons and through my own life I see something of God's incredible capacity for grace. The issue of being *willing* to turn away from sin can barely be emphasised enough. For the man or woman deeply convicted of their complete inadequacy and facing the truth of their sinful state, nothing can touch them apart from the assurance of a great big God who reaches down into and through our weakness when we just dare to turn our face towards Him. Why else would God use a man like Paul – previously the feared and murderous Saul, a man who persecuted those who loved and served Him – to start the worldwide Church? Such irony! In his first letter to Timothy, Paul writes:

> *But I was given mercy so that in me, the worst of all sinners, Christ Jesus could show that he has patience without limit. His patience with me made me an example for those who would believe in him and have life for ever.* (1 Tim. 1:16, NCV)

If only I could communicate how I, too, share this heart-cry. My life story, documented in *Taming the Tiger*[1] and *Cry of the Tiger*,[2] tells something of the depth of my sin. How could I be forgiven? How could I even hope to have a 'perfect record'? How could God ever use a scumbag like me to spread His word to millions of others? Is this what is meant by the foolishness of God, I wonder? So, basking in the purifying light of my Father's immense and amazing grace, I have to join with my brother Paul and exclaim, *'To the King that rules for ever, who will never die, who cannot be seen, the only God, be honour and glory for ever and ever. Amen'* (1 Tim. 1:17, NCV).

Finally, notice how our Gospel presentation calls for a very personal response. It illustrates God's redemption plan and makes clear the offer of Salvation to one and all, but it remains very personal throughout. At the end it calls for a response. 'How about you? If you die tonight where will you go?' It's a question that people often don't want to face, but it is one that demands a choice. There is no grey area, no compromise. This is the reality of the Gospel that we as God's 'fellow-workers' must present with urgency, with reverential fear, with expectation and longing because *'now is the time of God's favour, now is the day of salvation*' (2 Cor. 6:2).

- What obstacles prevent Christians proclaiming the Gospel? Consider the cause and effect of this.

- How confident are you in proclaiming the Gospel message?

- What are the benefits of learning and using a 'packaged' outline of the Gospel?

- What are the downfalls of a 'packaged' approach?

8

The State of the World

Remember we set out looking at the distinction between the 'works', the 'effects' and the 'words' of the Gospel? When Christians focus their attention solely on the works of the Gospel but ignore Jesus' mandate (Matt. 28:19) to speak the words of the Gospel, what separates them from the good Buddhist, the good Muslim, the good Hindu or the good atheist? Nothing. There are many compassionate people in this world engaged in good works, helping others, fighting for justice, standing up for the weak and oppressed and making our planet a better place. They are to be highly applauded.

Equally, whilst as an evangelist, the 'words' of the Gospel will always be *my* emphasis and focus, without the 'works' of the Gospel they are nothing (except of course that we are promised in Isaiah 55:11 by the Lord Himself that His Word, *'will not return to me empty'*). Preaching the Gospel is a high calling, but it is completely negated if we fail to 'walk the talk', to live out our words. That's why Jesus told the story of the Good Samaritan. I love the way Jesus deliberately chose a Samaritan, a despised, unclean heretic of pagan blood, for His illustration. Talk about an unsubtle dig at the righteous, those who thought they were God's chosen elite because of their good upholding of the law. To imagine that we can preach God's Word, share His Gospel, but not engage in compassionate deeds for our fellow human beings is nothing short of hypocrisy and is detrimental to the Gospel we preach.

We need to be very alert to propaganda.

Words and works, continually soaked in prayer, are God's perfect balance. With this at the forefront of our understanding I now want to begin to unveil what I, and many others, perceive as the truth behind the current breakdown of the Great Commission.

There are four key features of which we need to be aware. Firstly, we need to be very alert to propaganda. Just because something is written by a Christian or is printed in a Christian publication it does not automatically make it true.

Sadly, I know from my own experience that there are many reports about successful Christian missions, people being saved all around the world, which are highly exaggerated or, in some cases, simply not true. How often do we hear about the millions of converts in China, or in Africa? I travel a great deal and I often find myself wondering, 'Where are these people? Surely if there were millions of genuine new and excited converts there should be a greater impact on our world than we are actually seeing?' A fellow evangelist friend, Rico Tice, echoed some of my own experience in the sad testimony of a recent visit to India. Having faithfully accepted an invitation to lead a mission there he arrived only to discover that his hosts had very little interest in his work but were very eager to accept the financial gift he inevitably had for them. Similarly, I led a team of Avanti Ministries evangelists to South Africa. Having heard of our global work this particular group issued an invitation but, as in many of the developing countries, it was clear that we would need to raise the funds to travel to the country, pay for our accommodation and facilitate some of the meetings. Avanti's mission is to spread the Gospel to all the world and we readily embrace this need to fund our endeavours. However, when we arrived in the country for this particular trip it soon became clear that the promised crowds of thousands expected at our meetings didn't actually exist. It was soon brought to our attention that there were also extra hidden costs which we were expected to meet on the spot. Furthermore, the safety of our team was compromised through the accommodation we were allocated and, meanwhile, the organisers of the 'mission' were driving around in spanking new Mercedes cars whilst claiming poverty! It was very sobering to get out and work amongst the slum areas of Khayelitsha, one of the largest townships in South Africa. There we saw real poverty and met many people who needed very real help. It is a sad fact that on the mission field we need to constantly be on our guard against corruption in the Church itself. Excuse the rant – especially when the majority of our work is among very genuine, desperately needy, exemplary missions (I should add, that we have returned to South Africa a number of times and worked with such people) – but the point I'm trying to illustrate is that some reports of people being saved around the world are made up for propaganda, fundraising and sometimes very selfish means. They are not necessarily genuine cases of souls being saved. The danger here is obvious. Ordinary Christians believe the work of evangelism is being done, that there are people out there engaged in the Great Commission and all is going well. This is a belief that has catastrophic implications and consequences.

There is also another side to this. I was on a mission in Finland when I received an alarming text message from one of our team back home in England. It called for urgent prayer concerning persecution of Christians in India. It reported that on that very night twenty churches had been burned and a declaration had been made that a further two hundred churches were to be targeted in the same way. Of course, my first reaction to such news is to cry out to God; however, earlier in the day I had a received an email. It had the same disturbing news, although the report of this atrocity was in Pakistan. Another email from another source showed again, the same story, now from Afghanistan. What is going on here? I wondered. What is the truth of this situation? Now don't get me wrong, I'm not saying that we should not respond to such stories in prayer. No prayer is ever wasted and God acts in our turning to Him, crying out for our persecuted brothers and sisters, no matter what the facts of the situation. But this kind of 'Chinese whispers' among the Christian community can be dangerous. They also highlight the need for spiritual discernment among Christians. The Internet, email and other forms of modern communication can be wonderful devices in effectively calling the global community to prayer but they can also serve to intimidate and spread fear – 'If this is the fate of missionaries, then surely we should pull our people out of such places or temper our evangelistic endeavours in such regions.'

There was once a great hound that set about chasing a mighty stag. He pursued the stag down through valleys and glens undeterred by the speed and agility of the magnificent animal until, suddenly, a fox caught his eye. The fox ran off in the opposite direction to the stag and the hound immediately followed, now pursuing the brightly coloured creature as it darted through the ferns. But what was that? A badger suddenly appeared in the undergrowth, instantly catching the hound's attention. The chase was on, the badger ploughing through the scrub with the hound in hot pursuit until, suddenly, a mouse scurried across the hound's path. In a flash the hound leapt at the tiny creature but the mouse was too quick. Determined not to let it get away, the hound pursued the mouse until it darted down a tiny mouse hole . . . and there the great hound was left, staring at the mouse hole.

Just like the hound, we are so easily distracted. Though we are commissioned to chase the great stag, many other, smaller things completely turn our attention. Barely realising, we take our eyes off the mighty prize we should be pursuing and end up chasing something far less valuable. A similar parable is of the young boy who is desperate to see the circus. He comes from a poor family and knows his parents will never afford a ticket when the circus comes to town, so he sets about working to earn the money for himself. He does all sorts of odd jobs, every day gazing longingly at the posters and anticipating the day when the circus will come. By the time the day arrives he has earned enough money and can barely contain his excitement as he hears the rumble of the trucks pulling into the town. Within moments there's music, laughter, clapping and singing as people file into the streets to welcome the clowns, acrobats, dancers and circus trucks, all led by a marching band. Getting caught up in the crowd the boy squeals with excitement and claps and sings as he pushes himself to the front and gives his money to one of the clowns. Dashing home he is full of joy as he bursts in through the front door, 'Mum, Dad, I saw it! I saw the circus and it's amazing!' His parents looked at each other in confusion. Then, realising, what had happened his father ruffled his son's hair fondly. 'No, son,' he said, 'you didn't see the circus, what you saw was the parade.'

How often are we so caught up in the parade that we lose sight of the main event? As Christians we can be so enamoured with stories of great happenings – works of the Holy Spirit here, revival there, mass healings in that church, raising of the dead in another fellowship. Sometimes we dedicate our time and money to travel across the world in

How often are we so caught up in the parade that we lose sight of the main event?

pursuit of a piece of the action, in Toronto, in Pensacola, in South Africa . . . when all the time the mighty stag waits for us at home. The Great Commission is given to all who believe in the Lord Jesus Christ. It is a commission for us all, right where we are, every day and right now. This is the main event, so let's be careful of distraction.

Of course there are many reports of people being saved around the world that are completely genuine, and we need to rejoice in this. But here is the second point about the state of world evangelism today. When we hear these stories, how do we react? Do we really respond to the reality of what it means when a person – even just one person – gives their life to Christ.

I was on a mission in Australia on 25 April 2006 when news came through of an earth tremor in Beaconsfield, Northern Tasmania. On that fateful day three miners, Larry Knight, Todd Russell and Brant Webb, ended up hopelessly trapped inside a gold mine. The nation was transfixed as television news reported that the men were entombed almost 1km underground. Larry was crushed to death. Todd, almost completely buried, was struggling to cling onto life, as was Brant, buried up to his armpits. In one of Australia's greatest ever rescue missions, Todd and Brant were finally saved from their horrific ordeal some fourteen days later on 9 May. Everyone rejoiced. Journalists reported that family and friends celebrated with a well-deserved drink.

When telling the story of the lost sheep, Jesus said that there is more joy in Heaven over one sinner that repents than over ninety righteous people that do not need to. If Heaven parties when a soul is saved, how is it that we as Christians can be so apathetic when we hear such news? Where is the rejoicing, where is the celebration? A fellow human being, a friend, has just been saved from the grip of Hell and yet so often I perceive that many of us fail to grasp the momentous significance of such wonderful news. We go about our daily business as if we had just been told there's a sale on at the local supermarket or we'll be having steak for dinner! Please, put this book down a moment and think. How do you react? What does it say about your own Salvation if you barely release an expression of joy when you hear of entombed people saved and released?

Thirdly, we need to recognise that there are some great evangelists in our local churches today who we must rejoice in and support. In this sense we are talking of 'Ephesians 4:11' evangelists, those particularly gifted and called to work in spreading the Gospel and training others to do so. The difficultly is that so often church leaders and congregations fail to support and encourage such people. Forgive me a moment of generalisation, but I can't help notice certain shared character traits can often be observed in such evangelists. We tend to be highly driven, highly motivated, passionate and imaginative in our zeal to propagate the Gospel. However, the flip side of these things is we can appear impetuous, outspoken, possibly arrogant and too self-assured. We don't like being held back by church politics, administration and codes of conduct and we're too busy trying to get on with the job to be team players or think of the consequences of our actions. I'm generalising terribly of course, but I suspect this is ringing a few bells with some people. The sad fact is that often the local church doesn't recognise the need to support, channel, encourage and teach such people without quashing their enthusiasm, pouring cold water on their passion, halting their go-getting approach and stifling their God-given gift.

I knew the moment I met Neil[1] that he was a gifted evangelist. I also knew he would be a whole heap of trouble. He came to Avanti as a very new Christian. As a man he had more baggage than you care to know about, but as a newly-saved soul he had an infectious radiance and he simply couldn't help but tell anyone and everyone what Jesus had done for him. He had not been part of our team very long when I started to get complaints and queries about him – he was too mouthy, insensitive, lacking in compassion, too much of a loose cannon and sometimes spouting questionable theology. The rest of the team were right to be concerned, but one of the aims of Avanti is to train and nurture anyone who is willing to lay himself down for the Gospel, no matter how difficult that might turn out to be. Neil remains a tough case, with many personal issues to contend with, but God's grace continues to refine him and few men are more effective in bringing hardened alcoholics, the battered, the beaten, the broken, the bereaved and the dropouts to the foot of the cross. But what, I wonder, would happen to my friend if his gift was not recognised, if his fellow church members saw only his failings and, nervous of his blunt and outspoken zeal, relegated him to the coffee rota or some other less visible role where he couldn't be an embarrassment? The chances are he would soon be discouraged, as beaten by the church as by life. Finally he would abandon his gifting. Meanwhile the Church would lose a fantastic potential evangelist and many lost people would never hear God's plan of Salvation.

My point? We must recognise the gifted evangelists amongst us. If we fully embrace the unity celebrated in Psalm 133 and preached in Ephesians 4 we cannot allow church history to repeat itself by dispelling evangelists simply because we don't know how to handle them. As with all the gifts, leaders need to ensure that our evangelists are working to their full capacity, that we don't try to chop off their legs just because we don't like how fast they're running. Ultimately, when our evangelists are at work with the full support of their congregations, we should prayerfully expect souls to be added to the Kingdom day-by-day, week-by-week.

The fourth observation about world evangelism today concerns the fact that most Christians in their everyday activities no

When did you last speak the Gospel to someone? Earlier today? Yesterday? Last week? Ever . . .?

longer proclaim the full Gospel to non-Christians. For evidence of this you probably need look no further than your own backyard. When did you last speak the Gospel to someone? Earlier today? Yesterday? Last week? Ever . . . ? I often open my training meetings by getting people to put up their hand if they have shared the Gospel within the last twenty-four hours. In a meeting of 800 people recently only four people could raise a hand, and one of them was me! This is a very common percentage, and bear in mind that this is a crowd of people who have chosen to attend a meeting on evangelism training, so we might assume they have a good level of enthusiasm for the Great Commission! If it's a long time since you shared the Gospel with anyone I will assure you, you are not alone, but I will not say, 'Don't worry'! It has been suggested that today in the West 98 per cent of believers don't proclaim the Gospel. No wonder Billy Graham coined the phrase 'the unseeded generation'[2] to describe those who have never heard the good news of Jesus Christ. Why is this the case? Again I come back to perceived ignorance of the Great Commission. Remember, if you will, this is called the 'great' commission, not the 'miniscule', the 'optional', the 'suggested' or the 'if you can be bothered' commission. Yet in 1994 the Barna Research group found that among American adults who said they were born again, 75 per cent said they couldn't even define the Great Commission. As a result of their research the Barna Institute came to a definite conclusion regarding the state of the Great Commission asserting, 'How ironic that during this period of swelling need for the proclamation of the Gospel that the ranks of the messengers have dissipated to anaemic proportions.'[3]

We only need to look at a few statistics to wake up to the reality of people's interest in Christianity. The 2001 National Census in the UK suggested a healthy 71 per cent of people claim to be Christian (this same pole recorded 390,000 people claiming 'Jedi Knight' as their religion – a group that was larger than the Sikh, Jewish and Buddhist population!). However, dig a bit deeper and it becomes apparent just how many people in the UK are sincere or understanding in their claim to be Christian. Whilst a large proportion claim to be Christian, a massive 66 per cent of this group also say they have no actual connection to any church or even religion.[4] The Christian Research Group's fourth English church census reported that half a million people stopped attending church on Sunday between 1998 and 2005.[5] Similarly, the *Daily Telegraph*'s religious affairs correspondent Jonathan Petre says, 'While 1,000 new people are joining a church each week, 2,500 are leaving.'[6] Moreover a Tearfund 2007 report claims, '59 per cent of people never go to church and most of them are unreceptive and closed to attending church; church-going is simply not on their agenda.'[7]

Challenging, isn't it?

But if we, as Christians, struggle to define the Great Commission, how are we meant to be actively taking part in it? Let's consider the four elements that make up this mighty appointment. Jesus was very clear when he said:

> Go into all the world
> Preach the Gospel
> Baptise those who are saved
> Disciple those who are baptised

Why do we need to define the Great Commission? Imagine we gather all the Olympic athletes in the stadium then someone just shouts, 'Go!' What would happen? There would be utter confusion. 'What are we meant to be doing? Who are we meant to be doing it with? Where are we supposed to be? When will we end? Where do we get our refreshments?' If the athletes don't have guidance and know exactly what they're meant to be doing, how will they do it? It's the same with us. If, as Christians, we are uncertain, unconvinced and not at all confident of the Great Commission, then how can we take part in it. And if we're not taking part in it, then what are we doing? What is on the radar of our Christianity? We go to church, we do good works, we pray, we sponsor children, we worship, we have family time, make offerings, meditate on the Word of God . . . all great things, but what is at the centre of our radar? Is it a cup of tea and a muffin after church service on Sunday, or is it that great thing Jesus has asked us to do? What has happened to going into the world and proclaiming the Gospel? Why are only 2 per cent of believers actually doing it? We have a very serious problem here, and we need to come up with some very serious answers.

An old friend of mine once had a very disturbing vision of the Niagara Falls. In his vision the water was made up of people. There were millions of good people all swimming along, living their lives, caring for their family, keeping their bank accounts healthy, working hard, until suddenly they come to the point of death. This is when they fell over the mighty ravine, straight down into the depths . . . of Hell. I remember my friend relating this vision to me. I shuddered at the thought. 'But it didn't end there,' he told me. 'Back up on the river there were the Christians. They were in the nice still waters where all was pleasant. They were singing hymns and worship songs, enjoying fellowship together, praying and supporting one another and sometimes interacting with the other people on the periphery of the still water, but what I noticed was that they all had their backs to the falls. They were completely ignorant and happily oblivious to the millions of people tipping over the edge.'

When it comes to the collapse of the Great Commission today the evidence is unquestionable. It's been said that only 2 per cent of Christians actively proclaim the Gospel. But forget percentages and statistics and evidence. If the Great Commission has collapsed it is because it has little place in the hearts of those who claim to love the Lord Jesus, the One who gave it. What about you? Do you truly believe it? If Jesus Christ were to appear to you now and ask you in person to go into the world and proclaim the Gospel, baptise those who are saved and disciple those who are baptised, it is highly likely you'd say, 'Yes, Lord. With your help I will. I'll go and I'll go right now.' Let me remind you, He has and He does, so what's stopping you?

The story of Charles Blondin paints a real-life picture of faith in action. Blondin's greatest fame came in June 1859 when he attempted to become the first person to cross a tightrope stretched over a quarter of a mile across the mighty Niagara Falls. He actually walked across, 160 feet above the falls, several times, each time with a different daring feat – once in a sack, on stilts, on a bicycle, in the dark, and once he even carried a stove and cooked an omelet. The crowd 'Oooohed!' and 'Aaaaahed!' as Blondin carefully walked across, one dangerous step after another, blindfolded and pushing a wheelbarrow.

Upon reaching the other side, the crowd's applause was louder than the roar of the falls! Blondin suddenly stopped and addressed his audience: 'Do you believe I can carry a person across in this wheelbarrow?' The crowd enthusiastically shouted, 'Yes, yes, yes. You are the greatest tightrope walker in the world. You can do anything!'

'OK,' said Blondin, 'Get in the wheelbarrow . . .'

The Blondin story goes that no-one did![8]

- How confident are you in the Great Commission?

  Do you *know* it?
  Do you *believe* it?

- How convinced are *you* of the Gospel?

- Have you shared the Gospel with anyone in the last:

  24 hours?
  Week?
  Month?
  Ever?

- Think about whether there have been any opportunities you might have taken and why you let them pass by.

9

Itchy Ears

James Cameron's 1998 fictional romantic film depiction of the doomed *Titanic* captured the hearts of millions. Even the few who have never seen the multi-award winning movie recognise *that* certain scene and *that* certain song. Breaking all box office records, it frames a historical event in a compelling love story, thoroughly engaging the audience in what we know to be a real-life tragedy. Whilst many flocked to the cinemas in admiration of DiCaprio and Winslett, they left with their eyes opened to the utter horror of that ill-fated 1912 voyage. *RMS Titanic* was designed by highly experienced engineers using the most advanced technology of the time. Such faith undergirded its build that it is said lifeboats were attached more for decoration than for the purpose of saving lives in a disaster. Indeed, the *Titanic* was described as 'unsinkable'. Yet shortly before midnight, four days into the ship's maiden voyage, *Titanic* hit an iceberg and the 'unthinkable' happened. The sinking resulted in the death of 1,517 of the 2,223 people on board. There were simply not enough lifeboats and the film depicts all too graphically the dreadful scenes of people thrashing around in the icy water, grabbing hold of pieces of floating wood or anything that would keep them afloat a little longer. Who can forget those catastrophic scenes? Jack and Rose's final moments before he is overcome by hypothermia, the Irish mother trying to tell her children a story as their cabin fills with water, another mother soothing her children to sleep, knowing they are doomed. Few can watch this film with a dry eye or without a stab of outrage at the injustice of a system that saved first class passengers, leaving other women, children and the lower classes to their doom.

Are we outraged? Are our souls desperate to scream at the injustice of those who put their own comfort before the lives of others? I don't think it's a step too far to see some comparison here with the world and the Church. Aren't we all thrashing about grasping at fragments that we believe will give us security – our bank accounts, our respectability, our good job, our nice home . . . And don't we, as Christians, know the real truth about what alone can ultimately save us? Don't we have the lifeboats? Yes, we have the solution to the curse of death. Then why are we so reluctant to share? Is it that, like the upper class bigots of the *Titanic*, we don't want the personal discomfort of sharing our life raft? Is it that our own faith is, indeed, 'shipwrecked' (1 Timothy 1:19)? Remember those in the film who refused to cram their precious vessel full because it might be 'uncomfortable' for them. Yet what did it mean for those who didn't get on a boat? We know the answer, don't we?

In the previous chapter we touched on the state of evangelism in the West. Church attendance is in steep decline as a direct result of such a small percentage of Christians actually proclaiming the Gospel. It's also easy to understand when statistics and media reports show a decline in belief in God among the general population. There's no question about this, but the debate to be had is 'Why?' The Church may be in decline, but is *not* dead. There *are* 'real', free Christians in our communities, people who believe the Gospel, loving people who would want to see others saved. So what is going so wrong? If the church is in decline it is not a coincidence, it is a *consequence* – of blindness, reluctance or just plain ignorance – of not proclaiming the Gospel.

There is a particular church group in my home town that does a phenomenal job reaching out to our community through a feeding programme. Like any town or city in Britain there is a significant problem of homelessness and the Christians in this church serve these people by making nutritious soup and taking it out to those in need. These people see Christ at work through these Christians and, as such, are ripe and ready to give their lives to Jesus. When I first heard of this programme I was very excited and joined a group of others who wanted to go along and see them in action. It was wonderful to see so many being fed and responding to the warmth and love of the Christians who were serving them. There was the opportunity to talk and sometimes even pray and, on some occasions, Christians handed out pieces of literature. This was fantastic to witness, but I was curious about one thing. The church people talked about this work as 'evangelism', but when I asked about how and when they actually proclaimed the Gospel there was confusion between us. 'No, this *is* how we evangelise,' they told me. 'We just make soup and give it to whoever is hungry. We don't do much proclaiming the Gospel, we thought *you* did that.' To which I might have replied, 'No, we're not doing it because we thought *you* were doing it.'

Do you see my point? There is a tendency in church to assume that someone else is doing it. There is also, I perceive, very little accountability when it comes to proclamation of the Gospel. Many of us are accountable in other areas of our Christian life, at least on some level – we tithe, we turn up to church on time, we wear appropriate clothing, we sing the right songs, we're in the 'right' relationships – but in

In terms of spreading the Gospel in our daily lives, no-one holds us accountable.

terms of spreading the Gospel in our daily lives, no-one holds us accountable. When did your pastor, priest, vicar or elder last encouragingly ask you about how much and to whom you share the Gospel? Most of our leaders would have no idea whether people in their congregations are proclaiming the Gospel or not. Imagine how our approach to the Great Commission would change if we had a 'Great Commission offering' in the same way as we handle our tithing and monetary giving. What if, every week at church, a basket was passed round to collect pieces of paper each with the number of people we'd shared the Gospel with that week? There needn't be any pressure in the exercise. Maybe you'd be able to write tens, or hundreds, or even thousands of people (imagine your capacity through email, Facebook, Twitter, etc.). Maybe there would just be one. And one would be worth celebrating! What if the basket simply passes you by week after week because you have nothing to offer? Might it prompt you a little? Might it encourage you to offer just one small sacrifice, to maybe just hand over one tract to someone so that you could drop a piece of paper in the basket? How much more pleasing might that be to God than our monetary offerings? For the answer to this, think only on how many references there are in the Bible to monetary tithing in comparison to those related to the Great Commission.

Don't get me wrong, I'm not saying that in our efforts to proclaim the Gospel we should necessarily be answerable to our church leaders, but I simply want to highlight the fact that because we are not accountable (not even to ourselves, since for many of us it is not even on our agenda) the lack of activity when it comes to Great Commission goes largely unnoticed.

The significance of this is obvious but there are other consequences that are just as concerning. Perhaps one of the most serious is the increase in the spread of false gospels. The Bible tells us that God has *'set eternity in the hearts of all men; yet they cannot fathom what God has done from beginning to end'* (Ecc. 3:11). Certainly most people, at least at some point in their life, ponder eternity and the meaning of life. The notion that we are 'spiritual' as well as 'physical' beings is acceptable to most. Everyone appears to be looking for something and for a majority in the West this leads to the pursuit of 'happiness' through wealth, power and 'success'. Yet we need turn only to those who have their fill of wealth, power and kudos to find them unfulfilled and still searching.

Pop singer Madonna told a Los Angeles press conference, 'In these past few years of intense study of the Kabbalah I have felt an ever growing presence of the one, true light inside of me. I was pleased to discover recently that this presence is the higher being's way of letting me know I'm the Messiah, the chosen one of Kabbalah.' Dr Phil Abramowitz of the Task Force on Missionaries and Cults, a project of the Jewish Community Relations Council of New York, quite sensibly comments, '. . . it takes this whole Kabbalah thing out of the realm of Hollywood fad and places it firmly on the turf of first class la la land.'[1] I'm sure many of us smugly agree with Dr Abramowitz, and yet through her powerful celebrity status and funding capacity, many more of the Hollywood fraternity have turned their attention to Madonna's 'gospel'; just as others seek truth and fulfilment in the likes of Scientology thanks to 'authoritative' celebrity endorsement.

Such examples might seem extreme but it's probably fair to say that even in our everyday toils – our 'normal lives' in our streets, villages, towns, factories, offices and schools – most have some kind of God awareness and are searching for the spiritual. Where do they look? In generations gone by people in the West at least had some kind of grounding in the teachings of Christ. They might have been blighted by tradition, ritual and fear, but there are many testimonies of people who, at a point of true searching in later life called out to the God of their Sunday school days and found Him as their Saviour and friend. Of course there are many debates to be had here about the place of Christianity in modern society, but the question to really consider is what happens when non-Christians don't hear the true Gospel? When they don't hear the Gospel from Christians there is an innate tendency, albeit unconsciously, to make up their own gospel (a lifestyle, a feel-good, life-enhancing discipline) which, in turn, they start evangelising. More tragic still, some churches have been unwittingly influenced by such false gospels. There is a grave danger that ideas that have originated and circulated in the non-Christian community are adopted into our churches and accepted as though they are the true Gospel. Jesus knew of this hazard which I'm sure is why He was careful to say, 'Go into all the world and preach *the* good news . . .' He's not talking about just any old good news here. He has a specific message in mind and that message is clear and uncompromising throughout Scripture. The apostle Paul also recognised our inherent need for teaching that satisfies and endorses our own desires. In his second letter to Timothy, chapter 4:2–4 he gives the charge:

> *Preach the Word; be prepared in season and out of season; correct, rebuke and encourage – with great patience and careful instruction. For the time will come when men will not put up with sound doctrine. Instead, to suit their own desires, they will gather around them a great number of teachers to say what their itching ears want to hear. They will turn their ears away from the truth and turn aside to myths.*

So what are some of the false gospels that seem to prevail in our society and some of our churches? There are a remarkable number of people who subscribe to a liberal gospel that claims that everyone, unless they declare themselves Muslim or Hindu,

Buddhist or any other religion, is a Christian. This closely links with the belief that 'we are born in a Christian country, therefore we are Christian'. How many people when filling in a hospital admissions form declare themselves 'Church of England'? Similarly, some have been christened as a baby or gone through confirmation or first communion or some other kind of church ritual and therefore believe themselves to be Christians, even though they might give God very little thought at all. Some believe wearing a cross as a piece of jewellery or attending church at Christmas offers them passage to Heaven. Others adopt a 'fingers crossed' mentality or a 'just say a quick prayer and you're in' gospel. Equally, there are those who hold the misguided idea that 'I belong to a particular denomination', or 'my grandfather was a preacher, so I am saved'.

Then there's the widely-held notion that 'surely all the good I have done outweighs all the bad, so I'll be OK'. It's amazing how many people, even devout church attendees believe in being saved by good works. It's easy to see where this idea comes from, isn't it? It makes a lot of sense and Jesus spoke a lot about loving one another and living a good life. But when we confuse this teaching with the biblical message of Salvation and our true God-given purpose on this planet we are in danger of missing out on God's almighty provision for us and of plunging into Hell, sincerely holding on to a false gospel. Someone once shared a powerful analogy with me to illustrate how no matter how 'good' we are or how hard we try there is nothing we can *do* to earn eternity with God.

We are in danger of missing out on God's almighty provision for us and of plunging into Hell, sincerely holding on to a false gospel.

Imagine that everyone in the United States is lined up on the shore of California and told that they have to swim to Hawaii, or die. There would be all kinds of people from all walks of life and many different shapes, sizes and levels of fitness and ability. There's the 500 lb man who can barely walk across the room without getting out of breath. As he begins to walk out into the water, a big wave knocks him over and he can't get up. He gargles salt water and quickly drowns.

Then there's the middle-aged man who used to be a great swimmer. He begins to swim, but it isn't long before he begins to get tired. He practises survival techniques he learned in the Boy Scouts and tries to keep going, but eventually the water overcomes him.

Next there's the girl from the high school swimming team. She has been swimming most days of her life for the past ten years and is in excellent physical condition. She paces herself, starting slowly and steadily. One mile, two miles . . . ten miles. But soon she begins to get cramps in her tired muscles. She can't go on. She too gargles the salty water and drowns.

Following on is the marathon swimmer who regularly swims the English Channel just for fun. He starts out strong and steady, soon passing the ten-mile mark, then the twenty. At fifty miles he is feeling the struggle and it's not long before the waves take their toll. Finally he succumbs to the power of the water.

Although some swimmers are much better than others, there is not a single swimmer who can cover over 2,500 miles, all the way to Hawaii. In the same way, even the best person in the world can't get into Heaven on the basis of his or her good works. Only God's grace makes the journey to Heaven possible. Doing good things and being helpful to other people is the 'fruit' of the Gospel, not the root of it.

This 'good works' gospel is just as false as the notion that 'Christianity is a bed of roses' or the 'Come to Jesus, He'll make you rich' gospel or the 'Jesus loves you' gospel that seems to ignore any need to respond to Him through change or sacrifice on your part.

Another worrying trend I perceive in some modern churches is what we might call the 'join the Church as a lifestyle option' gospel. In recent times there has been great work in changing the 'face' of the Church. What does your average person in the street think of when asked about church? Quite often you'll hear descriptions like 'cold, stuffy, miserable, morose, judgmental . . .' What a shock then when they're introduced to vibrant modern venues with state-of-the-art lighting, dazzling PowerPoint greetings and a top-class band blasting over the sophisticated PA system. Beautiful, well-dressed, smiling people are testimony to just how good church can be and a stuffed social calendar of all manner of events keeps everyone securely in the happy fold. Forgive my slight air of sarcasm here. The fact that many churches have embraced a contemporary, open approach and encouraged relevant and natural expression for the modern disciple is to be celebrated, but there's also a certain danger here. Sometimes people can be so caught in the razzle dazzle of belonging to a caring, vibrant and beautiful community that they forget the horror, the degradation, the loneliness and the sacrifice that is Jesus on the cross, dying for our sins. It is real blood on that cross, real suffering that whispers, 'Come follow me.' It's easy to preach good news about God, but unless we preach *the* Good News we are preaching a false Gospel, just as the apostle Paul feared in his

People can be so caught in the razzle dazzle of belonging to a caring, vibrant and beautiful community that they forget the horror, the degradation, the loneliness and the sacrifice that is Jesus on the cross, dying for our sins.

warning to the Galatians (chapter 1:6–9). *'As we have already said, so now I say again: If anybody is preaching to you a gospel other than what you accepted, let him be eternally condemned!'*

I'm sure you'll recognise some of these false gospels. Maybe you're confident you don't uphold any of them yourself, but do you tackle them? Do you seek them out and expose them with the truth of *the* Gospel? When we study these disturbing truths and meditate on them, big considerations emerge. The reality is that many sincere people will plunge into Hell holding onto false gospels because they have never heard the truth. And yet there's no natural or logical reason why Christians find it so difficult to proclaim the truth. It's not as though we can't get access to training on evangelism. This book is just one of many on the subject. We have the worldwide web, video, DVD, television, radio, satellite, phenomenal graphic design and print capabilities. What did Wesley and Luther have? Just a horse, a Bible and the Holy Spirit!

It's not as though we lack the finance to do it either. Certainly all ministries struggle – and we could do much more training and resource funding if caring Christians gave more sacrificially for the cause – but, at the end of the day, lack of money is no excuse if someone has a genuine heart to proclaim, or train in how to proclaim, the Gospel. It's not as though we lack the power to do it. There is no lack of God's power. In the book of Acts the believers were given the Holy Spirit so they could be 'witnesses' (Acts 1:8) and we know that it is the same Holy Spirit that dwells within every true believer today. Is it, then, that the command is too complicated to understand? No. It is plain and simple: *'Go into all the world and preach the good news to all creation'* (Mark 16:15). And let's face it, there are plenty of people in the world to share the message with. Think about the scale of our mission. There are now nearly seven billion people on the earth. Overwhelmed? We needn't be. We have Jesus' promise to claim as our own: *'I am with you always, to the very end of the age'* (Matthew 28:20). We cannot allow fear or lack of resource or low self-confidence to stop us.

When we consider these issues it's hard to understand why the Great Commission in the West should have collapsed. There seems to be no natural or logical reason why we have come to the point where Christians don't know how, or don't believe they need, to proclaim the true Gospel. However, the more one studies Scripture and prays about this situation, the clearer it becomes that driving the collapse of the Great Commission are principalities and powers and their leader, Satan. Chilling isn't it? Well, maybe, but we have already highlighted that we, as Christians, are in a war and as we move forward we should, as the early church is reminded, be secure because we are *'sons of the light and sons of the day . . . since we belong to the day, let us be self-controlled, putting on faith and love as a breastplate, and the hope of salvation as a helmet. For God did not appoint us to suffer wrath but to receive salvation through our Lord Jesus Christ'* (1 Thess. 5:5–9).

So are we ready to go into battle? Are we ready to wage war in the heavenlies by seizing the mantle Christ offers? With our eyes fully open – knowing that the souls of our friends, family and other fellow human beings are at stake – let's now move on to look at practical ways in which we can build the Great Commission back into our hearts and back into the Church.

- Do you recognise any of the 'false gospels' in your own church life? Which do you feel is the most common?

- Has there been a time in your life when you believed or trusted in some of these false gospels? How did this come to happen? How did you realise that you were putting your trust in something less than the full true Gospel?

- What is your reaction when you consider the consequence of false gospels and the millions of people who have never heard and understood the true Gospel?

10

The Man in the Mirror

If we believe in the message of Jesus Christ, if we 'put on Christ' for ourselves, if we accept the grace of God, knowing that whilst we were still far off, he came to meet us with his arms of unconditional love, then we too are called and compelled to love. And if we are compelled to love, then we are compelled to save – not that we ourselves save, for that is the work of God alone (Mark 2:7; 1Thess. 1:5), but we are determined to do anything our Lover asks so that more might be offered the gift of life. We cannot be disciples of Christ without being committed to Him. To be committed to Him we must engage in His work of redemption to bring glory to His name.

> *It is written: 'I believed; therefore I have spoken.' With that same spirit of faith we also believe and therefore speak, because we know that the one who raised the Lord Jesus from the dead will also raise us with Jesus and present us with you in his presence. All this is for your benefit, so that the grace that is reaching more and more people may cause thanksgiving to overflow to the glory of God.* (2 Cor. 4:13)

We have demonstrated, in the 'Words of the Gospel', that the decision between Heaven and Hell is an issue of free will and of 'justice'. But let's not be mistaken here, the Gospel itself is fundamentally and completely an issue of 'love' – a sacrificial, redemptive and unconditional love that is bigger, deeper, wider than any human mind can comprehend – a love that, we are promised, will never leave us nor forsake us. The apostle Paul in his letter to the Romans has much to say about what it means to live as a co-heir with Christ, to share His righteousness and to see the world through new eyes as the Spirit within us ordains. It makes sense then that when we find ourselves in a position of proclaiming the Gospel to another it is because of a genuine heart for that person, a deep love and a driving passion to save them from the grasp of evil. What does love look like? We need only turn to the famous passage 1 Corinthians 13 to see all that love is and is not – it is patient and kind, it keeps no record of wrong but rejoices in truth; it trusts, hopes and always perseveres. It does not envy or boast, is not proud nor is it rude, self-seeking or easily angered.

So again I find myself coming back to a personal challenge, because if love is not genuine, it is worthless. Do *you* believe the good news? Do *you* accept that you are loved and saved by Almighty God? Do you *know* Him as your Saviour, your Lord, your advocate, your bridegroom, your friend? Don't be mistaken here, I'm not enquiring as to the depth or quality of your relationship with Jesus. Remember, Jesus didn't call the spiritual giants, the highly learned or the apparently 'righteous', but the weak, the vulnerable, the uneducated, the failing, the apparently insignificant. Even those who lived with Him, who witnessed the miracles, felt His touch, ministered, hung out with Him and experienced His magnetism, abandoned Him when the going got tough. Would we not have fallen asleep in the garden of Gethsemane? Would we not have denied our beloved friend three times and maybe more? These are the weak, frightened and lacking men who Jesus knew all too well. He knew they would fail Him, He knew they would let Him down and deny Him, but He still chose them to be the founders of the church He was to establish here on earth. No, Jesus didn't expect His disciples to be spiritual giants. He didn't then and He doesn't now.

Remember in Chapter 7 when we looked at the 'words' of the Gospel? The seeker need be nothing more than *willing* to turn and surrender to God, so that God might run out to meet His lost son or daughter with arms open wide. When those first disciples chose to follow Jesus they did so with nothing other than willing hearts. They had no idea what they were to see, do or experience, or what they might ultimately become. Willingness to surrender is all that is required when we first turn to Jesus, and this genuine passion and honesty that leads to our first conscious decision to follow Him is all that need remain throughout our Christian walk. Certainly, it is sometimes battered in the harsh waters of life. How often do we feel that we take one step forward and two back in our faith? But if we return again and again, in repentance and submission, that simple willingness to 'let go and let God' inevitably grows into deeper trust as we walk the narrow path and cling to his cloak. Even the apostle Paul, with all his experience and all his 'knowledge' of his Saviour, exhibits a sense of continued longing for more. *'I want to know Christ and the power of his resurrection and the fellowship of sharing in his sufferings, becoming like him in his death, and so, somehow, to attain to the resurrection from the dead,'* he says to the Philippians (chapter 3:10–11) as he encourages them to 'press on towards the goal to win the prize . . .' Paul, in all his apparent strength and marvellous communion with Christ is still aware that he lacks 'knowledge' of Him. He knows that there is always *more*; that what we see now and have now is nothing compared to the magnificence of *knowing* Jesus when we are united with Him in glory.

Time and again in the New Testament we are shown that God seeks a genuine, sincere heart above all else. This was what Jesus saw when He looked into people's faces. When I look at my own young children I often see mischief, sometimes temper, sometimes dishonesty, but when I really get their attention and we look into one another's eyes I more often see pure love and unwavering trust. It's no mistake that Jesus tells us we must become like children. All He requires from us is our love and our trust, which in turn leads to devoted obedience. Then, out of this genuine heart – however weak, flawed and floundering – we can begin to persuade, rather than manipulate, other people towards our Father.

I can't labour this point too much. So often I find people say to me, 'Well it's all right for you, Tony, you have a really strong faith,' or 'You know how to do it,' or 'You've seen God move in power, so of course you can convince others . . .' This kind of talk upsets me a great deal and in telling my story in *Taming the Tiger*[1] I was determined to illustrate the Gospel through the testimony of other supposedly more 'normal' Christians. I recounted the testimony of my friend Mike who was raised in a Christian family, who couldn't name a day or an hour when he had given his life to Christ. He just knew that Jesus was his Saviour and as he grew in years he came to trust Him more. My wife Sara has a similar story and many other friends testify to a natural, yet no less determined, faith in God, even though they have never had the kind of 'Damascus Road' conversion experience that was mine. Why do we insist on measuring ourselves as Christians? We compare ourselves to others and find ourselves inferior, inadequate and wanting. Jesus never measures, never compares, never asks for more than we can give. We all have a heart, we all have the capacity to love

Jesus never measures, never compares, never asks for more than we can give.

because of, and through, Him who first loved us. Where does love lead? Love leads to obedience and a life in all its fullness. And a passionate life, it stands to reason, will attract others to want to know what it is that makes us different. In short, when we are seen to be 'walking the talk', when everything about our lives is motivated by Love and the Spirit living in our hearts, we are attractive and are given time and space to 'talk the talk'.

Before Christ was born, the philosopher Aristotle (384–322 BC) laid the groundwork for successful communication and expression – the shifting of attitude that is called 'persuasion'. In his classic work *The Art of Rhetoric* he outlines three forms of persuasion that can apply to the way we witness to others about Christ. The most persuasive message would aim to blend all three elements in order to achieve our goal effectively.

The first form is *ethos* (character), which interestingly is the root word for 'ethics', that is, a set of moral principles. *Ethos* relates directly to the speaker and his or her character, as revealed through what they are trying to communicate. For the message to be believable there must be 'credibility' in what a person is saying. This is something that a listener is constantly looking for in order to identify some form of trustworthiness and sincerity. We only need to turn to the world of politics to see this in action. In 2009, trust in British politics hit an all time low following the 'MP's expenses' scandal. A MORI poll reported that 'Politicians are now the group of professionals least likely to tell the truth' with only 13 per cent of people believing them to be trustworthy.[2] As Christians we must be vigilant, being good examples through our words, attitudes and actions. If our lifestyle doesn't match up to our words then we are nothing more than hypocrites or sales people trying to flog a product that we do not use and simply do not believe in.

Henry Stanley said of Scottish missionary and explorer David Livingstone, 'He never tried to convert me, but if I had been with him any longer I would have become a Christian.'[3] What a testimony! When people around us see the reality of Christ in our lives, our words are taken more seriously. Think how important the issue of trust (*ethos*) is to politicians, or closer to home in our own families and relationships. When we find that someone has lied to us or not fulfilled their promises in the past, it's very hard to believe them or trust them again. In 1 Thessalonians 4:12 the believers are exhorted to live *'so that your daily life may win the respect of outsiders . . .'* This issue is something that should be at the forefront of our minds in all our dealings in everyday life.

'Always be prepared to give an answer to everyone who asks you to give the reason for the hope that you have. But do this with gentleness and respect, keeping a clear conscience.' (1 Peter 3:13–15)

When we live a holy life, we will attract attention that, in turn, will lead to questions. It is then that we are to be ready to speak the Gospel. As Peter instructs us, *'Always be prepared to give an answer to everyone who asks you to give the reason for the hope that you have. But do this with gentleness and respect, keeping a clear conscience'* (1 Peter 3:15–16). Remember again Francis of Assisi's instruction as he finished preparing his disciples for their work of evangelising the world? He strongly emphasised to them that their words would be most powerfully received when delivered through the positive witness of their lives and actions.

Pathos (feeling) is the second of Aristotle's forms of rhetoric and is the root for 'sympathy' and 'empathy'. It is *appeal* based on recognising and understanding someone else's *plight, their emotions, their viewpoint and struggles.* Think about television or print advertising. Many of the most successful adverts engage the emotions on at least some level. Reports of war or famine in a far off land are suddenly more meaningful to us when pictures of suffering innocents are broadcast into our living rooms.

Care, compassion and empathy are vital parts of communicating the Gospel. A person is far more easily persuaded if their emotions are stirred by a message. Of course, only God can bring conviction for a person to give their life to Christ (John 6:65), but it benefits us to recognise that in such God-ordained situations human emotion is fundamental in how a listener engages and responds to the message. The Alpha Course has seen many people turn to Christ because they have been introduced to the Gospel in a setting that is comfortable and engaging. The meal and social time that usually accompanies the course often sets a certain dynamic of camaraderie within a group. Discussion then is more open, free, honest and relevant. Time and time again it's revealed that people make close and lasting emotional bonds with others within their group, especially if they step forward in commitment to Christ together.

I recently heard a story of a group of students from a Christian college who, whilst touring Europe, witnessed to their bus driver. One girl tearfully pleaded, 'If you don't accept Jesus, you'll go to Hell. Please, please trust in Jesus.' It was an emotional appeal that reminds me of Paul's impassioned plea and its effect on King Agrippa in Acts 26:28. Perhaps the bus driver would dismiss the young girl as just some crazy Bible-basher, but I would hope that her witness, along with that of her fellow students might have stirred something in the bus driver and that her genuine tears and honest words might have caused a warming in his heart for the Holy Spirit to begin a work in him. Genuine *pathos* is hard to ignore, for it is this uniquely human condition that naturally resonates with our fellow men and women.

There was once a Shakespearian actor who was known far and wide for his one-man show of readings and recitations from the classics. He always ended his performance with a dramatic reading of the twenty-third Psalm. Each evening, without exception, as the actor began his recitation – 'The Lord is my shepherd, I shall not be in want . . .' – the crowd listened attentively. And then, at the conclusion of the psalm, they always rose in thunderous applause in appreciation of the actor's incredible ability to bring the words to life.

One night, just before the actor was to offer his customary recital of Psalm 23, a young man from the audience spoke up. 'Sir, do you mind if tonight I recite the twenty-third Psalm?' The actor was quite taken aback by this unusual request, but he allowed the young man to come forward and stand in the centre of the stage to recite the psalm. He was confident that the ability of this unskilled youth would be no match for his own talent.

With a soft voice, the young man began to recite the words of the scripture. When he finished, there was no applause. There was no standing ovation as on other nights. All that could be heard was the sound of weeping, the audience had been so moved by the young man's recitation.

Amazed by what he heard, the actor said to the youth, 'I don't understand. I've been performing the twenty-third Psalm for years. I have a lifetime of experience and training, but I've never been able to move an audience as you have tonight. Tell me, what is your secret?' The young man humbly replied, 'Well, sir, you know the psalm . . . but I know the shepherd.'

It's not enough to just know the content of the Bible – its stories, its sayings and its teachings. Unless you know the Author, the Bible is nothing more than just another book. But when you put your faith in Jesus Christ and enter into a personal relationship with God the Father, the Bible truly becomes *'living and active – sharper than any double-edged sword'* (Heb. 4:12).

To speak the words of the Gospel in genuine power we need to *know* their source. *Logos* (reason), which is the third of Aristotle's forms of persuasion, translates into 'word'. For Aristotle, *logos* – the very content of what we say – was the primary element. The words and the content of our communication are to be backed up and verified through *ethos* and *pathos*, but it is critically through what we *say* or write that we deliver the entirety of our message. To me this also appears biblically consistent, since the Bible asks every believer to proclaim the words of the Gospel. At the end of the day, we can be the most upright and caring person in the world and people might think we're wonderful, but they're unlikely to become Christians if they don't hear the Gospel message.

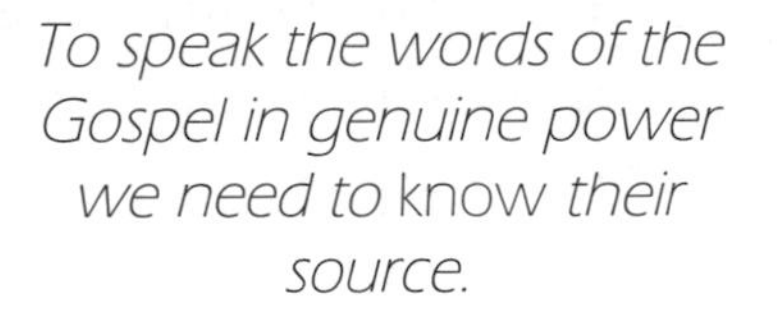
To speak the words of the Gospel in genuine power we need to know *their source.*

Words are crucial to our work of spreading the Gospel and it's a powerful thing when we recognise where words come from. When we are confident in the authority of God's words spoken through us we can be released from our own self-consciousness about speaking the Gospel. A short Bible study should excite and inspire us as we recognise that through God's words, creation came into being. All tangible and intangible things are held together by His word. Psalm 33:6 tells us that *'By the word of the LORD were the heavens made, their starry host by the breath of his mouth.'* Note that God said, *'"Let there be light," and there was light.'* He said, *'"Let there be an expanse between the waters, to separate the water from the water." . . . And it was so'* (Gen. 1:3,6–7).

Even when Christ – who Himself was the *Word* manifest in human form (John 1) – was tempted by the devil in the wilderness

He anchored Himself in the Word of God. Matthew 4:4 reports, *'Jesus answered, "It is written: 'Man does not live on bread alone, but on every word that comes from the mouth of God.'"'* Jesus' response here indicates that we are not just biological machines, but that God's words are a prerequisite for life. The Roman Centurion (Matt. 8:8–9) also seemed to understand this. When he asked Jesus to '*just say the word, and my servant will be healed*', he recognised that Jesus' word carries greater weight that anything in the physical realm. Verse 10 in this passage shows us Christ's reaction, *'When Jesus heard this, he was astonished and said to those following him, "I tell you the truth, I have not found anyone in Israel with such great faith."'*

When we submit ourselves under the authority of God our words can be used, in His authority, over creation. Jesus emphasised that there is no end to what we can do by the Word of God, so long as we have faith: *'You can say to this mountain, "Move from here to there" and it will move'* (Matt. 17:20). Right from the very beginning God wanted human beings to have such spoken authority over creation. He chose us to be part of His creation work when He invited Adam to name the animals. The act of naming implies a type of ownership and enforces God's desire for mankind to be set apart, above all creatures, created in His own image and bestowed with the honourable task of taking special care of His marvellous creation. It is as though a father wants to share the delights of his brand new and very precious sports car with his son, so he gives him the car keys: 'Go ahead,' he says, 'I put your name on the registration documents too and filled it with petrol for you. Have fun and enjoy yourself, just be careful not to scratch it!'

Unfortunately, because our hearts are corruptible, our words become fallible. Because of the effects of sin we cannot control our mouths. Our words are made imperfect and we step outside of the authority granted to us under Christ. James reminds us *that 'no man can tame the tongue. It is a restless evil, full of deadly poison'* (James 3:8). Romans 3:13,14 embarrasses us more when it talks of throats being as open graves and tongues that practise deceit, poison of vipers on lips and mouths that are full of cursing and bitterness. Serious stuff indeed! But the notion of original sin and our fallen state is no excuse for us. As Christians we must obey God by maintaining the integrity of our words. Proverbs 4:24 instructs us to *'Avoid all perverse talk; stay away from corrupt speech,'* and there is plenty of warning throughout Scripture about lying and false testimony.

Since we can't fully trust our speech, we must address a second component at work in our words. If our words are the overflow of our hearts, we should think about the intent in our hearts as we speak words. So again we are back to our need to have our hearts right with God. When our hearts are aligned with Him, God's words speak through us because we are under His authority.

Alongside authority, authenticity is another key component at work in our words. Aristotle's notion of *ethos* highlights the necessity of good character and trustworthiness when it comes to the art of persuasion, but in the work of sharing the Gospel we're looking at a much bigger picture. Being authentic is crucial to our relationship with other people, but it is more important still when it comes to our relationship with God. The authenticity of our commitment to Him is what our judgment is based on and where our eternal destiny lies. Our authenticity doesn't just make us effective at sharing the Gospel, it ensures that we ourselves qualify. Using the analogy of an athlete training for a race, Paul tells the Corinthians how he disciplines himself so that *'after*

Our authenticity doesn't just make us effective at sharing the Gospel, it ensures that we ourselves qualify.

preaching to others I myself will not be disqualified for the prize'. Similarly Matthew's Gospel records Jesus' warning that on judgment day *'Many will say to me on that day, "Lord, Lord did we not prophesy in your name and in your name drive out demons and perform many miracles?" Then I will tell them plainly, "I never knew you"'* (Matt. 7:22–23).

The right heart towards sharing the Gospel is not something a person one day 'gets' or something they indefinitely 'have'. It is found through deep conviction and gratitude for Christ's work on the cross and our recognition of who we are in Him. I had the privilege whilst in Canada of accompanying a good friend to his regular meeting with Alcoholics Anonymous. Sitting in the circle I listened as each person shared intimate experiences and stories from that week. Before each person spoke they addressed the rest of the circle with, 'Hello, my name is [Gary], and I'm an alcoholic.' Having never had a problem with that kind of addiction I found myself wondering how I would introduce myself if asked to speak. I came to the conclusion that I could say something like, 'Hello, my name is Tony, and I'm a sinner.' From what I understand, the success of the AA rehabilitation programme is the premise of tough love, based on the conviction that no effective recovery can be initiated until a person admits they are powerless over alcohol and their life has become unmanageable. Isn't it this same bare-faced, broken recognition of ourselves as sinners – useless and doomed to destruction – that we come to when we sincerely turn to Christ? When this happens the 'programme' of recovery – our Salvation – can take place. When we become real with ourselves, and real with God, then, and only then, we can authentically help turn others towards Him. Indeed, Charles Spurgeon once said that evangelism is just like one beggar telling another beggar where to find food. Isn't that just so?

So the right heart towards sharing the Gospel is a result of our very own, everyday relationship with Christ, as we die each day in response to His sacrifice. If our relationship with Christ is not genuine and authentic then concern for the eternal well-being of others is fraudulent and turning them to the Gospel virtually impossible. Rather, we are doing no more than spouting a sales pitch to join a religious club that most people will see through and close down even before we open our mouth. Proverbs 13:17 (NLT) tells us, *'An unreliable messenger stumbles into trouble, but a reliable messenger brings healing.'* We are messengers of Christ, carriers of the Gospel, and it is only right that we should please, rather than frustrate Him; that we should be genuine for the sake of others, for our own sake, but most importantly, for Christ's sake so that He gets that which His blood paid for – a soul made right for His glory.

'An unreliable messenger stumbles into trouble, but a reliable messenger brings healing.' (Prov. 13:17, NLT)

The key element to evangelism is harder (yet paradoxically much simpler) than memorising any Gospel script or handing out any tract or standing on a stage or pulpit with a pre-baked message. The primary – indeed the only – component necessary to share with others the good news of Jesus Christ is nothing but a genuine, authentic heart for God, freshly cooked!

Author Robert Fulghum tells this story of one of his professors, a wise man whose name was Alexander Papaderos:

> At the last session on the last morning of a two-week seminar on Greek culture, Dr Papaderos turned and made the ritual gesture, 'Are there any questions?'
>
> Quiet quilted the room. These two weeks had generated enough questions for a lifetime, but for now, there was only silence.

'No questions?' Papaderos swept the room with his eyes.

So, I asked.

'Dr Papaderos, what is the meaning of life?'

The usual laughter followed, and people stirred to go. Papaderos held up his hand, and stilled the room and looked at me for a long time, asking with his eyes if I was serious and seeing from my eyes that I was.

'I will answer your question.'

Taking his wallet out of his pocket, he fished into a leather billfold and brought out a small round mirror, about the size of a quarter. And what he said went something like this:

'When I was a small child, during the war, we were very poor and we lived in a remote village. One day, on the road, I found the broken pieces of a mirror. A German motorcycle had been wrecked in that place.

'I tried to find all the pieces and put them together, but it was not possible, so I kept only the largest piece. This one. And by scratching it on a stone, I made it round. I began to play with it as a toy and became fascinated by the fact that I could reflect light into dark places where the sun would never shine – in deep holes and crevices and dark closets. It became a game for me to get light into the most inaccessible places I could find.

'I kept the little mirror, and as I went about my growing up, I would take it out in idle moments and continue the challenge of the game. As I became a man, I grew to understand that this was not just a child's game but a metaphor for what I might do with my life. I came to understand that I am not the light or the source of the light. But light – truth, understanding and knowledge – is there, and it will only shine in many dark places if I reflect it.

'I am a fragment of a mirror whose whole design and shape I do not know. Nevertheless, with what I have I can reflect light into the dark places of this world – into the black places in the hearts of men – and change some things in some people. Perhaps others may see and do likewise. This is what I am about. This is the meaning of life.'

And then he took his small mirror and, holding it carefully, caught the bright rays of daylight streaming through the window and reflected them onto my face and onto my hands folded on the desk.

Jesus said, *'I am the light of the world'* (John 9:5) and as His followers, we are to be like that little mirror, reflecting the light of Christ into the dark corners of the world. That is the meaning of the Christian life.[4]

That is authenticity and, ultimately, persuasion.

Let your light shine before men, that they may see your good deeds and praise your Father in heaven. (Matt. 5:16)

So is my word that goes out from my mouth: It will not return to me empty, but will accomplish what I desire and achieve the purpose for which I sent it. (Isa. 55:11)

- Jesus described the Word as 'seed', the source of life and growth. Do you trust that when you speak the Gospel your words will have such impact?

- The world speaks of weapons as a means to defeat enemies. What effect does it have on you when you consider the power of your words (the Gospel spoken through you) as a two-edged sword? (Heb. 4:12; Rev. 1:16)

- What kind of responsibility does this carry when you reflect on personal authenticity?

- How do you believe non-Christian onlookers view your church? Is it an authentic reflection of what a group of followers of Christ would hope to be?

11

Leaning Towers

If personal authenticity is crucial in being able to draw others towards Christ, we must also be sure that we are able to continually keep the bigger picture in mind. Remember our artists at the opening of this book? Each was working on his or her own little part. They had no idea what picture they were creating. That was OK because the 'master artist' had a plan and knew how it would all come together at the end to make the perfect whole picture. But still, the success of the project relied on each individual paying particular attention to the careful detail of what they were asked to do. If any one of them deviated at all from the precise instruction of their own painting, the whole picture would not have worked when it was finally assembled. The crux of the entire project relied on everyone being, if you will, 'truthful' to the master's instructions.

When it comes to proclaiming the Gospel it's vital that we have a clear understanding of its *truth*. What is truth?' Have you ever stopped to really consider what you believe the truth of the Gospel to be? It's an interesting exercise to have a group discussion and see if you can actually agree on *the* 'truth'. We've already considered that false teaching has infiltrated our churches and, in some cases, been incorporated into our understanding of what the Gospel is and what the Great Commission is all about. So how do we, as Christians, ensure that what we believe is God's actual intention? What is truth? Well, the answer should be simple: 'God's word, because the Bible is truth.' Yet if we ask twenty Bible-believing Christians what evangelism is, we will probably receive twenty quite different answers. Who is telling the truth, and how can we find out? Hopefully we study the Scriptures for ourselves and we pray and ask the Holy Spirit to enlighten us. But it's not always that simple, is it? If it were, we wouldn't have quite so much disagreement in our churches and split denominations would be an anomaly.

So what do we do with our twenty different definitions? Should we just go on with our own hunches, make it up as we go along, hope for the best and ignore the issue?

No. When a builder sets about building a house he has to get the foundations right if the project is to succeed. He draws on the authority of an architect who carefully calculates the measurements, dimensions and materials. The plans are defined at the earliest stage. Without this groundwork the builder might have nothing more than random sections of brickwork that make no sense and are of no use to anyone. The Bible calls us to be like master builders, knowing we must be accurate as we study biblical words. 2 Timothy 2:15 implores us: *'Do your best to present yourself to God as one approved, a workman who does not need to be ashamed and who correctly handles the word of truth.'*

'Do your best to present yourself to God as one approved, a workman who does not need to be ashamed and who correctly handles the word of truth.'
(2 Tim. 2:15)

The leaning tower of Pisa is a fabulous example here. Since its construction in 1173, the tower has become a world-renowned icon, but it's hardly the straight, erect tower that its planners intended. Somewhere along the line something went drastically wrong. The foundations were poorly laid and nobody anticipated the shifting substrata that very soon allowed the tower to start its famous tilt. What can we say? It's a bell tower, it has done its job – and even brought a wealth of tourism to Pisa down the ages – but it does not stand to the truth of its intentions. It is not particularly honourable to its designer or builder.

Maybe the 'what is truth' issue is often at the forefront of my mind because of the many people I meet on my travels. I'm constantly aghast at how many seem to sign up for ideology or lifestyle based on very little knowledge or exploration. I'll never forget a particular conversation with a London taxi driver who told me of his experience with a Ouija board. He was excited and enthusiastic after a first 'session' where the board revealed information to other members of the group. 'I have a really difficult decision to make,' he told me, 'and I just don't know what to do. Whatever I decide it's going to cause damage to someone, so I need a message to tell me which is the right way.' I listened sadly, incredulous that his trust in the board was instant and unwavering. Deeply disturbed I longed to share the Gospel with him and carefully picked my way around the conversation trying to expose the false trust he was placing in the séance. 'How do you know this to be true? Where do you think this information comes from?' I asked him. 'What if you're wrong?' They were questions he hadn't even considered. Ultimately it paved the way for me to share *the* truth with him, but the point is that many people seem to casually base their eternal future on whatever is offered to them, without thorough investigation, without seeking the truth.

Where do we go to find truth?

A man is suffering with a heart problem. He's referred to a top cardiologist who runs a range of high level, sophisticated tests and reports that surgery is required. The doctor assures the man that he is in good hands and that he has performed the same operation many times before on other similar patients. The man goes home and tells his neighbour. The neighbour takes hold of his friend's wrist and fumbles around until he finds his pulse. The friend waits expectantly as the neighbour counts ten seconds. 'Nah, don't worry about it mate, there's nothing wrong with you, forget about it, seems to me that you're fit and well,' he announces. Who does the man trust? He's not sure, so he looks at the evidence. The cardiologist is one of the most respected and renowned in his profession. He has thirty years' experience and has read and written many books on his subject. The neighbour, on the other hand, has no idea what he's talking about, except for some good pointers he's gleaned from a *Reader's Digest* article on how to keep the heart healthy. Who does the man trust?

It's a simple and rather farcical example, but hopefully this opens up the idea that, when we are uncertain, it's important to turn to an 'authority', or an expert, someone who is entitled to speak on the matter. After all, that's why the New Testament demonstrates a need for leadership and authority within the Church. We should be thankful that today we are blessed with numerous such people and all manner of communication through which they can expound their God-given wisdom. The apostle Paul came across difficult issues in the early church as the young Christians began shaping their corporate worship. In his first letter to the Corinthians 14:29, he recommends *'Two or three prophets should speak, and the others should weigh carefully what is said.'* This idea of 'carefully weighing' is, I believe, even

'Two or three prophets should speak, and the others should weigh carefully what is said.' (1 Cor. 14:29)

more imperative today. We live in a time when liberal ideologies concerning the Bible and Christian belief are rife and there are many issues on which respected authorities disagree. The church has enough hot potatoes to feed a heavenly banquet for all eternity, but you might be surprised to learn that when it comes to the definition of evangelism, there is remarkable agreement between scholars across denominations and cultures.

Why is it important that we should be bothered to seek out a definition of evangelism and what it means to evangelise? Well, as we saw with the example from my friends' soup kitchen, there are many good-hearted Christians who believe they are engaged in evangelism, yet they are not actually doing evangelism at all. That is, they're involved in all sorts of activities in the name of evangelism but rarely do their efforts include the proclamation of the Gospel. Then again, you might ask, 'Who says evangelism is "the proclamation of the Gospel"?' Here's where we should turn to some of the 'authorities' on the matter. Two of the world's leading Bible scholars are Dr John Stott and Dr J.I. Packer. Both assert that evangelism is very simply 'the proclamation of the Gospel'.[1] Furthermore, in acknowledgement of the importance of this issue, modern history has seen the establishment of the Lausanne Conference on Evangelism. This conference seeks to define terms and determine agreement and understanding across the broad spectrum of the Christian Church. When the conference first met in 1974 it universally agreed their first statement, 'To evangelise is to spread the good news.'[2]

'To evangelise is to spread the good news.' (Lausanne Conference on Evangelism)

Interestingly enough, the word 'evangelism' appears very infrequently in the actual gospels, but down the ages the church has embraced it as suitable description for the Great Commission, the proclaiming of the Gospel. In its original context an 'evangelist' was the runner who carried 'the good news' of a military victory. He would run from the battlefield to the king, kneel at his feet, unroll a scroll and announce the victory. He was essentially a messenger of good news. The scroll on which that good news was written was known as the 'evangel' and 'evangelism' was the word used to describe the act of announcing the military victory to the ruler.

Using this terminology in the Christian realm, then, we can legitimately claim that the act of actually announcing the Gospel to non-Christians and ensuring they understand it is called 'evangelism'. Something important to note here is that, in this context, the message has a beginning, middle and an end. It is therefore an 'event', not a 'process'. Let me say that again. Evangelism is an event, *not* a process. Now I know that this is a pretty heavy statement that flies in the face of many people's thinking about evangelism. But consider it this way: if we plant seeds in the garden we prepare the soil, then put the seeds in, then cover them over and water them in. We don't then go back the next day with the hoe and start digging up the soil and planting seeds again. Nor the next day, nor the next. The seeds have been planted, once. Though much preparation might go into preparing the soil and creating the right conditions for the seeds to grow, and though much more tender care will be needed for them to flourish, the act of actually putting the seeds into the ground is a 'one-off'. In the same way, if we are sowing the Gospel into someone's life, we either sow or we don't. The relevance of this cannot be underestimated and it will become clearer as our discussion unfolds.

Evangelism is an event, not a process

So, by our definitions, it follows that anyone who is proclaiming the Gospel is 'evangelising' and acting as an 'evangelist'. However, Scripture teaches us that some people in the Church have what is commonly understood as 'the gift of evangelism'. Paul wrote to the church in Ephesus of the special gifts and calling that God has on the lives of certain individuals in the Church, '*It was he who gave some to be apostles, some to be prophets, some to be evangelists, and some to be pastors and teachers, to prepare God's people for works of service, so that the body of Christ may be built up*' (Eph. 4:11–12).

'It was he who gave some to be apostles, some to be prophets, some to be evangelists, and some to be pastors and teachers, to prepare God's people for works of service, so that the body of Christ may be built up.' (Eph. 4:11–12).

When I study the work of John Wesley, Charles Spurgeon, Hudson Taylor, Smith Wigglesworth and, from a more modern era, Billy Graham and Luis Palau among others, I resonate with the same heart-cry. Such men are certainly what we might call 'Ephesians 4:11–12' evangelists. What a privilege to be able to address hundreds and thousands, from street corners to stages and stadiums, witnessing God turning many souls for His glory! Avanti Ministries has over 176 'associate evangelists', men and women who believe themselves called by God to make proclaiming the Gospel their life priority. Circumstances and cultures vary tremendously, but what such people share is a deep compulsion to respond to their vocation and gifting. Many other people around the world also share this calling, some who have aligned themselves with evangelistic mission organisations such as Avanti Ministries or Open Air Campaigners, Youth For Christ, Campus

Crusade, Teen Challenge or Youth With A Mission to name just a few. But there are also others who simply go about their everyday lives and everyday jobs 'being' evangelists. My friend Chris is a window cleaner by trade. He has no call to address masses from a stage and any spark of limelight sends him running for cover, yet all who know Chris recognise that he is a gifted evangelist, the very kind Paul was highlighting in his note to the Ephesians. Few days pass without God placing someone before him who needs to hear the Gospel from this most humble, yet powerfully gifted, individual.

I sometimes imagine that evangelists can be parodied with dogs. We're all the same species, yet all so different. Some are the yappy terrier type who just can't shut up, no matter where they are or who they're with. Some are bulldogs, strong determined and fiercely charged. Some are sheepdogs, working diligently for the master, attentively going only where and when He leads. Others are show dogs that can stand up in front of an audience and present the Gospel with confidence. Others are like greyhounds – fast, furious and focused, burning themselves out to win the race. Then there's the good old faithful Labrador – gentle, trustworthy, sensitive, good with children, leader of the blind. All are different, yet all are 'man's best friend'. Indulge me if you will in this analogy that evangelists are called to be 'mankind's best friend'! The point I'm making here is that all share the same passion and mission, but it's important to recognise that our personality types will always try to dictate the way we do our job.

This was something that became very clear to me on one of my first missions in New Zealand. I was invited, along with a fellow evangelist, to lunch at the home of one of the couples organising the mission. It's always nice to be invited to join someone's family, but our new friends were honest in declaring that our invitation came with something of an agenda. They were deeply troubled that their eldest daughter was not a

Christian and hoped that in meeting us she might be challenged. As the lunch appointment approached my evangelist friend and I were like soldiers preparing for war. We prayed together and built ourselves up in anticipation of powerfully sharing the Gospel. Both being of a certain bulldog-like personality when it comes to our passion for evangelism, we were determined almost to the point of aggression. I should probably confess that there might also have been a degree of competitiveness between the two of us as to who would actually win her for Christ!

The family were very welcoming and all was well as we began eating together, but I could tell that my friend was itching to 'get stuck in'. It wasn't long before he turned the general pleasantries into a more direct challenge aimed at the young girl. No wonder she quickly grew tense and resistant as my friend pursued a hard line of questions about her lack of belief. In good faith and passion for her Salvation my friend pressed on, confronting her with the Gospel message, but I soon realised that in this case a very different approach was needed. Against all my natural instincts I kept my mouth shut and decided that I would not even try to speak the Gospel to her, at least not on this occasion. Instead, I simply caught her eye and offered a smile. When I could get a word in edgeways from my friend I turned the conversation to other things, asking about her job, her friends, her life, sharing stories and photographs of my children, but deliberately avoiding anything to do with Christianity. Lunch was good and after a relaxing afternoon my friend and I left to prepare for the mission that evening.

The next day, I received an excited, emotionally charged call from our new friends. Despite her parents being the organisers of the mission the young girl had vowed that she would not be attending the evening meeting. I shouldn't have been surprised that by deliberately not preaching, I had intrigued her. She had warmed to the friendship connection we had made earlier in the afternoon and had been interested to hear bits and pieces of my story. Of course that evening I told my story, as always, as a vehicle to give a clear, compelling presentation of the Gospel. I must admit to shedding tears myself when her dad told me that she, along with a group of friends, had attended the meeting and she had responded to the message and stepped forward to accept Christ.

When we present the Gospel we must do so with love, grace and tenderness. This is the premise that was summarised in the second statement of the Lausanne Conference of 1974, 'Our Christian presence in the world is indispensable to evangelism, and so is that kind of dialogue whose purpose is to listen sensitively in order to understand.'[3]

Sometimes I perceive that we 'Ephesians 4' evangelists can be so caught up in our determination to share the Gospel that we fail to embrace this truth. Like bulldogs, terriers or greyhounds we can tend to focus a great deal on us and our mission to the detriment of those we are supposed to be ministering to. Similarly, it's a sad fact that show dogs can battle with ego and begin to believe in their own power and ability, rather than the Master's. There's a story of John Bunyan who, when he had finished addressing a large crowd, had a man approach him. 'Sir, let me be the first to congratulate you on a wonderful sermon,' the man said. 'No, you are not the first,' replied Bunyan. 'The devil has already done that.' Then there are others, the less 'showy' breeds who are driven by evangelistic calling, but easily become heavily burdened, prone to depression and bogged down by everyday life, despite the passion for evangelism that still burns in their belly.

There are many pitfalls in the work of a 'called' evangelist. Most evangelists I know, when being really honest, will admit to significant struggles. Many of us suffer significantly with feelings of discouragement and isolation. Too often we find that our home churches are not particularly supportive of us in our role as evangelists. And sometimes the fact that not every Christian appears to share the same passion to see the lost saved just gets too depressing. Many of us suffer with frustration over the workings of our ministries or organisations or we struggle with money management or spiritual disciplines such as Bible reading and praying. The devil always attacks through our close circles, and that usually means through family, friends, health, church and those who would support us in ministry – all the things closest to our heart and most needed so that we can function properly in our calling. My friend and mentor George Verwer pulled me up sharp one time when I was seeking his support in a mission to India. 'We can work on India,' he told me, 'but I think there's somewhere else you need to put in some time first.'

'Where?' I asked him eagerly.

'Bedspring Baptist,' came his cheeky reply.

When you think about it, there's no wonder the devil tries to throw all manner of curve balls. When we're on the front line of battle we can expect full-on attack with sling and arrow. There's no easy answer to this, other than to be aware and to be on guard against the evil one. 1 Peter 5:8 warns us, *'Be self-controlled and alert. Your enemy the devil prowls around like a roaring lion looking for someone to devour.'* This means being especially careful to protect our relationships and to be constantly in check of our morality in thought and deed and in witness to others.

'Be self-controlled and alert. Your enemy the devil prowls around like a roaring lion looking for someone to devour.'
(1 Pet. 5:8)

I'm sure that if you're not such an evangelist yourself you recognise some of what I'm talking about in those you know.

One thing is clear, though, evangelists are certainly called to be man's best friend and, according to Scripture, that means more than just proclaiming the Gospel to unbelievers. Remember the *second part of that verse in Ephesians 4: 'some to be evangelists, and some to be pastors and teachers, to prepare God's people for works of service, so that the body of Christ may be built up . . .'* Here's an area that I perceive can be very lacking in our churches and in the lives of so-called 'evangelists'. As we know from our earlier discussion, and from the clarity of the Great Commission, *all* Christians are called to engage in the work of evangelism. All are called to spread the good news of Jesus Christ, yet not all have the gift of being able to naturally proclaim the Gospel. This is where the work of the gifted evangelist comes in. It is his or her commission to train the church, to 'prepare God's people for works of service'. I am sure that when God places an evangelist in a particular church it is so that he or she can train the rest of the congregation in the art of proclaiming the Gospel. Meanwhile others are engaged in the jobs that require other giftings – teaching, preaching, discipling, tea-making . . . The reality is that most Christians don't know how to share the Gospel. Is it because they have never had any kind of training? Is it because those who seem to be called to evangelism don't fully embrace their biblical remit? Is it because other leaders in the church don't recognise them as such?

All are called to spread the good news of Jesus Christ, yet not all have the gift of being able to naturally proclaim the Gospel., This is where the work of the gifted evangelist comes in.

Only God can give the 'gift' of evangelism. But when someone with the gift trains others in how to proclaim the Gospel, they begin to function as an evangelist. When this happens the wider church is faithful to what Jesus asks of *all* of us through the Great Commission.

Defining our terms, knowing the truth, trusting the correct authorities and knowing our calling is fundamental to the propagation of the Church. Are you an 'Ephesians 4' evangelist? If you believe this is your gifting are you fully aware of the responsibility of your role? Are you regularly proclaiming the Gospel to non-Christians and are you training and encouraging other members of your church? Are you a minister or church leader who needs to recognise the gifting of others in your congregation? You may be a great pastor, preacher or teacher, but you will struggle to successfully equip your congregation with the skills or the impetus to share the Gospel in the wider community without utilising the evangelistic gift. Do you need to identify those with the gift of evangelism and set out to mobilise them to somehow fulfil their biblically ordained job? And what about everybody else? What if your gifting is hospitality or teaching or reading, praying, making tea, cleaning the carpets after everyone else has gone home for Sunday lunch . . . what if you're pretty sure that you are not an 'Ephesians 4' evangelist? Well, the answer, as I hope you're coming to understand, is that as a follower of Christ, you are still called to engage in the Great Commission – you just need a little help to set you on your way.

- Why is it important for Christians to clearly and accurately define key terms like 'evangelism'? Read 2 Timothy 2:15.
- How do we deal with so many different interpretations of 'truth' in the Bible?
- Might you be an 'Ephesians 4:11–12' evangelist? Are you living in your full potential as such?
- Do you recognise any 'Ephesians 4' evangelists in your church or local community? Are they training others in the spreading of the Gospel? Do they receive support and encouragement? If not, why do you think this might be?

12

Called and Qualified

God doesn't call the qualified, He qualifies the called. The previous chapter focused on the importance of recognising, empowering and supporting the 'Ephesians 4:11–12' evangelists amongst us. Yet if there is a driving purpose to this book it is to ignite the passion of *all* Christians; to inspire and equip all who claim to love the Lord Jesus Christ to embrace the Great Commission on a very personal level.

In Acts 1:8 Jesus promised His followers, '*But you will receive power when the Holy Spirit comes on you; and you will be my witnesses in Jerusalem, and in all Judea and Samaria, and to the ends of the earth.*' Let's examine again some of the instances in which we see Jesus commissioning His followers to 'go out' in His name. I have made frequent reference to Mark 16:15 and Matthew 28:18–20 but there are key passages in the Gospels of both Luke and John that many understand as the Great Commission:

> *He said to them, 'This is what I told you while I was still with you: Everything must be fulfilled that is written about me in the Law of Moses, the Prophets and the Psalms.' Then he opened their minds so they could understand the Scriptures. He told them, 'This is what is written: The Christ will suffer and rise from the dead on the third day, and repentance and forgiveness*

> *of sins will be preached in his name to all nations, beginning at Jerusalem. You are witnesses of these things. I am going to send you what my Father has promised; but stay in the city until you have been clothed with power from on high.'* (Luke 24:44–49)

> *On the evening of that first day of the week, when the disciples were together, with the doors locked for fear of the Jews, Jesus came and stood among them and said, 'Peace be with you!' After he said this, he showed them his hands and side. The disciples were overjoyed when they saw the Lord. Again Jesus said, 'Peace be with you! As the Father has sent me, I am sending you.' And with that he breathed on them and said, 'Receive the Holy Spirit. If you forgive anyone his sins, they are forgiven; if you do not forgive them, they are not forgiven.'* (John 20:19–23)

There can be little doubt that the Great Commission is given to *all* disciples of Jesus Christ. It was originally given to His first followers in the period shortly before His ascension – essentially outlining what the Lord expected His disciples to do in His coming absence – but, because it tells them to teach others to obey everything they were taught by Jesus, it is *perpetual.* The very fact that Jesus specifically refers to preaching the Gospel to 'all creation' broadens the timeline from the first believers up until today, and onwards until the Lord returns. This is truly a task for the full legacy of the Christian Church.

> We cannot pick and choose which commands of our Lord we will follow. Jesus Christ's last command to the Christian community was, *'Go into all the world and preach the Good News to all creation'* (Mark 16:15). This command, which the Church calls the Great Commission, was not intended merely for the eleven remaining apostles (or preaching the Gospel would have stopped when they died!), or just for the apostles, or for those in present

> times who may have the gift of evangelism. This command is the duty of every man and woman who confesses Christ as Lord. (Dr Bill Bright)[1]

We return then to Acts 1:8 and recognise that here we are presented with very clear evangelistic strategy. If ever we were unsure just who Jesus is asking us to 'witness' to, the answer is easily found by unpacking this powerful piece of Scripture. The Lord first promises us that the Holy Spirit will give us authority and strength for the task ahead. When He speaks about being 'witnesses', He means we are to be just that, people who tell what they have seen and experienced to others who have not yet seen and experienced.

Where are these people? Jesus addresses this next. They are first in Jerusalem, secondly in Judea, thirdly in Samaria, and finally, throughout the ends of the earth. What does that look like for us today?

Let's first consider Jerusalem. One reason the Lord Jesus instructed His disciples to start in the city was because it was where they were, it was their home, and what better place to start than on your own doorstep. Our Jerusalem then is our immediate circle of friends and family, neighbours, colleagues and so on.

Take heart here. Jesus knows that our Jerusalem can be a huge challenge.

Consider what the disciples' track record was like in Jerusalem. When Jesus was taken into custody the disciples deserted Him and ran away. Peter denied Him three times (Matt. 26:56,69–75). Jerusalem was a tough call for the disciples stepping out on their mission but Jesus explicitly instructs them to start here, their place of greatest failure. The uncomfortable but essential fact for us to grasp then is that we have to start sharing in the place where we might have been least effective as a witness.

If we can witness in our Jerusalem, we can witness anywhere! So don't ever imagine that God doesn't call us to share our faith amongst those with whom we feel we have failed.

Easier said than done? Many of us have family or friends with whom we've never been able to share our faith, or those with whom we've tried and seemingly got nowhere or even been rejected outright. When it seems such a tall order to begin at close quarters, I believe our first step has to come through loving these people and through persistent prayer.

A helpful way to witnessing amongst such people might be to apologise. Say, 'I'm sorry – I've never shared with you the thing that is most important to me,' or 'I'm sorry that I've been too pushy in sharing with you what is most important to me.' If we are genuine in what we are saying, the other person will sense that and put us, and what we say, in a different light. Demonstrating love, respect and gentleness is crucial.

In some cases there are people we might have known for years but somehow the subject of our faith has just never come up. Is it too late to start now? Maybe we feel that our lifestyle and the way they see us doesn't match up to what we'd like to preach. It isn't uncommon to feel awkward and embarrassed. But consider Jesus' instruction to a new believer:

> *Go home to your family and tell them how much the Lord has done for you.* (Mark 5:19)

Jesus constantly taught that if we are His followers, our lives will bear the stamp of profound love – to God, to ourselves and to our neighbours. Our sociology ought to reflect our theology. Amongst our close family and friends we would hope to be the 'living' Gospel from which should spring questions and discussions about what and why we believe. How we treat others will be the clearest signal of what we think God is like. I always remember my dear missionary friend Michael Wright pointing out, 'You might well be the first Bible a person will ever read.' It's true, isn't it? Most people will read our lives, long before they ever read the Book. You and I are a witness whether we want to be or not. Either we are a good one or a poor one. We may bring good news, or bad news.

Just how do we go about introducing the subject of the Gospel if it has never naturally come up in conversation? Jesus would have us step out in boldness. I have found a useful strategy is to go to the person in question, or write or phone, saying something like, 'Could I just talk to you about something? It's only really just occurred to me that we've known each other for a long time now – and I know you see me go off to church and I'm what you might call religious – but I've never really told you about the most important thing in my life. I'm sorry, it seems silly to be so close and yet I've never really explained it to you . . .' Of course it's then up to me whether I weave the Gospel message into the testimony of my own story or use a more 'packaged' explanation of the Gospel of the kind described in Chapter 7 or at the back of this book.

What will the person's reaction be? If they value me as a friend, they should certainly respect me coming to them in this fashion, particularly as I'm asking them to forgive me for not speaking up before. This should certainly get a reaction and earn their 'ear'. An apology can be endearing and is a big indication that something major has happened in my life. By approaching a friend in this way the biggest message I'm giving is, 'I value you, now let me share the most important thing in my life with you.'

So when we think about our 'Jerusalem', we must consider whether we can care about someone and *not* share these things. Remember we are not going to preach at them, far from it. The hope should always be that there will come a time when we are asked to fully explain our hope in Christ and the glorious

Gospel. A never-to-be-underestimated point, however, is that often in Jerusalem we are called to do no more than the ground work (a most crucial task!). Many Christians seem to find their influence and testimony nudges a friend or loved one towards someone else who God uses to lead him or her in a full step of commitment to Christ.

For all Christians, Jerusalem is the place where we must be aware at all times of the potential to share a few seeds of the grace of God we know at work in us. It is undoubtedly where the majority of 'ordinary' believers are most effective in evangelism. If we believe that God has created us *'for such a time as this'* (Esther 4:14) then we must trust that all our encounters may be of divine purpose. By reminding ourselves of that and by praying each day, 'Lord, help me do Your will,' we will inevitably grow more bold and more loving in our approach to those we see as being placed in our circle as part of the 'big picture' agenda. Whilst some 'Ephesians 4:11–12' type evangelists might make a lot of noise in the public arena it is again the 'foot soldiers', the ordinary men and women of faith who can make the biggest, longstanding impact on someone else's journey towards God. But our journey does not begin and end in Jerusalem. Jesus would have us look beyond the city . . .

Judea was further afield for the disciples, and it's the same for us. Judea represents the evangelism of those friends and contacts we don't see so regularly, our wider family perhaps, and those who we would perhaps call acquaintances and distant colleagues rather than close friends. The process, however, is the same. Wherever there is conversation, there is opportunity:

'How was your weekend?'

'Great thanks. We went to the cinema on Saturday night, then on Sunday we went to church as usual . . .'

This kind of dialogue is always very useful. Never be afraid to sandwich something about church or something that indicates you're a Christian into a normal conversation. It might be that the person you are talking to completely ignores the fact that you've just mentioned you're a churchgoer and you should always give them the space and choice to do that. On the other hand, since this is no longer the Sunday morning pursuit of most people, you'll probably find it gets a reaction that can kick off a further conversation.

If Jerusalem and Judea posed a challenge to the first disciples they would feel especially in need of the power of the Holy Spirit when Jesus mentioned Samaria. I can just imagine a few hard gulps as they swallowed this piece of the command. Samaria, where the Samaritans lived, represented the enemies of the Jews. What does this mean for us? I suggest that this means Jesus asks us to evangelise amongst people we might find it very difficult to like and get along with, and people who might not care too much for us either. This might be very tough but, again, where there is relationship, even poor relationship, there is communication, and where there is communication there is the possibility of the Gospel. Jesus told us, *'Love your enemies, do good to those who hate you, bless those who curse you, pray for those who ill-treat you'* (Luke 6:27–28). John's epistle should also provoke our heart:

> *We love because he first loved us. If anyone says, 'I love God,' yet hates his brother, he is a liar. For anyone who does not love his brother, whom he has seen, cannot love God, whom he has not seen. And he has given us this command: Whoever loves God must also love his brother.* (1 John 4:19–21)

The more we love God, the easier it will become to love people, whoever they are. And we cannot love other people without caring for them. Perhaps in some cases a prerequisite for 'love' will be the need for 'forgiveness'. Jesus was very clear on this matter in his parable of the unmerciful servant recorded in Matthew 18:21–35. Here a servant pleads for mercy at the feet of his master over a huge debt he cannot pay. Taking pity on him, the master cancels the debt, letting him go free. But no sooner has this happened than the servant, we are told, goes to a fellow servant who owes him a relatively small debt. Despite this man's pleas, the first servant is unforgiving and has him thrown into prison. The master of course hears about this wicked act and confronts the servant:

> *'You wicked servant,' he said, 'I cancelled all that debt of yours because you begged me to. Shouldn't you have had mercy on your fellow-servant just as I had on you?'* (Matt. 18:32)

We get a forgiving heart when we have a forgiven heart. The crux of the Gospel message is forgiveness: forgiveness of sins, my sins. And the direct consequence of God forgiving me is that I am compelled to forgive others: *'Forgive as the Lord forgave you'* (Col. 3:13). True forgiveness in human terms is extremely hard and in some cases impossible. Yet the forgiveness of God, by its very nature, makes all things possible. For some people it will be the experience of your genuine forgiveness that speaks louder than any other words as to the truth of the grace of Christ abounding in your life. Perhaps then 'Samaria' has the most powerful potential for evangelistic efforts and for the power of the Gospel to be doubly revealed by our witness of forgiving as we are forgiven.

Samaria might present a challenge to the early disciples and to us today, but once again we can only look at Jesus as our example. People whom many others would have labelled 'difficult' or undesirable surrounded Him day by day. Yet He was labelled 'a friend of sinners' (Matt. 11:19). One of the many so intriguing things about Jesus in the Bible is that He was comfortable with 'sinners' and they were comfortable with Him. Keep in mind here that He didn't just spend His time having a social chit-chat with such people, He also taught them about the kingdom of God, He confronted them.

The 'danger' with our family, friends, colleagues, neighbours, acquaintances and, yes, even enemies, is that sometimes we are so keen on maintaining the relationships that we ignore the evangelism. There is no relationship on earth that takes priority over our loyalty to Jesus Christ and we must remember His example above all others. Jesus lovingly pointed out to Nicodemus, an older man with considerable prestige and knowledge of the Scriptures, that he was ignorant of heavenly things (John 3). Jesus also lovingly told the Samaritan woman that she could never worship God without facing up to her moral sin (John 4). What does this tell us? I believe it shows us that the relationships that Christ formed – close and distant – led directly to confrontation and sometimes rejection. This is a potential consequence for us too and, as we have already discussed, we know there are spiritual powers and principalities at work. When we're looking at matters of the soul, we are very much in a war zone. Rejection and even persecution shouldn't exactly surprise us. But what is the Lord's example? 'Jesus looked at him and loved him,' we are told of our Saviour in His encounter with the rich young man who couldn't handle His message (Mark 10:21). And what greater love in the face of rejection was ahead: Jesus praying, 'Father forgive them,' while the crowd hurled abuse as He died on the cross.

Our message will be rejected, and sometimes that will mean personal rejection too but please take heart and persevere; for whilst we sometimes walk on stony, rocky ground we are also surrounded by rich fertile soil that is ready and waiting for the seeds of the Gospel to be sown.

'Jerusalem', 'Judea' and 'Samaria' are areas that require serious personal investment. Just as Moses found himself wandering the desert with his people so, too, we might have to prepare ourselves to persevere long and hard in the hope and expectation that our witness will lead our friends, loved ones and acquaintances to the promise of God.

Our desert quest continues but now let's pack our bags with a new set of skills and step out into new territory. Just what did Jesus have in mind when he talked about . . . 'the ends of the earth'?

- Who are the people in your Jerusalem, Judea and Samaria?

------------------------ ------------------------

------------------------ ------------------------

------------------------ ------------------------

- Pray about these people and ask God to show you those whom you should persevere more for in prayer. Ask Him to create opportunities for you so that you can 'witness' effectively in the power of the Holy Spirit.

- Consider how you can give the message of the Gospel through the story of what God has done in your life. It is sometimes helpful to write down some key points in your own story so that you can be sure you're covering the full Gospel message in your testimony.

13

The Ends of the Earth

To witness '. . . to the ends of the earth' represents evangelism to those we do not know; people who don't know us, who might not particularly care about us and could care even less about what we believe we have to say to them.

Why is sharing the Gospel with a stranger such a heavy and daunting task? Why would we rather run a marathon than contemplate such an endeavour? Let's look again at our definition of evangelism. The Lausanne Conference on Evangelism stated their categorical agreement that 'to evangelise is to spread the good news'[1] and this is generally accepted as a fair definition amongst the vast majority of biblical scholars. So before we tighten the laces on our running shoes, let's look at some ideas of how we might just possibly put this 'spreading the good news' into practice, without breaking into a sweat.

Firstly, then, let's consider an approach that requires no skill at all. It is easy, anonymous and not intimidating to anyone. All we have to do is drop a tract – a small piece of literature that contains and explains the Gospel message. There are many good tracts available. They can be discretely hidden in your overcoat, ready to be 'dropped' on your seat as you get off the bus, or left on a park bench or restaurant table. They could be left in a library book or on a cinema seat. If you're really worried about being identified, why not drive to another city in the middle of the night to do your drop. We can even supply false beards and fake car number plates so you can be totally anonymous! Avanti Ministries produce a tract that looks like money (although these are produced quite legally and are not so close as to be considered counterfeit notes. We have all types of currencies: sterling, euros, dollars, Malaysian ringgit . . .). Who can resist picking up a currency note off the floor? I often drop these things around then stand by to see people picking them up. It's really interesting to watch people's different reactions. Many will quickly pick it up and shove it into their pocket without looking at it properly, carefully glancing round so as not to be seen. Another will look around to see if anyone obvious has dropped the note before keeping it for him or herself. When they open up the note it says, 'Don't be fooled, Jesus is the real thing.' As they turn it over they then read a concise Salvation message. There are a great variety of tracts that can be dropped in this way, but I have found this one is often received in good humour wherever in the world I have used it. I should of course issue a word of caution here for fear of encouraging activity that might be seen as littering. We must practice wisdom and discretion in everything we do. Would dropping a note of currency be classed as littering? Not by the fortunate person who picks it up! I would suggest, of course, that a Gospel tract has far more value than this, but I am in no way endorsing a random scattering of tracts in a way that compromises decent social behaviour. I thoroughly believe in the value of scattering seed in the hope that some, or even just one, might land in fertile soil. There's a suggestion that Communism spread more quickly in some countries than Christianity simply because they had more literature. There might be some truth in this.

Some time ago I was on the London Underground travelling home from Epping on the Central Line. It seems commuters are in the habit of leaving newspapers on their seat, which other people are accustomed to picking up to read. The cycle continues until a cleaner sweeps through, consigning the particularly dog-eared copies to the trash. This particular day I deliberately bought a new newspaper and placed a tract inside the fold. The carriage I chose wasn't very busy and no-one noticed as I placed the paper down on a seat hoping someone might be drawn to the fresh copy. I chose another seat for myself across the aisle. At the next stop a lady got on the train. I quickly prayed, 'Please, God, let her choose the seat next to my newspaper.' Sure enough, she did and I watched the tract fall onto her lap as she picked up the paper to read. To my delight she put the newspaper down and started reading the tract. I could hardly contain my grin as I watched her turn the pages, obviously engrossed in the message. All the time I praised God and prayed that the message would stir her heart. From where I was sitting, if I leaned up against the window I could surreptitiously put my hand on the reflection of her head in the glass, praying over her for the conviction of the Holy Spirit. As she read the tract it was almost as though I was speaking the Gospel to her myself. After some time the lady put the tract in her handbag. I knew a seed had been planted.

Would you be surprised to hear that a few days later our office took a call from a lady who had picked up a tract on a train? She wanted to become a Christian and was looking for a church. She called the number on the back of the tract. The Avanti Ministries office was able to put her in touch with a local church. Tracts work and dropping a tract *is* evangelism. Some people might think that tracts are terribly unfashionable, but they communicate the whole Gospel to anyone who will read them. If you think about it, most businesses produce small leaflets or booklets that promote their product or company message. Why shouldn't Christians promote the Salvation message in similar innovative ways. I have a colleague who has been known to unroll the toilet paper a little in airport restrooms. He places a tract within the roll and puts the paper back in place. The mind boggles, but what a way to reach a lost soul!

The possibilities for this kind of drop are endless. I always leave a tract on a seat as I leave the bus. Many times I've witnessed someone I've been anonymously sitting next to pick up the tract and start reading it as the bus pulls away. It's so easy. Why not consider dropping a tract on the floor in your workplace, the restroom, the canteen, the kitchen and stationery cupboard. Tracts can be left in lockers at the gym, at ATM machines, in coffee shops, libraries, elevators, on stairs, in telephone booths and even post boxes. You could even get a little braver and hand one to someone in the guise of 'Is this yours?' or 'Does this belong to someone here?' OK, so this might be a bit cheeky, but at least the person is sure to examine it for a few moments!

Tracts can be left in lockers at the gym, at ATM machines, in coffee shops, libraries, elevators, on stairs, in telephone booths and even post boxes.

Dropping tracts is a very simple and easy way of engaging in evangelism. They leave you free from any kind of confrontation, embarrassment or questioning. If you feel a little more confident but don't want to actually start a conversation about the Gospel you can still use tracts, but try handing them over personally. I pay a hotel or restaurant bill, I hand over a tract to the receptionist or waiter. I get out of a taxi and put a tract in the driver's hand, along with the fare. Similarly at the fast food 'drive-through' or ticket office, toll booth or supermarket checkout. All that is required is a simple comment such as, 'This is for you,' or 'I think you might be interested in this.' This approach is very non-confrontational. Both parties know that something has taken place but there is still freedom to keep the action private.

Nothing more need be said. I generally find that people in this kind of situation rarely refuse a piece of literature. They might put it straight in the bin when they realise what it is, but unlike simply handing out leaflets in a street where people consciously give you a wide birth, when you're making this kind of low-level personal contact people are usually happy to accept something from you – especially if you hand it over at the same time as giving a tip! A friend of mine when driving through the manned tolls, often pays for his own car and asks if it's OK to pay for their friend in the car behind them. They then ask, 'Do you mind passing this note to the driver as he comes through?'

What ideas can you come up with?

Do we have any excuse not to have a go at this? As long as we have breath in our body I believe we can do something to get the Gospel message in front of others. I came across a lady in Auckland, New Zealand who is a quadriplegic. Almost every day she gets her friend to position her wheelchair out on the city streets. She has very little movement but is able to hold a tract between two fingers and shout out in a very distorted way, 'Tract, tract!' At first it's quite a distressing sight, but this woman is a real warrior for God. Despite her severe disability she is able to grab the attention of passers by and some, of compassionate disposition, have the guts to take what she is offering from her twisted hand. What a witness! What an inspiration to those of us who are so much more physically able.

My old friend and fellow evangelist Jon and I were heading off on a mission in the UK and we stopped at a motorway service station. Jon came out of the shop having bought a couple of drinks with a big smile on his face. 'Tony, have you got any tracts on you?' he asked. I rummaged around in my trouser pockets, but I had left my jacket in the van. 'I really feel I should give a tract to the lady at the till,' Jon said. 'I believe God made a connection there,' he said, continuing to turn out his pockets in hope. Of course we had thousands of them in our van so, when we got to the car park, Jon decided to go back to see the lady. As I waited I casually prayed, but the more I thought about the shop, the more my mind wandered. My chocolate-loving reputation goes before me and discipline just doesn't come into it when I get a craving. I passed Jon in the doorway as I headed back inside. 'She was really pleased,' he reported, still grinning. 'I just went up to her and said, "God has asked me to give this to you," and handed over the tract.' I smiled at him, recognising the pleasure he felt through this small act of seed-sowing.

As I went back into the shop I had the privilege of seeing what Jon couldn't have seen. When I went up to the counter the lady had the tract in her hand. She didn't take much notice of me as she was so busy telling her colleague about the gentlemen who had just given her this leaflet because 'God had told him to'. I didn't care that she was a bit distracted as she took my payment and handed me the chocolate and change. Instead I looked forward to telling my friend what an impact he had made. Who knows whether she has become a Christian yet. Who knows whether she even read the whole tract – though I suspect she did. Perhaps that was just another step along a long road for her but, either way, Jon's small gesture meant something that day. I suspect the incident will remain with her for the rest of her life.

There are many social instances that allow us to evangelise using tracts. We really don't need to work hard or sweat over making an approach to a stranger. On the other hand, it can also be a lot of fun, particularly in a group of believers, to work out some strategies that get people's attention.

Jon's small gesture meant something that day. I suspect the incident will remain with her for the rest of her life.

We have had a fruitful time at the Southend Air Show. This is a local community event close to where I live and in the last few years the show has drawn half a million people from all over the country for a great day out. We sometimes have a stand in one of the exhibit tents, but our team like to get out among the people and use a survey approach to practise evangelism. Engaging a stranger in conversation by using such a method is really not as intimidating as you might think, especially when you have a good reason for people to want to talk to you. One of our strategies is to hand out free bottles of water and balloons for children. There are always huge queues at the refreshment tents so when we approach people they are usually very happy to accept a bottle of water and a balloon in exchange for answering a few questions. The questions themselves are usually very general and straightforward:

1. What's your first name?
2. Is this your first time at the air show?
3. Where have you travelled from to be here today?
4. Are you enjoying the day?
5. What do you think are the best things about the Southend Air Show?
6. Is there a way you think the air show could be improved?
7. Is there something more the local community could do to improve the show?
8. Is there something the local churches could do to improve the air show?
9. Do you ever go to church yourself?
10. Has anyone given you one of these free booklets before?
    'Thank you very much. Have a great day!'

These are all very light and easy questions and generally we find that people are very willing to offer their opinions. The object of the exercise is two-fold. Firstly, it hopefully means we can put a tract in a person's hand that they may read later. Secondly, the key benefit of this approach is that it gets members of our team into the habit of approaching and talking to people. They don't necessarily have to speak the Gospel themselves, so in that sense it requires no special skill, but it does ask them to go up to strangers and offer them something. If you're reading this and cringing at the thought of it, then it's obviously not for you, so please try one of the other ideas. This is an approach that I have found works best as a group activity, especially for young people interested in street evangelism. We've seen youth groups having a great time engaging with the crowd, all in matching T-shirts or caps.

The beauty of something like the questionnaire method is that you don't feel pressurised to speak out the Gospel yourself. This idea simply allows you to hand out a tract at the end of your conversation.

Another approach that we have used at events like the air show is where we are asking a different set of survey questions leading to an opportunity to verbalise the Gospel.

Our dialogue often goes something like this: 'Excuse me, can you help me? I work with mainstream churches, and I am conducting a short survey asking people ten quick questions to measure how good you are as a person. Then I'd like to show you the best presentation you've ever seen about the Bible, but you've got to be honest. Can you help me?'

We find that the majority of people we approach are willing to take a few minutes to do the survey:

On a scale of 0 to 10, where 0 is 'never', 5 is 'sometimes' and 10 is 'always', how would you rate yourself on the following statements:

I give to charities
I pray
I help strangers in need
I read the Bible
I forgive people when they hurt me
I love and help family members
I am loyal with my friendships
I put other people first when they need me
I am totally honest in the things I say and do (the liars usually score 10!)
I see the best in people

The person is then scored and rated:

68 – 70 Angelic
64 – 67 Saintly
35 – 63 Good
25 – 34 Struggling
Under 25 Seek help!

The scores of course are all a bit of fun but we then go on, using the tract, to say, 'You're obviously a very good person! Now let me tell you what the Bible says to a person like you.' This then leads on into a Gospel presentation similar to the one presented in Chapter 7 or one of the others at the end of the book.

Let me emphasise that this is simply one approach and there are many other ways of engaging the attention of strangers and many other Gospel illustrations that could be used.

There are countless opportunities that allow you to be bold and verbalise the full Gospel with a stranger. For some this might be a terribly intimidating thought, in which case, stick with the tracts. On the other hand it is my hope that, with the right tools, more people might be encouraged to develop the skills to boldly speak out about the love of God and the good news of Jesus Christ. I'm not talking here about stopping a stranger in the street and bashing him or her with a Bible. No! Many situations in life put people in our path with whom we can share the greatest story ever told.

I love the opportunities offered by air travel. I'm sure everyone shares similar concerns as they board the plane. Who will I be sitting next to? Will I have enough elbow space? There are always those few moments of trepidation as you watch people filing by while you secretly plead that the seat next to you will be left vacant. We've all been there, haven't we?

Surely it's just good manners, when you're going to be sitting next to someone in a very confined space for the next however many hours, that you at least make pleasant conversation. On the whole I find that people are happy to talk about themselves. Some are even hard to shut up when they find someone prepared to take an interest in them. Generally, people like to be listened to. It only takes a few questions – about their journey, why they're making it, their family, their job – and before you know, they're relaxed and happily engaging in conversation. You'll end up hearing about their grandson's friends, the hazards of keeping a pet hamster and why it's so hard to grow carrots in their garden! Ask enough questions and, unless they really do want to be left alone, they will ask something back. In my case it's easy to steer the conversation, simply because of the job I do and the reason I am travelling. I usually say something like, 'I'm an author and I speak in maximum-security prisons around the world. We find that the message I share is really changing so many people's lives and it's having a massive effect on re-offending crime figures.' This usually gains their interest and I might talk more about my life and what brought me to the work I do now, incorporating the Gospel message through the story of how I became a Christian. Like many air travellers I often have my laptop in front of me so instead of using my own testimony I sometimes refer to the 'message' that I told them was having an effect on crime figures: 'I have it on my computer here. It's only a ten-minute presentation and I'm always looking at ways to improve it. Would you like to see it and maybe you could give me your opinion?' If they show interest I take them through an interactive Gospel presentation using the same illustration included back in Chapter 7.

I'd encourage anyone who uses a laptop or any similar handheld technology to get a good Gospel message presentation on their gadget. People are often curious to see something new on a screen and it's an easy tool, perhaps a less 'threatening' way of presenting the message. You can download one from our website: www.avantiministries.com/think. I have used this presentation with so many people on my mobile phone using headphones, with great success.

Let me issue here another word of warning. I use such Gospel presentations a great deal and find that they can be very effective. However, there are dangers in a 'packaged' approach to the Gospel and here I have to remind you of our teaching on 'pathos' back in Chapter 10. Let me reiterate. Whenever we present the Gospel we must do so with care and sensitivity and, when possible, a sense of understanding of the position of our hearer. I believe we should all learn some kind of Gospel presentation, but this is as much for our own use – so that we can get the message clear in our head as a foundation – as for use as a public tool. Think of it as stocking up your armoury. When you are confident in the Gospel message you will be able to use it and adapt its telling according to circumstances. When I get into a taxi and the driver engages me in conversation about the terrible disaster of the Haiti earthquake, do I recite to the driver the text of the Gospel presentation? No! And yet as we weave our way through our dialogue I can hopefully get to the point where I am naturally sharing my hope and belief in the sovereignty, justice and love of my Creator. And in this situation am I going to push my driver friend to a point of decision for Christ? No, probably not. But hopefully I will have offered something of the light of the Gospel and hopefully, for him or her, there will be another time . . .

I really believe that God opens up opportunities for us and they usually spill out from our everyday encounters. When you live constantly alert to this fact you find that you're always looking to be one step ahead of a situation, always looking for a way to naturally get into a position where you can share the Gospel. The key, as I'm sure I've already stressed, is to be real and genuine so that you might earn a listening ear when it comes to presenting the all-important message. When Jesus meets the woman at the well He opens the conversation in a natural way. He asks for

> *God opens up opportunities for us and they usually spill out from our everyday encounters.*

water. Of course it doesn't take long before the Lord starts talking about the water of life, but His first approach is through friendly, polite, everyday conversation. Later, when Jesus, just after the Resurrection, appears to the two travellers on the road to Emmaus He opens up a conversation. Luke 24:16 reports *'they were kept from recognising him'. 'What are you discussing together as you walk along?'* Jesus asks. The gospel tells of Cleopas's incredulity that this stranger did not appear to know: *'Are you the only one living in Jerusalem who doesn't know the things that have happened there in these days?'* Jesus still chooses not to reveal Himself, but asks, *'What things?'* The account goes on with the two friends telling their new companion about the events that Jesus of course knew only too well, first-hand. Why would Jesus do this? Might it be because He wants to meet them in a spirit of openness? He wants to engage with them, hearing their concerns, listening to their interpretation of the events that are troubling them so much. As an apparent stranger He wants to show interest in them, to meet them on their level and allow them the space to reveal something of themselves before making Himself known to them, at the right time in a way that is most meaningful.

What made the apostle Paul such a great communicator of the Gospel? Undoubtedly it was his passion for it; *powerful* passion not born out of 'emotion' but fuelled by the conviction that every man and woman faces either Heaven or Hell. What do we see when we are dropping our children off at school, or when we're in our place of work or out doing the shopping? What do we see when we look at people? Is it just their fashion sense, the car they drive, their financial status? Do we ever give a thought about what they face after death? Paul did. In fact he seemed to see this before and above anything else. Take for example his visit to Athens. Paul wasn't impressed by the greatness and the grandeur of Greek society. Neither the towering Acropolis nor the magnificent Parthenon overwhelmed him as he made his way around this most civilised and educated cultural centre. What Paul saw was the individual Athenians, individual, misguided and lost souls.

Another key aspect of Paul is that he was constantly looking for a way to connect with people.

> *Paul then stood up in the meeting of the Areopagus and said: 'Men of Athens! I see that in every way you are very religious. For as I walked around and looked carefully at your objects of worship, I even found an altar with this inscription:* TO AN UNKNOWN GOD. *Now what you worship as something unknown I am going to proclaim to you.'* (Acts 17:22–23)

Notice how Paul engages the people on common ground. He talks to them about being 'very religious', introduces the issue of one specific idol they have and then tells them he knows *that* God. Paul then goes on with a clear presentation of the Gospel. Read Acts 17:22–31. This is Paul doing what he does best! So in the same way as Jesus communicated with the woman at the well, or the friends on the Emmaus road, Paul finds the hook. He takes something from his hearer so that he might give the Message in meaningful context. I am convinced that the Holy Spirit gives us these same kinds of openings and opportunities every single day. We just need to look for them and recognise them. Another point to draw out from this piece of scripture is the simplicity of the apostle's Gospel presentation. He speaks around three simple points. First, God is the Creator and Owner of the universe. Secondly, God wants everyone to know Him and thirdly, all people everywhere must repent because the judgment day is coming. Paul didn't make the Gospel more complicated than it is, and neither should we.

Finally, we must also take comfort in this report of Paul's activity in Athens. The apostle must have recognised that everywhere he preached this message he would be faced with ridicule and rejection. He was therefore realistic in his expectations. We are told in verse 32, *'some of them sneered'*. Did this discourage him? Did he give up? No. He knew there were others who wanted to listen and, sure enough, we are told that a few men became followers and believed. In the same way, when we share the Gospel with strangers we put ourselves on the line and set ourselves up for rejection. But we must never give up for there will always be those who want to hear.

On a flight home from Hungary I found myself in conversation with a Hungarian girl, Timi, who was travelling to London to find work. She started telling me about her life in Hungary and her hopes for her future and, before long, she pulled out her camera and started showing me pictures of her family and her village. We were seated on a row of three with the spare seat in the middle of us and it was hard to see the pictures on the tiny camera. Noting I had my laptop on my knee she said, 'Maybe you could view the pictures on your computer.' Instantly my heart sank. My computer was showing only twelve minutes battery time left and I had no means of plugging into the mains in our economy seats. I had been hoping that I could use those precious minutes at some point in our conversation to show her the Gospel presentation. Of course I didn't want to be impolite and she seemed so keen to share her pictures with me, so I took the memory card and put it into my laptop. There was picture after picture: her home, her mum and dad, her beloved grandfather, her boyfriend, the local cake shop where she met with her friends, her holiday in Tunisia . . . Timi seemed so pleased to talk to me and I was careful to show as much interest, despite my dismay at the failing battery. Finally her show came to an end. 'Would the computer hold out?' I wondered. I absolutely *had* to share my message with her. 'Thank you,' I said, 'that was lovely. Would you mind if I showed you an amazing presentation that I have on my laptop?' Timi was instantly warm to the idea. 'It's just a fun presentation that shows why I believe in God and about my faith in Him,' I said as I typed her name into the interactive box.

As we neared the end of the presentation Timi appeared thoughtful. It came to the point of challenge and, as her name came up on the screen, I quietly asked, 'So, Timi, if you died tonight, where would you go?'

'I'm not really sure,' she said, her voice uncertain and a little shaky.

'Well let me show you the rest of the presentation so you can be sure.'

I recapped about the fact that you need a perfect record to get into Heaven. There are two ways you can get a perfect record: you can be a perfect person, but we've all blown that one; or you can ask Jesus for His perfect record. The presentation reminded her that we need to accept Jesus' perfect record to be forgiven. 'To be forgiven we need to be willing to turn away from the things that are wrong in our life and say sorry to Jesus,' I gently showed her. 'The second thing is to surrender our life to Jesus, in every way we can.' Timi looked as though she was trying hard to understand. 'Unless you do those two things, Timi,' I said, 'it's impossible for you to enter Heaven, and that's such a shame because that's why Jesus died for you.' The presentation ended.

Timi told me about her eighty-two-year-old grandfather who was severely ill in hospital in Hungary. She was very close to him and was deeply saddened that since losing her grandmother the previous year he was looking forward to death himself. 'I'll probably never see him again,' she told me sadly.

'Could I pray for you,' I asked tentatively, 'and perhaps I could pray for your grandfather, too.' She looked at me, her eyes watery, and smiled willingly. I closed my eyes and prayed quietly, trying to be sensitive as I heard her starting to weep. When I finished she seemed very upset. 'I'm so sorry,' I said, worried that I had pushed too much. 'No,' came her reply, as she smiled through her tears, 'it's just that no-one's ever prayed for me before, and no-one has ever bothered to tell me about God like this.'

The young woman was very moved by the Gospel message and the prayer. I could see she wasn't at the point of dedicating her life to God there and then but she began asking so many questions and I knew she was on a new path. The amazing thing is that the computer battery held out just long enough for me to type her address into an email back to my office so one of the team could send her more literature. I hit 'send' and the machine shut down. I'm sure God was smiling.

A beautiful analogy of our relationship with the Lord can be found in our solar system. The moon does not actually shine by itself, it only reflects the light given off by the sun. The sun is the source of the light. When the world gets in the way of that light, the moon reflects less than it is fully capable of, as is seen in an eclipse. Likewise, God is the source of light and truth, and when we put the world in front of Him, we reflect less of His light than we were designed to. We were intended to fully reflect the radiance of His glory in our lives. It's not always easy, though, is it? By natural instinct we try to manipulate and work things out in our own way. I recognise that personally I am very burdened to spread the Gospel, to see souls saved. It might seem like a worthy mandate, the motivation of a 'good Christian', but not when I try to do this alone, in my own strength. How can that bring glory to Christ? No, to truly reflect Christ I need to slow down, to simply 'be', to let Him shine through me as I seek Him in all that I do and all that I am. The result is that I am more compassionate to others. I give time, I seek to level with their concerns, recognising that if my life reflects Christ, my words will be effective.

The John Hancock Tower is the tallest building in New England. It stands sleekly on its own in Copley Square, away from the high-rise area of Boston's downtown. This modern building stands 60 storeys high with a glass curtain wall, which is a stark contrast to the nineteenth-century Romanesque Trinity Church of multicoloured granite, and the Italian Renaissance-styled Boston Public Library across the street.

However, despite its enormity in its local area, its presence is made less overpowering by its pure, crystal-like geometry and reflecting glass skin. The architect's intent was to honour these landmarks by reflecting them first, and then building his architectural statement around them. In the final analysis, the dominant view when you are close to the building is of the nearby historical buildings reflected with subtle distortions of colour and shape in the Hancock Tower's glass.

Unless we can present the Gospel message to people in a way that enables them to see themselves in our communication, they will always struggle to assimilate what we are trying to say. To motivate people we need to help them see themselves in what we are talking about. Our communication must be at their level, reflecting their concerns. Unless they see themselves reflected in our message, our words end up being nothing more than what our own ears want to hear.

To motivate people we need to help them see themselves in what we are talking about.

Whether in Jerusalem, Judea, Samaria or out at the 'ends of the earth', this is perhaps the most vital point to remember as we interact in the hope of sharing the Gospel.

- The early part of the chapter mapped out a range of activities and ideas based on confidence and skill level. The object of this exercise is primarily to instil confidence, to illustrate that evangelism is purely the spreading of the Gospel – an activity in which anyone can, and everyone must, engage. Can you see yourself attempting any of these ideas in the grid opposite?

- Can you come up with any other ideas that could help you proclaim or spread the Gospel?

Ideas to spread the Gospel	Activity	Skill Factor	Christian Identity Level	Engaging a non-Christian in conversation
1	Dropping **Tracts**	Nil	Private and invisible	No
2	Dropping **Tracts**	Nil	Public and invisible	No
3	Giving **Tracts**	Low	Public and visible	Yes 'Have you been given one of these?'
4	**Survey** One-to-one with strangers	Low	Public and visible (Give out a tract at the end)	Yes 'Have you been to a church in this area? (zero confrontation)
5	**Survey** One-to-one with strangers	Moderate	Public and visible	Yes (present the full Gospel at the end)
6	**No Survey** One-to-one with strangers	High	Public and visible	Yes (verbalising the full Gospel to people)
7	**Proclaiming** to groups	Moderate to high	Public and visible	Yes (verbalising the full Gospel to groups)

14

Call Me Crazy!

Timi's story is, of course, unique, but not particularly unusual. I love to share my computer presentation of the Gospel with people. The more I use it, the more I love it, and the more I love it, the more I want to share it. Whether we use a tract or a technological presentation or our own telling of the Gospel message we must always be prepared to share it with sensitivity and love. I've said it before, the Gospel is a matter of the heart and a young woman's emotional response to hearing the message and being prayed for should come as no surprise. There are millions of Timis out there – people who have never been prayed for and never been listened to by someone with God's compassion. Whoever I find myself seated next to on an aeroplane I pray that I see them through God's eyes, not my own. At one time I might have hoped for a vacant seat so that I could stretch out, relax and enjoy the free elbow space. Now I ask my Master to seat me next to someone who needs to hear the message of Salvation and, no matter what my initial preconceptions and judgments, I remind myself that I am called to be 'Jesus with skin on' to whoever I encounter.

What must it have been like to look into the face of Jesus? His compassion for people was something beyond what I could ever imagine. So much of our approach with strangers rests on us showing interest in them as human beings. If we cannot smile at them, listen to them, appear interested in their life, how can we expect them to listen to us so that we can share our message? The Gospel message is the greatest story ever told and if it's ours to tell then it should flow easily through us like fresh water pouring from a swollen spring. Part of this flow is in *who we are* and the compassion we have to make connections with our fellow human beings. Talking to a stranger becomes an altogether different experience if we can look them in the face and think, 'God loves this one and He wants him or her for His own.'

On another flight I had the pleasure of sitting next to a well-known Rastafarian reggae musician, 'Demolition Man'. We quickly got into conversation and he explained that he had turned from a life of drugs and was travelling around the former Eastern Block performing and holding reggae-music workshops, encouraging others to live positively and turn from substance abuse. I listened excitedly to his aspirations and mission to help others. 'We share so much common ground,' I told him. It was easy to lead the conversation and, like the young Hungarian girl, he, too, was very willing to hear my message. As I drew to a close there were tears rolling down my new friend's cheeks and he wept openly as he prayed and gave his life to Christ there and then on the aeroplane.

Each of the ideas illustrated at the end of the last chapter are, I believe, very easily attainable for any Christian. Please don't get me wrong, however. They are not designed to be a series of steps on which we should try to climb. The point of the chart (p. 167) and our discussion in the last chapter was to demonstrate that if we are able in body and mind there is no reason why we shouldn't be engaged in at least some basic activity that builds an evangelism habit into our lives. Ideas 1 to 6 are all activities that can take place easily and casually in everyday life. Idea 7 might, at first sight, appear to be very much the realm of the Ephesians 4-type evangelist we talked about in Chapter 11. It involves proclaiming the Gospel to groups of people. It calls for moderate to high skill in verbalising the message and is very public and visible.

Might you be surprised that after all my years in public ministry I still quake as I stand up to address an audience? I still get the butterflies in my stomach, still sweat, still fantasise a last-minute escape and am still, quite often, physically sick. It doesn't matter who the crowd is, how big it is or what the circumstances, my ministry remains a massive dichotomy between my call and passion to share the Gospel and the flight instinct of the shy and cowardly flesh.

The 2005 Southend Air Show was wet. It had been a glorious morning but as thousands of people filed into the showground the sky began to darken and spots of rain could be heard pitting the canvas of the exhibition tent. Avanti Ministries had a small stand in a tent where a number of other charities were showing their wares. It was a nice place to be. It never got too crowded and the people who came in were usually polite, caring folk who were mostly happy to add our leaflets to their collection of worthy-cause literature. Most of all, our stand was a base for our team who were excited at the idea of getting out among the crowds with their clipboards, handing out lollipops and bottles of water, chatting to friendly people who took part in our survey and handing out Gospel tracts. As the rain grew heavier the temperature dropped noticeably and we all grew more despondent. Despite waterproofs, people didn't want to stand in the cold and rain answering questions. The bottles of cold water lost ground to a quest for hot chocolate in a dry refreshment tent. We sat miserably at our stand, straightening literature, smiling at those who walked by. The wind started to whip up a gale, beating noisily at the side of the tent. It was then that it occurred to me. We didn't need to go out to the people any more. Here they were, pouring into our tent to keep warm and dry. Before too long the place was packed with steaming bodies and there was quite a commotion as men battled to secure the large door that was flapping precariously in the now gale-like winds.

I began sweating, but it was nothing to do with the sudden humidity in the tent. This was home turf. There were people there I recognised from taking my children to school, or from the supermarket and bus queue. I pushed the thought away but it wouldn't lie still. I tried to ignore what I knew God was saying to me, but the more I fought, the more I knew I had to put my money where my big mouth is. It was a captive audience. These people had come for a day out. They wanted to be entertained. If I were a singer or a dancer, magician, musician or political activist it would be a prime opportunity to showcase my talent, to win a crowd. But that day there were no singers or dancers, no performers in the tent. There was just me, with a powerful message to share. When I looked at the rest of the team I realised they were no longer despondent. They, too, recognised the situation for exactly what it might be. What bothered me was the way they were looking so expectantly at me! My old friend Jo Martin pushed a chair forward and eventually, feeling sick to the core, I climbed up to stand on it and began to address the crowd . . .

I learned many lessons from that experience. First there was shame – shame that I would hesitate at a God-given opportunity. Shame at the hypocrisy that, whilst I encouraged a team to get out there and take part in the Great Commission, my fear of embarrassment would have me shy away from speaking out the Gospel to a captive crowd. But when it comes to shame all I can console myself with is the knowledge that He has been there and done that. The shame of the cross is beyond measure and didn't Christ Himself falter in the garden, knowing what public humiliation lay ahead of Him? Didn't Peter, our Lord's close friend, run and hide rather than speak out for the One he loved. When I remember the fear and the temptation to hide under the

God knows that we will let Him down, He knows there will be times when we fail, but like the loving father He invites us still to have a go.

table rather than stand up on that chair, I only need think of the way the apostles also feared being publicly identified with Christ. I have said it before, and will again that God knows that we will let Him down, He knows there will be times when we fail, but like the loving father He invites us still to have a go. Though we wander away and let Him down badly, He still prepares a banquet for us when we come back and say sorry. He doesn't *need* us to paint His picture. He is the Author and Finisher of all things, the Creator of colour and texture and all that is beautiful. But still, He invites us to pick up the paintbrushes and have a go and, as we make smudgy marks on His perfect canvas, He carefully refines and tweaks and loves the scene into something spectacular.

If I still feel those pangs of shame about my hesitation that day, what I feel more is the absolute euphoria of it. As I began to stutter and stammer through my message the crowd fell respectfully quiet. They were willing to listen and gave me the courtesy of their attention. I kept my message short and succinct, but invited anyone who was interested in learning more about why I had taken this opportunity and why the rest of the Avanti team had given up their family time to be at the air show that day, to take home a free copy of *Taming the Tiger* or any of the other Gospel tracts we had on our stand. To my surprise and delight people clamoured to come forward and we soon had no literature left. Isn't it amazing how we underestimate how much people *do* want to know about God? Only He knows the effect of that day. As Jesus foretold, there would be many seeds that fell on rough ground or got tangled up by weeds or blown away in the wind, but I'm sure there were also seeds that became embedded in good soil that have since grown and prospered. Either way, that is God's business, not mine. All I can ever hope to do is be faithful to my call to cast seeds, so that the Holy Spirit can work wherever they fall.

I tell this story not to brag about the one day I happened to be faithful. I'm ashamed to say there are probably many more where I gave in to the flight instinct. Rather I tell this story perhaps to throw down a gauntlet, to challenge you to discover for yourself the biblical link between proclaiming the Gospel and the 'fullness of life' the Gospel promises for those who fully partake in its message. *'I pray that you might be active in sharing your faith, so that you will have a full understanding of every good thing we have in Christ'* (Phlm. 6). Can you imagine how that feels? So often I think we live in a twilight world, going about our business with only a tiny taster of what it means to have 'life' in Christ. Yet here, we are promised *'full understanding of every good thing . . .'* if we are only prepared to share what we know. I know through my own experience that this is the case. When I describe my feelings that day at the air show as 'euphoric' this barely touches the surface of the joy that was in my heart. Charles Spurgeon sums it up brilliantly as far as I'm concerned:

'I pray that you might be active in sharing your faith, so that you will have a full understanding of every good thing we have in Christ.'
(Phlm. 6)

> Even if I were utterly selfish and had no care for anything but my own happiness I would choose, if I might, under God, to be a

> soul winner, for never did I know a more perfect, overflowing unutterable happiness of the purest and most ennobling order, till I first heard of one who had sought and found the Saviour through my means. I recollect the thrill of joy that went through me! No young mother ever rejoiced so much over her first born child, no warrior was so exultant over a hard won victory![1]

Let me stress again my belief that anonymously dropping tracts is a commendable act of evangelism, but in the same breath I must also encourage anyone who might dare to consider engaging in idea 7 on our chart: public proclamation to groups of people.

Here's a really crazy idea: why not set up a phone call the next time you're on a train, in a doctor's surgery or in some other public place? Speak the Gospel to the 'person' on the other end of the phone and rely on everyone's natural instinct to eavesdrop. Believe me, I've done it and it's amazing how a whole train carriage can become transfixed. Even if no-one has the guts to respond, it's great practise for you!

There are, of course, many less contrived, very natural opportunities. Proclaiming the Gospel to groups of people doesn't need to involve a stage, a pulpit or a chair in a crowd. It doesn't need to involve a stranger either. Most of us have some kind of social circle or an environment where we are able to speak to a small gathering about ourselves. And if we can speak about our life, we can – even if only in pieces and over time – speak about the Gospel. Do you attend a sports club, a school PTA, a mother and toddler group, retirement club or any type of hobby or interest group? Maybe you go out for lunch with a regular group or find yourself congregating in the kitchen at work as you wait for the kettle to boil? Think about how you can steer the conversation next time you find someone asking about how your week has been, or what motivates you to do what you do. If

Christ is in you, then I challenge you to let the Gospel pour – or even trickle – out from you and you'll probably find there's more than one person interested to listen.

In the last few years I've seen my face plastered on billboards and posters all over the world. I've seen myself on TV, heard my voice on radio broadcasts, been recognised by people I've never met and asked to sign books as though I'm some kind of celebrity. It's something I don't think I'll ever feel comfortable with. In fact the thought that people are attracted to come to an event to see and hear me, Tony Anthony, makes me quite sick. Why are they coming? What do they think they will find – Kung Fu demonstrations, stories of depravity? Sometimes I feel a little like Russell Crowe in the film *Gladiator*: 'Are you not entertained? Are you not entertained? Is this not why you are here?' he cries, as he slaughters yet another gladiator, sending the bloodthirsty crowd wild with excitement.[2] I understand, of course, that my story carries a lot of interest for people, but I often think how wrong it is that large crowds of people would come to hear this pathetic and shameful story rather than that of the greatest rescue plan ever, packed with incredible stories of redemption. At the end of the day my events are just a form of public confession, and yet people still come! I pray for the day – though I fear it will not come – when people like me will not be invited to speak, for the simple reason that there will be so many more ordinary Christians willing to stand up and share their stories of faith. What about John Smith, or Barbara Jones or A.N. Other Christian? They might be men and women who live very 'unremarkable' lives, yet if they are followers of Christ they, too, have a compelling, thrilling, dramatic, action-packed, life-transforming story to tell. I love the testimony of Angus Buchan, whose experience is told in a book and film, *Faith Like Potatoes*.[3] Buchan is a humble Zambian farmer. He is not a celebrity, a famed theologian, a celebrated evangelist or public speaker. He is a farmer, trying to make a life for his family in harsh cultural and environmental conditions. Through him God has demonstrated miraculous provision and today thousands of people all around the world flock to hear his story.

Imagine how wonderful it would be to see people filing into stadiums, not to hear some dumb story from a 'worldly-famed' personality, but to hear the best news in history – the story of Jesus Christ? And who would tell it? Well . . . why not you? Again, I remind you of Michael Wright, the ordinary man with an ordinary story who led me, and many others, to Christ because of his relationship with the finest Author and the greatest Performer of Miracles this world will ever know.

As I write this chapter I realise more and more the dichotomy of what I am doing. My job has many blessings. I get to travel the world and meet wonderful people. Yet when I travel I'm separated from the ones I love. Every time I walk out the door for a long mission I leave my wife Sara to manage as a one-parent family. For my boys it must often seem like an eternity before Daddy's home to tuck them into bed again. I miss their swimming lessons, their football practises, their parents' evenings, Christmas shows, harvest festivals and many of the precious things that ground and secure a family. I leave behind the comfort and strength of consistent fellowship and when I travel I am alone, yet constantly in the spotlight . . . and all this for a job I don't really want to do. In fact, I've been known to rant about how much I hate evangelism. Yes, that's the truth. I hate evangelism.

Why do people need to be persuaded from the road to destruction?

I hate evangelism in the way that the paramedic hates arriving at a road traffic accident to be met with dying people in desperate situations. Hate in the way that I wish this dreadful situation had never occurred. Why do people need to be persuaded from the road to destruction? And yet this is also the thing I love with relentless passion. Love in the way that the paramedic knows he can get in there and save those lives. The adrenaline kicks in and it doesn't matter how broken, how bloody or how dangerous, he sets aside his own agenda and dives right in there to do his job. A mother, trapped in the driver's seat, is screaming for her children. The paramedic brings first aid and life-giving oxygen. 'They're OK, I can see them, they're alive, we can save them,' he assures the distraught woman. 'You just need to listen to me. You just need to let me help.' In the midst of the drama his mind flashes back to his own children, left at home, and he knows he will do everything he can to save these little ones. The paramedic hates that this has happened, hates the sacrifice, but loves his job.

Like the paramedic, I will fight with all I have to save lives. I will battle for Timi and Demolition Man, the ones who come expecting a Kung Fu demonstration and all the others with whom I have the privilege of sharing the Gospel. Will you join me in the battle? Will you drop a tract next time you leave a tip in a restaurant? Will you hand over a tract to someone you've got chatting to on the bus? Will you talk to your buddies in the work's canteen about why you went to church on Sunday morning, or tell them about a great book you've just read about how God is real and impacts people's lives today? Might you ask for the privilege of sharing your story of faith at your next tennis club social or mother and toddler meeting? I ask you right now to secure yourself in the spiritual armour that is yours for the claiming. Come with me, if you will, to the front line . . . we're about to take a look at the enemy.

- Was it a surprise for you to discover that acts of mercy and charity, Godly living and caring for our neighbours are not evangelism?

- Do you know what your friends believe evangelism to be?

- Reflecting on this chapter, do you believe you could build more evangelism into your life?

- *'I pray that you may be active in sharing your faith, so that you will have a full understanding of every good thing we have in Christ'* (Phlm. 6). Do you know the blessing that Paul is talking about here?

- If more Christians realise there is a connection between proclaiming faith and fullness of life, do you think they will proclaim the Gospel more?

15

Salty Tea

We've already discussed the fact that we're in a spiritual war. As Christians we are engaged in the heavenly battle that has raged since the Fall, since the time that God, in complete love, bestowed men and women with freedom and we, in proud independence, chose to turn from the perfect relationship He ordained for us. As Christians, restored into that relationship through our trust and surrender to Jesus Christ, we are equipped with heavenly armour and are required to join our leader in fighting for the souls of those who are still lost. Who are we fighting? Well, it's unfashionable and it doesn't sit well in many of our modern feel-good-lifestyle churches of today, but when the old revivalists preached hellfire and damnation, they were surely closer to the mark than we comfortably care to mention today.

I was once openly challenged during my Gospel presentation by a pastor. He had invited me to address his church but when it came to my presentation he objected to its assumption of the reality of Hell, the devil and the certain cost of what comes with walking with God. I'm sure Satan was having a field day. If we believe the devil doesn't exist, then we don't pay any attention to him. And if we don't pay any attention to him he can quietly get on with his stealth-like corruption under our very noses. We have our church meetings, sing our songs of praise and do the things

Many people doubt the existence of God. Many more doubt the existence of the devil, and that's just the way he likes it for now.

that 'good' Christian people do. Meanwhile, the devil's back there in the church kitchen sneakily switching the sugar and salt labels around without anyone noticing. Then we wonder why our tea tastes so bad . . . or worse still, we simply acquire the taste without even flinching! This is how Satan operates. By switching labels for words like 'Gospel' and 'evangelism' we are quickly duped into thinking we are spreading the Gospel and 'doing' evangelism, when actually we are not.

Many people doubt the existence of God. Many more doubt the existence of the devil, and that's just the way he likes it for now. While we don't believe in him, he can continue to wheedle his way unacknowledged and undeterred into the fabric of our lives. The devil was real to Jesus. Each of the synoptic Gospels is keen to tell us of their forty-day and night meeting in the wilderness. I'm sure it's no coincidence that these accounts resonate with the forty-year wilderness experience of the children of Israel back in the Old Testament. Was the same devil present then? It was certainly not God's plan that His chosen people flounder and turn to idolatry. I think we can imagine that when the Spirit led Jesus into the desert it was perhaps a revelation of what should have been, what might have been for God's Old Testament children if only they had remained faithful and trusting. OK, so Jesus was Jesus, but the lesson is that when the devil tried to tempt Him – and boy did he try hard! – Jesus grounded Himself firmly in Scripture and in the promises of God and used that as His shield and protection.

Yes, the devil was real to Jesus. He appeared to Him, tempted Him, and tried to toy with Him. To imagine that he can't, or won't, or doesn't do the same with those who follow Christ is naïve at best. Let's be straight here. The devil is our enemy and like any serving military officer, it's important that we know a little bit about our enemy so that we can be ready for the battle, so that we understand his motivations and recognise his strategies and weaponry.

Church historian and author Dr Michael Green, in his book *I Believe in Satan's Downfall*, reveals why the devil is fanatically committed to hindering the Gospel:

> What is the motivation which goads the Tempter into continually seeking the downfall of man? The answer is ambition. His God is no longer the Lord, but himself. He must replace the Almighty. He must have pride of place. Therefore his aim is to get every man, woman and child to owe him suzerainty. His success is phenomenal. There is an important passage in 2 Corinthians 4 which sheds light on his ultimate strategy. He blinds the minds of unbelievers so they cannot see the Gospel. Satan is the great unseen adversary. He does not take kindly to seeing his kingdom assailed and his captives released. He has, for all practical purposes, taken the place of God in the lives of many people. His great concern is to keep the light of the Gospel of Jesus Christ who is the likeness of God, from breaking in upon them.[1]

So if we go along with Dr Green's assertions, we recognise that the devil has several motives for preventing the spreading of the Gospel. First is ambition and glory. He wants pride of place in the universe. He wants to take glory from Jesus. Secondly, he works on territorial advantage. He wants to keep non-Christians in spiritual prison. They were born into his kingdom and he wants to keep them there. The Bible is clear that there is no grey area here. It might be a tough one to swallow, but we are all currently serving either the devil or Jesus. Christ himself said, *'He*

> *'And this gospel of the kingdom will be preached in the whole world as a testimony to all nations, and then the end shall come.' (Matt. 24:14)*

who is not for me is against me' (Luke 11:23). Thirdly, the devil is supremely motivated to stop evangelism by life preservation. Read again the account of the devil trying to entice Jesus in the wilderness and we see just how well he knows the Scriptures. He quotes and uses its prophecy and reads, as plainly as you and I can read, that there is coming a time when he will ultimately be defeated. This 'time', it appears, begins with the worldwide preaching of the Gospel. Jesus' words in Matthew 24:14 reveal the great divine plan, '*And this gospel of the kingdom will be preached in the whole world as a testimony to all nations, and then the end shall come.*' What happens at the end? Flick forward to the book of Revelation 20:10 . . . '*And the devil, who deceived them, was thrown into the lake of burning sulphur, where the beast and the false prophet had been thrown. They will be tormented day and night forever and ever.*' No wonder our great adversary is fighting with all his might to delay the coming of *that* day!

War is always more than just the battle scene. Behind every war is strategy and stealth. The numerous resistance movements in operation in World War II are now legendary and can surely be credited for victory against Nazi dictatorship. Such 'underground' manoeuvres took place right in the heart of occupied territory – hiding of Jews, forging documents, sabotage and intentionally substandard work by those forced to labour for the enemy, disruption of communication, provision and supplies to enemy lines . . . The success and power of any resistance movement relies on intelligence, stealth and deception so that maximum disruption is caused long before the enemy realises and is able to respond. Isn't this just the way of the devil? His mission is to stop communication of the Gospel, to distort it, disrupt it and put a halt to that which will ultimately win the war. Certainly there are circumstances where his hand is highly visible, where the full force of battle can be identified – in poverty, corruption, starvation, depression, abuse, illness, moral decline, not to mention manifest attack on families and individuals etc. – but Satan is also cunning and his most successful form of assault is in a society where he goes unnoticed, where he doesn't exist in the minds of the people and, more importantly for him, where the Gospel of Jesus Christ is nowhere close to their agenda; where *'our gospel is veiled, it is veiled to those who are perishing [because] the god of this age has blinded the minds of unbelievers, so that they cannot see the light of the gospel of the glory of Christ'* (2 Cor. 4:3–4).

Where 'our gospel is veiled, it is to those who are perishing [because] the god of this age has blinded the minds of unbelievers, so that they cannot see the light of the gospel of the glory of Christ'. (2 Cor. 4:3–4)

Would you be surprised to learn that just as these unbelievers are blinded, so too are most Christians? Certainly the devil has his bases fully covered. What better way to keep the blind in sightless oblivion than to also keep the children of light from believing they can or should show them the Way? Sometimes when we watch television reports, a person's face might be obscured to conceal or protect their identity and I often think on this when I consider how many Christians read and interpret the Scriptures. Take, for example, a very famous Bible passage in Mark 8:35 where the Lord is talking about what it really means to follow Him. Often in my training seminars I ask people to

'For whoever wants to save his life will lose it, but whoever loses his life for me and for the gospel will save it.' (Mark 8:35)

quote this verse from memory and many of them in unison will typically recite: 'For whoever wants to save his life will lose it, but whoever loses his life for me will save it.' I suspect you have probably just skimmed over this quotation and not realised the deliberate error. Let's just focus on the verse, this time looking at the truth of the words: *'For whoever wants to save his life will lose it, but whoever loses his life for me and for the gospel will save it.'* Did you spot it? For some reason, when people recite this verse they very often omit these crucial words, 'and for the gospel'. That, to me, is daylight robbery. It's subtle, and it so often goes unnoticed, but it ultimately alters the message of the Scripture.

How do we interpret 'losing our lives'? We don't necessarily mean the loss of physical life do we? (Although it did mean this for the early believers and too many of our contemporaries in other cultures do face dreadful persecution and sometimes execution today). Rather, I imagine that for most Western Christians this 'loss of life' is played out in our sacrifices – our going to church, giving ourselves in prayer and worship, serving the community, giving of time and finances. As Christians, hopefully these are things motivated by our love of God, more than our love of self. We do God-related things like sacrificing our Sunday morning lie-in or family time by getting up and going to church, like giving our tithe rather than spending the money on ourselves, like committing to a prayer group when we could be simply going to the cinema or meeting up with friends. We do many 'good' things because of Jesus, but if we take Matthew 8:35 in its fullness, we are also called to make sacrifices for 'the gospel'. And what is the gospel? No more or less than 'good news', news that must be heard, spread, proclaimed, communicated. So if we serve our neighbours, if we give to charities, if we attend house groups and church services galore but never give a thought to communicating the Gospel, then we are only being faithful to half of this verse and, therefore, half of Jesus' message. Jesus asks us to lay our life down for the Gospel. This would seem to mean giving our *all* for it . . . surely the very least we can do then is mention it, don't you think?

Too many Christians are blinded to this kind of robbery. We go on with our lives, doing our best, not even realising that we are not seeing and living in full truth of Jesus' commands and promises. Then we wonder why we get distracted or depressed – by credit crunch or latest natural disaster – tired or burnt out by the same routine, the going to church every Sunday, singing the same songs, hearing the sermon, praying the same prayers, or by endless 'giving of ourselves', discouraged that though we long for and pray for revival, our churches remain the same. Is it, I wonder, because we build comfortable lives for ourselves that incorporate a version of Christianity so sanitised from the true grit of the Gospel that we are likely to one day wake up and find it sadly lacking. When life deals its next big blow, our faith does little to sustain us because it is 'faith' in *our* strength, or even the faith of our fellow churchgoer, more than *the* Truth. The Church can be very good at supporting people. Things like sending flowers or cards or food or helping with childcare and other needs show God's love in action through people. As the song goes, 'we all need somebody to lean on', and this is where the church can really shine. But the truth of the Gospel is much more than that. As Christians we need to lean on Christ, not just our church friends. We need to be built up by the power of God, the transforming power of the Gospel and genuine truth. Ravi

Zacharias, reading the stern warning of Romans 1:18, tells a fun story that highlights exactly this:

> A man was looking for a job. He was a body builder by training, with strong, bulging muscles. Disillusioned with the lack of opportunities that seemed to come his way he finally responded to an advert for a job at the local zoo. When he got there he was horrified to discover that the job was to play the part of a monkey. The zoo had run out of monkeys but didn't want to disappoint the hoards of children who would be expecting to see them. The man was reluctant, but money was tight so he took the position. Before sunrise, so nobody would see him, he got into his monkey suit and slipped into the monkey enclosure. All he had to do was move around the enclosure impersonating a monkey, swinging between the trees and eating the peanuts and bananas as they were thrown at him. All was OK for a time, but after eight hours of this the bananas were getting the better of him and he was beginning to feel sick and exhausted. He set about another round of swinging from tree to tree when, suddenly, he slipped and fell into the lion enclosure next door. Terrified, he cried out, 'Help! Help!' as a lion quickly approached. But to his amazement the lion suddenly said, 'Shut up! If you don't shut up we're both gonna lose our jobs!
>
> It's a farcical story but the point is that human beings carry on this game of pretence in many arenas of life. We look to build civilizations when we don't know what it means to be civilised. We try to be philosophers when we don't know who the Master Philosopher is. We try to portray artistic perceptions without knowing who the Master Artist is. We moralise on life when we don't know who the moral Law Giver is. We try to build utopias and bring about dreams only to find that time and again they come crashing down, making havoc of all our ambitions. Then,

> at that moment when the human being shouts out 'Help, help!' he discovers the one he's shouting to is only playing the same game himself.[2]

When we look at Christians who are living in full truth, leaning on Christ in all things, it's easy to see a difference. Some are persecuted, some live and serve in abject poverty, some live wholly by faith to serve others with the Gospel. Mother Teresa left a world-renowned legacy through her work among the poor of Calcutta. What did she say of her motivation? 'I am a little pencil in the hand of a writing God who is sending a love letter to the world.' Here was a woman who truly seemed to understand what it means to lose her life for the Gospel, not just because of what she was able to bring to others, but because of the riches with which she, too, was rewarded. The joy she experienced in living out the works of the Gospel, in laying down her life in Christ's service, serving people in India's stinking slums was undoubtedly from the same source as Paul wrote of in his letter to the Corinthians concerning the Macedonian churches: *'Out of the most severe trial, their overflowing joy and their extreme poverty welled up in rich generosity'* (2 Cor. 8:2). It's reported that Mother Teresa died with only a pair of sandals and a bowl of beans to her name, but I'm sure she died a rich lady.

'I consider my life worth nothing to me, if only I may finish the race and complete the task the Lord Jesus has given me – the task of testifying to the gospel of God's grace.' (Acts 20:24)

The apostle Paul was also clear in his intent to lay down his life for the Gospel. *'I consider my life worth nothing to me, if only I may finish the race and complete the task the Lord Jesus has given me – the task of testifying to the gospel of God's grace'*

(Acts 20:24). Paul hardly had an easy time did he? In 2 Corinthians 11:23–27 we see something of his trials:

> *I have worked much harder, been in prison more frequently, been flogged more severely, and been exposed to death again and again. Five times I received from the Jews the forty lashes minus one. Three times I was beaten with rods, once I was stoned, three times I was shipwrecked, I spent a night and a day in the open sea, I have been constantly on the move. I have been in danger from rivers, in danger from bandits, in danger from my own countrymen, in danger from Gentiles; in danger in the city, in danger in the country, in danger at sea; and in danger from false brothers. I have laboured and toiled and have often gone without sleep; I have known hunger and thirst and have often gone without food; I have been cold and naked.*

Yet Paul speaks of joy that knows no bounds!

I imagine a water tap in Africa. It stands alone in dry, hard land. It's old and rusty, but it's turned on once a year. Who in their right mind would drink the first glass of water from that tap? What will the water be like? It will be stagnant, stale, old, rusty, dirty and possibly the source of nasty, potentially fatal disease. Then there's another tap in a nearby village. This one is turned on virtually all day long, every day of the year. The people use it to bathe and to wash clothes. Children play in its fresh spring and the whole village drink from it. The water is moving all the time; it is fresh and full of life. If you had a choice of drinking from the first or the second tap, which would you choose? You'd choose the second one, of course. Surely we Christians should be like that tap, constantly switched on, constantly ready to share the Gospel, allowing that Living Water to flow through – cleansing and refreshing us – and out to the people we encounter.

When we look at our society in the light of 2 Corinthians 4:3–4 it's clear to see how much the devil appears to be having his way with unbelievers. Yet in my mind, the equally great travesty is in Dr Green's fourth point that the devil's plan is to rob Christians of life. Remember Charles Spurgeon spoke of 'perfect, overflowing unutterable happiness of the purest and most ennobling order'?[3] Actually, we know that Spurgeon battled terribly with depression and yet he is still able to speak of unutterable happiness when he recalls the joy of being a soul winner. We're not talking here about the Christian life as a bed of roses, but my challenge here is to ask, 'Am I like that old rusty tap, harbouring only septic water, or do I know something of what it means to be continually running over with fresh water?' For Spurgeon, high euphoria came as a direct result of being a 'soul-winner'. But this privilege isn't just for him or the apostle Paul or any other great evangelist who has made the connection between proclaiming the Gospel and 'life in all its fullness'. It is a privilege that I am sure is afforded for me and for you and every ordinary Christian with a willing heart to give it a go.

The devil's plan is to rob Christians of life.

Proclaiming the Gospel can bring incomparable life to any believer who delivers it. This 'life in all its fullness' is available to us now, here on earth. It is the promise of God and yet for so many of us we still attain just a glimpse, a small taste, a slight aroma. I believe that for Christians eternity starts now. From the moment we turn over our lives to Christ we are living our eternity. Surely this is something of what Jesus alluded to when he said, 'The Kingdom of God is near.' So whilst we might look ahead to great things and unimaginable happiness when we are with Him in glory, so, too, we may hope right now, here on earth, for a good sized portion of 'full life' (even if we suffer with depression and life is tough) the more we recognise ourselves as co-heirs with Christ.

The early Christians found this 'life' through proclaiming the Gospel to the point that they were willing to be martyred for the cause of the Great Commission. To get to that point surely requires more than bull-headed bravery. Surely these precious believers were *living* the experience of life in all its fullness. For them the veil between the physical and heavenly realm must have been so thin that they would willingly step out of their flesh to embrace even more of the fullness on which they were already feasting. I can only guess here and make assumptions and yet as I taste more and more of the euphoria, as I realise for myself the link between proclaiming the Gospel and fullness of life, I, too, begin to resonate with those who willingly laid down their lives rather than keep quiet about Jesus Christ: Philip stoned to death in Phrygia, AD 54, James clubbed to death in Jerusalem and John abandoned on the Isle of Patmos in AD 63; Barnabas burned to death in Cyprus and Mark dragged to death in Alexandria in AD 64; Paul beheaded in Rome in AD 69, Andrew crucified in Achaia, Thomas speared to death in Calamino, Matthew beheaded in Ethiopia in AD 70, and Luke hanged in Greece in AD 93. Were these the first to know the reality of this link between proclaiming the Gospel and life in all its fullness? If so, they paved the way for a legacy that runs down the ages to our present day. What of William Tyndale, Jim Elliot, John Bunyan and the many others we can name who have been persecuted and given their lives for the Gospel? And what of the many more thousands of Christians whose stories will never be told? For a brief time in October 2008, the world headlines reported the outrageous slaughter of Gayle Williams, a thirty-four-year-old aid worker, killed in Afghanistan. Whilst the authorities were quick to deny any obvious 'proselytising' of the Christian faith, those who knew Gayle recognised her heart to help young disabled people in a Muslim country was motivated by her own deep conviction, love for Jesus Christ and willingness – if it came to it – to lay down her life for the Gospel. Which tap were these believers like?

Surely what we're talking about here is more than 'life' as the majority of us know it. When the Scriptures tell us in John 1:4 that *'In him was life, and that life was the light of men,'* the Greek word here for life is *zoe* (zoh-ay). More directly translated this means 'a life that is real and genuine, active and vigorous'. Sometimes I fear that we miss out on some of the priceless riches of Scripture because we are limited by our translations. We often refer to the knowledge that in the original language of the Scripture there are several notions behind our singular word for love (*agape* – the fatherly, intimate love of God for mankind, mankind for God and Christians for one another; *phileo* – friendship and fondness, and *eros* – sexual longing). Understanding the difference here can put a different light on our reading and understanding. So, too, with *zoe*. In general we have reduced the word into something more functional and less vigorous. When we look up the word 'life' in the English dictionary we are told about 'capacity for growth' and 'functional activity'. The application the Greeks had was something much bigger, much wilder, more vigorous, deep and active. The life that John is speaking about here at the beginning of his gospel is something far more than many of us have come to settle for. And I'm not just talking here about building up a sweat as we jump up and down vigorously to the latest praise and worship music. Rather this is 'life'

The life that John is speaking about here at the beginning of his gospel is something far more than many of us have come to settle for.

where life just isn't important anymore, where you're willing to lay your life down for Christ, where you're willing to talk to your friends or go up to a complete stranger and attempt to persuade them of the Gospel. This is a life that moves you to do something exceptional and to do it out of '*agape*' and abandoned gratefulness.

If we have a life any less than a '*zoe*', when non-Christians look over the fence they will not bother to look any further. If, when they look into our lives they see little more than a mundane existence that amounts to nothing more than churchgoing, there will be nothing to attract them from one spiritual prison to what is, in effect, just another. When non-Christians see nothing of the vigour and the joy, the genuine active life that the Bible is talking about, we are doing the devil a favour. There is little need for him to try to stop our efforts to spread the Gospel. We are already our own – in fact the Gospel's – worst enemy. We might attend Bible teaching, worship seminars, prayer meetings, conferences on caring for our local communities, summer camps, retreats and other such good things, but I question whether any of these things offer us the fullness of life that Christ intends for us in these days. Remember Philemon 6? *'I pray that you may be active in sharing your faith, so that you will have a full understanding of every good thing we have in Christ.'* Here Paul gives us the solution. He doesn't say 'If you go to a five-day seminar, if you do another course, if you study the latest material or attend another conference, you will understand every good thing . . .' Please don't get me wrong. I'm certainly not demeaning these things. It is very

'I pray that you may be active in sharing your faith, so that you will have a full understanding of every good thing we have in Christ.'
(Phlm. 6)

important that we study and tap into the wisdom of God-gifted teachers. Indeed we should celebrate that so many lay people in the modern church have woken up to the error of trying to survive on spiritual baby milk and mushed-up biscuits. Yet if we attend these things to make us smarter, better people but we aren't living it out 'for the Gospel', then it's pretty pointless. We might as well still be drinking our milk from a teated bottle. In the meantime the few who bother to fully embrace Jesus' commands will feast on steak and join with the apostle Paul who, after listing his many persecutions still declares, *'in all our troubles my joy knows no bounds'* (2 Cor. 7:4). When it comes down to it, all these great courses and teaching facilities that our churches offer are just a means to an end, and that great end is to evangelise the whole world.

'In all our troubles my joy knows no bounds'.
(2 Cor. 7:4)

In closing this chapter, I hope it might leave you contemplating your life. Are you living a life of existence and function or do you have '*zoe*' – a life of vigour and abundance, a life with 'edge', the kind of confidence and joyful assurance that drives you to take risks for Christ? Paul had edge, and plenty of it. So did the Old Testament prophet, Elijah. I laugh out loud just about every time I read the story of his challenge to the prophets of Baal. Elijah's tongue-in-cheek ridicule of the pagan ritual in 1 Kings 18:27 is superb: *'Perhaps he is deep in thought, or busy, or travelling. Maybe he is sleeping and must be awakened,'* Elijah taunts them as they call upon their false god. The story goes on to tell us that the crying out to Baal grows more frantic and intense as the dancers move into sacrificial mutilation to try to rouse the deity, but the scripture recounts, '*But there was no response, no-one answered, no-one paid attention.*' At this Elijah continues the mockery, suggesting that they pour water on the ruined altar of the Lord. Again and again he orders that they drench the wood, rendering the sacrificial fire impossible to light. Then what happens? Elijah prays to the One true God. He calls on Him to demonstrate His almighty power so that the people might turn their hearts to Him. I wonder what Elijah was feeling in those moments? He had taunted the people to the point of being arrogant about his confidence in God. Some would say it was one mighty risky task he set. And yet we read in verses 38–39, '*Then the fire of the LORD fell and burned up the sacrifice, the wood, the stones and the soil, and also licked up the water in the trench. When all the people saw this, they fell prostrate and cried, "The LORD – he is God! The LORD – he is God!"*'

The Bible has many accounts of people who were prepared to take these kinds of risks for God, people who knew life in all abundance. People who lived '*zoe*'. People who were not afraid to step forward into battle and live to shine this light of Life in the darkness, to show this Life as the Light for all men (John 1). No matter what else brings you 'life' in your Christian walk, please ask yourself, 'Am I settling for second best? Am I living God's second best? Do I believe that by actively and regularly proclaiming the Gospel to strangers or the people I know, I will begin to taste something more of this '*zoe*' life? All I will conclude is, if you're not sure, why not put it to the test? Go on, prove me wrong!

- How do you feel about the following statement?

  'A Christian life without regularly proclaiming the Gospel to non-believers is settling for, and living in, God's second best.'

- When you look at the lives of the early Christians how does it make you feel?

- Have you ever experienced the thrill of personally sharing the Gospel with a non-believer? Could you encourage others by sharing that experience?

- Imagine if every Christian in the world was consistently spreading the Gospel on a daily basis.

  What impact would this have on our world?
  Do you think we would see the Church grow?
  What impression would non-Christians have of the Church and its message?

16

One Degree Off

Good Will Hunting is one of my favourite films. As a young man, Will Hunting has a photographic memory, exceptional intelligence and an unprecedented talent for mathematics. Yet despite such profound gifting, his highly abusive upbringing renders him incapable of any professional and emotional life. Instead, he clings to his macho, working-class persona and his life revolves around low-skilled jobs, hanging out with his tight gang of friends, fighting and getting into trouble. The story is one of rescue, hope and healing as Will eventually learns to trust and open up to others who love and care about him. For me, one of the most memorable scenes is when his childhood friend Chuckie chastises Will about his wasted life. At the risk of his own loss of macho face and incurring Will's wrath he confesses his recognition of Will's potential and his hope that his friend will someday take his ticket out of the wasteful life to which he himself is forever destined.

> Every day I come by your house and I pick you up and we go out. We have a few drinks, and a few laughs, and it's great. But you know what the best part of my day is? For about ten seconds, from when I pull up to the curb and when I get to your door, 'cause I think, maybe I'll get up there and I'll knock on the door and you won't be there. No goodbye. No see you

> later. No nothing. You just left. I don't know much, but I know that.[1]

Put simply, the moral of the story is not to let your past prevent you from grabbing the full potential of your life. When Will finally decides to move on it is at great personal risk. By leaving his current downtrodden situation and heading off to California to follow his estranged girlfriend, he opens himself up to love and life, and we get the feeling that he will begin to flourish as he embraces the truth of what he is and could be. I'm retelling this story in very simple, way too trite terms, but its beauty is that it exposes the human condition in all its complexities, its hurts, its reluctance to trust, its fear of failure and its instinct to stay in the safe and secure even when that means incredible waste.

Will Hunting was blinded to his potential (or at least running away from it) because he had grown up with an abusive foster father who had told him he would never amount to anything. Perhaps you see why this film speaks so much to me? Maybe you're beginning to see for yourself that this is exactly where the devil has us – in a place of darkness, blinded to the potential of the 'zoe' life. Indeed, when you look at this with enlightened eyes it's easy to recognise just how much Satan blinds non-Christians – and regrettably many Christians too – to the truth of the Gospel: the reality of existence after death on this earth, the sacrifice Jesus made to save people from Hell, the love and power of the cross, the miracle of the resurrection and the gift of forgiveness. For non-Christians there are crucial and pressing issues that don't even appear on their

For non-Christians there are crucial and pressing issues that don't even appear on their radar.

radar. They are truly blind to the brevity of life, the gravity and seriousness of their sin, the reality and horror of sin's power to enslave and the coming judgment for those who die without Christ: *'Man is destined to die once, and after that to face judgment'* (Heb. 9:27). John 10:10 warns of *'the thief who comes only to steal and kill and destroy'*, and it would certainly seem to be the case that Satan blinds non-Christians to his hidden agenda for their lives. Will Hunting had no idea just how bound he was to his situation. From the depths of his wounded self and the cocoon of his small, self-preservation fuelled existence he could not look beyond to the reality that others could perceive might be his. Thankfully for Will there were those – motivated by friendship, professional determination and love – who committed themselves to releasing the young man to the truth of his potential, those who could take his hand and guide him onto a path of freedom and light and truth and life in everything it should be for a man of his gifting. Isn't this just the same for us as Christians – we who see that there is so much more, we who know the truth about sin and judgment and death and Jesus and forgiveness and Salvation? Is it not our duty and our honour to do what Christ would have us do for his glory?

Only when we recognise and are suitably grateful for our Salvation, when our eyes are opened to the reality around us and we see the truth of our 'prisons', then we begin to take risks; then we begin to trust our Master and speak out for him in love and desperation for others. Then we begin to listen and act in obedience, gratitude and love.

There is the wonderful true story of Quaker missionary Stephen Grellat. About a century ago Stephen Grellat was led one day to go out to a heavily forested area of America to preach. It was a strong inward compulsion of the Holy Spirit. When he arrived at the loggers' camp, he found they had moved to another location, and their shanties were deserted. However, he was so sure he was sent by God that he went into an empty shanty and preached to the bare walls the sermon God had placed upon his heart. He then returned to his home. He could never understand why God would send him to preach to an empty shanty.

Many years later, as he walked across a bridge, a man grasped his arm, 'I found you at last,' the man said.

'I think you are mistaken,' said Mr Grellat.

'No, didn't you preach in an empty shanty in the woods years ago?'

'Yes,' Mr Grellat admitted, 'but no-one was there.'

'I was the foreman in charge of the loggers,' the stranger explained. 'We had moved to a new location but before long I realised I'd left one of my tools behind. I returned to get it and heard a voice in one of the shanties; I peered through a crack between the logs and saw you. You never saw me, but I listened to the rest of the sermon. God touched my heart that day and I became so convicted of my sins, that after some time I purchased a Bible, repented of my sins, and became a Christian, then I began to win my men to Christ. Your sermon has led over a thousand people to Christ, and three of them have gone on to become missionaries!'

This story thrills me. First of all, imagine having such conviction! Isn't this the relationship we should all expect with our Lord, that He would so lead us? I wonder what was going through Grellat's mind as he made his way into the forest? The suggestion is that he fully expected to be doing God's work there. He was simply being obedient to a familiar calling. I'm sure he expected a large number of men. Many would be tough, worldly, perhaps not too interested to listen to his preaching. Perhaps he prayed for protection and that the Holy Spirit would soften their hearts . . . But what did he think when he got there and found the area deserted? He must have been rather taken aback. I suspect if it had been me I would have been quite distraught to find the place empty. I'd probably have turned right around and given up in frustration and anger. Yes, I know and believe that scripture about God's word never returning void, but this would have seemed like a step too far. Not for Grellat, though. Did he doubt God? Did he doubt himself? No. He obediently got on and did what he believed God had asked him to do. He preached his sermon of Salvation to an empty shack and bare walls. We are not told whether his mind was in turmoil and confusion as he left that day. Maybe this was the case, although I suspect more that he left – though not understanding – with peace in his heart, knowing that he'd done his master's will. Perhaps the incident remained on his mind for many weeks to come before slowly fading in his memory. Then all those years later, a stranger approaches him on a bridge and reminds him in a most glorious way of one afternoon when he chose to be faithful. What a blessing that God should choose to reveal the truth of the situation to him! Sometimes God surprises us this way, letting us see the fruits of our words or actions, even many years later. Imagine Grellat's joy, knowing that his obedience, his apparent foolishness, had led to the winning of so many souls, more indeed than he could ever know about. We should never be surprised to hear such stories and always be expectant that when we do God's will, when we are obedient to His calling, we are part of the 'eternal' picture, a picture that we may not recognise or understand at the time or, indeed, ever in this lifetime.

The reason I tell this story is to emphasise that faithfulness to our calling is paramount and that we should be careful to never stray away from the truth or to be misguided by what we think we see. Though the devil might try to blind us, might tell us there's no-one in the shack to listen, we must set our sights, in gratitude-driven obedience, on proclaiming the Gospel with the soul purpose of glorifying Him who sees the bigger story, because He is the Author of the book.

The thing we need to recognise is that the devil is cunning and clever. Remember the sugar swapped for salt in the church kitchen? Where best to centre the attack than among God's own foot soldiers – the Church herself. Can this really be?

In my work as a bodyguard I did basic training with many different intelligence agencies. The people who dealt with fraud and counterfeit money always fascinated me. It was interesting to discover that the way they learn to identify counterfeit notes is not to study counterfeits, but to study the real thing. They study and study the tiny details so that when a note comes along that has the smallest of differences they can identify it immediately as false. That kind of job requires a supreme eye for detail and lots of patience!

In the last few years I have spoken to the Church all over the world about the 'one degree off the truth' principle, showing how very small falsehoods have been infiltrated into our Christian lives so that we barely realise them as counterfeits. Perhaps in the light of this you'll understand why this book has gone to significant lengths to look at the importance of truth and correct definitions of words such as 'evangelism' and 'the Gospel'. I think you'll be surprised by what lies ahead.

Back in Chapter 11 we defined evangelism as 'the proclamation of the Gospel'. You'll remember, this was based on the scholarly opinion of Bible teachers and theologians from across Christian Church denominations. Yet there is a definition that the devil would have us believe which is:

> Evangelism is the winning of souls.

Maybe you need to read that last sentence again. Yes, I do assert that this definition 'evangelism is the winning of souls' *is not*

> *Satan covers the hook of error with the bait of truth.*

correct. It is, indeed, a fabrication widely accepted among many well-meaning Christians, yet perpetrated by the devil through his one degree off the truth strategy. Satan covers the hook of error with the bait of truth. Imagine a fish. On first appearance we see nothing but honest bait, yet inside there is a hook – a device that leads to destruction. The devil's cunning plan is that he covers the error in something that seems like the truth. Our greatest desire as Christians is to win souls for the glory of God. Of course that's the truth, yet the error occurs *when we call evangelism the winning of souls.*

Writing on how the devil mixes truth with error in order to dupe us, Christian statesman J.O. Sanders writes:

> His strategy is to include enough truth in his teaching to make error appear both credible and palatable. So much seems good and true that injection of error is not obvious. To achieve this end, Satan will quote or misquote Scripture as best suits his purpose. He is ingenious. He employs orthodox language, while giving the old words new and heterodox content. That is especially true in theological circles, where theological double talk confuses the issues and conceals the error.[2]

Do you see that by making this slight, one-degree change, damaging falsehood can slip under our heresy radar without being noticed? Once there we even find that the devil can manipulate Christians to use Scripture to validate his new definition of evangelism. Unaware of his devices, Christians look at passages such as Luke 19:10, saying, 'Didn't Jesus say that He came to seek and save the lost? Didn't Paul say, "I have become all things to all men so that by all possible means I might save some?" Don't the parables of the lost sheep, the lost son and the lost coin talk about seeking and saving people? Surely, then, evangelism is the winning of souls.'

Indeed, this new definition of evangelism as the saving of souls does sound so right and many scriptures seem to back up this definition. No wonder the devil's own stealth heresy bomber has flown undetected under our radar and unloaded its cargo on the Church with stunning accuracy and success. Ask the majority of Christians if evangelism is 'the winning of souls' and most will reply with a resounding 'yes'!

The truth is that every genuine believer wants to seek and save the lost, but the tragedy is that the devil takes this goal and uses it to help collapse the Great Commission. This is nothing new. Jesus Himself knew of His adversary's cunning ability to sow heresy into the church, as He demonstrates in the parable of the wheat and weeds in Matthew 13:24–30: '*"Sir, didn't you sow good seed in your field? Where then did the weeds come from?" "An enemy did this," he replied.'*

But, you might ask, what is wrong with this definition of evangelism as 'the winning of souls'? I don't think we have to dig too deep to see that this seemingly small issue of semantics is actually having catastrophic consequences for the Great Commission. In my own experience I can clearly see at least five ways in which defining evangelism as 'the winning of souls' actually stops Christians proclaiming the Gospel. Firstly, we set Christians up for failure. When we share the Gospel message with someone it is, of course, in the hopeful expectation that they will come to receive Christ as their own. But it is a fact that most people are not saved immediately when they first hear the Gospel. There are all sorts of interesting statistics about how many times a person has to hear the message before they respond sincerely. The danger then for the Christian sharing the message is that since they do not witness an immediate conversion, it appears that they have failed. The Gospel has been shared, yet with no soul won the teller may feel he or she has done something wrong and been 'unsuccessful' in evangelism. This kind of experience only leads a person to believe 'evangelism is not my thing, it's not my gifting, I never seem to do it properly. I've never been able to lead someone to Christ, I might as well give up and leave it to the experts.' You've probably been through this yourself. Many Christians fall into condemnation and feelings of inadequacy when they find they are unable to meet the impossible and unbiblical expectation of having to win a soul every time they share the Gospel. The result is simply that they are reluctant to set themselves up for failure again – or they believe their inadequacy endorses an idea that evangelism is exclusively the territory of the 'gifted' – and they give up.

Secondly, defining evangelism as the winning of souls can actually lead to bullying. It puts Christians in the position of being high-pressure sales people. I've heard testimonies from many who say they felt pushed, manipulated and coerced into 'saying the prayer' by a well-meaning but over forceful Christian. The result is that a non-Christian can be put off for a very long time, or end up being bullied into making a commitment they are not ready for. In doing this, the Christian is trampling over any sense of conviction by the Holy Spirit, in a bull-headed mission to get a result.

Leaders can also unwittingly propagate this wrong definition of evangelism by the way we only ever talk about our successes. When we speak of our evangelistic endeavours we often count those who have apparently given their lives to Christ. In this way we are endorsing the message that evangelism *is* the winning of souls. We also give the impression that people are saved every time we share the Gospel. I can promise you, this is simply not true and I often feel it benefits people to hear of the times when I've been rejected whilst trying to share the Message. Many times

I've shared it to apathetic disinterest and many more times I've shared the Gospel knowing that it would be highly inappropriate to persuade them into a prayer of commitment. Am I discouraged, downhearted and ready to give up? I might be if I believed that evangelism is the winning of souls.

The third danger in this wrong definition is the notion of 'watering down'. In order to 'win a soul' we might feel compelled to water down the Gospel message. This is incredibly common, especially in contemporary society. People don't want bad news. They don't want to hear about sin and death and judgment, so instead we tend to 'sell' a sugar-coated gospel that perhaps concentrates on the love of God and the social benefits of being part of a church. This unleashes a whole legion of dangers. Non-Christians find it easy to say 'yes' to this watered-down, diluted gospel, but it is not the Gospel of truth. They are deceived and the tragedy is that we may well have inoculated them against the true Gospel and against Christ. When someone approaches them later with the real Gospel they will say, 'No thanks. I've tried that already. It didn't work!'

What is our motivation here? Is it love for a non-Christian? Is it to glorify God? Or is it the satisfaction of chalking up a 'success' in evangelism? Watering down is a serious business. When we water down the message, the essential powerful life-giving ingredients of the true Gospel go down the drain. A lesser gospel involves deception and takes glory away from Christ. Moreover it causes grief to the Holy Spirit and may leave a friend back in the devil's prison forever.

Inevitably the pressure on the Christian becomes too much – on one hand the man-inflicted pressure to win souls, on the other, the conviction of the Holy Spirit to tell the whole truth of the Gospel, even when it apparently means 'no result' in that instance. When the pressure is too great, it's easy just to bow out of the action and not engage in the Great Commission at all.

Non-Christians who have 'said the prayer' under pressure or in half-truth will show none of the fruits of true Salvation and are likely to fall away very easily.

Bullying and watering down tactics are easily recognisable in hindsight, but by then the damage has already been done. Non-Christians who have 'said the prayer' under pressure or in half-truth will show none of the fruits of true Salvation and are likely to fall away very easily. Seeing so little good fruit from their proclamation efforts, Christians soon become discouraged and quickly give up proclaiming the Gospel at all. In this, the devil utters a resounding 'perfect result!'

Finally, I perceive that this belief that evangelism is the 'winning of souls' has caused millions of church leaders to be discouraged and, like dealing with foul play in a football match, they spring a red card and put a stop to many good evangelistic efforts and schemes. When they see that an evangelism method or strategy does not lead to *souls immediately being harvested* into their church they believe it to be 'not right' or 'not of God'. Yet what did Jesus teach in Mark 4:26–29?

> *This is what the kingdom of God is like. A man scatters seed on the ground. Night and day, whether he sleeps or gets up, the seed sprouts and grows, though he does not know how. All by itself the soil produces corn – first the stalk, then the ear, then the full grain in the ear. As soon as the grain is ripe, he puts the sickle to it, because the harvest has come.*

Here we see Jesus teaching specifically that we should expect a time delay between planting the seed of the Gospel and reaping a harvest. Note also that the only part the man plays here is scattering the seed. Everything else happens by the power of the unknown, while the man goes about the rest of his business.

Time and again we see such error in our churches. Worst of all, some leaders who don't see immediate results from their proclamation efforts spread a bad report to other church leaders about their 'failed' strategy. This isn't in any way out of bad intent, but so often it is through ignorance deep in their hearts. If they understood evangelism as sowing seeds they would see their efforts as highly productive, but whilst we continue to look at the wrong statistic in this way we continue to be discouraged. Very soon the wider church becomes wary and reluctant to embrace what may well have been a strong, truly evangelistic, programme. Having ruled out genuine Gospel proclamation because it often doesn't lead to an immediate result, many abandon it completely. A red card is issued and the player sent off the pitch! Instead perhaps the church turns to slick marketing gimmicks, or even genuine Christian programmes, to attract the lost to church. That's all very well – the church is filling up, people are being cared for, but is this at the expense, I wonder, of the full and genuine Gospel message being proclaimed? Are we being too 'fruit focused', rather than 'root focused'? Are we too busy counting the number of people we have in our congregations rather than keeping our attention firmly fixed on the root, which is Jesus Christ and His words. Have we redefined the Great Commission as: 'Go into the world and attract non-Christians to church', rather than 'Go into the world and proclaim the Gospel'?

Once again, we have truth and error mixed together. The *truth* is that there are many good schemes we can use that break down the walls between the Church and the wider community. The *truth* is that everything we do should be done with a level of professionalism and excellence. (I, for one, am a great fan of technology and state-of-the-art visual presentation.) The *truth* is that we desperately want the Church to be attractive to non-Christians and we always need to work on creative and innovative ways of reaching out. It is also *truth* that we want everything about our Christian life to positively and powerfully impact non-Christians. But the *error* here – and it is a very grave one – is when we engage in all these things but somehow discard the actual proclamation of the Gospel.

Does all this mean then that we are not to be concerned with the winning of souls? Absolutely not! When we evangelise we must always do so with the supreme hope, faith and intention that we will see souls won. That is what we should pray for and work passionately towards in expectation that our efforts will eventually lead to a harvest. But ultimately, evangelism is not the winning of souls. Evangelism is the proclamation of the Gospel – nothing more, nothing less and nothing else.

Evangelism is the proclamation of the Gospel – nothing more, nothing less and nothing else.

Martin Luther defined evangelism as, '. . . nothing other than preaching, the speaking forth of God's grace and mercy, which the Lord Jesus Christ has earned and acquired through his death'.[3] Hundreds of years later, contemporary theologian J.I. Packer suggests that the way to tell whether you are in fact evangelising is not to ask whether conversions are known to have resulted from your witness. Rather, it is to ask whether you are faithfully making known the Gospel message.[4]

My prayer is that in contemplating the content of this chapter you will be liberated from a sense of failure; from the need to pressure non-Christians to make a decision; from the temptation to water down the message of the Gospel. With enlightened eyes I pray that you will no longer be discouraged by apparently fruitless results. Nor will you support the issuing of a red card to evangelism programmes that don't immediately bring people falling to their knees in commitment. I pray that with renewed vigour and confidence you will move forward in truth, leaving the harvest to the Master, but being a willing worker of His fields and doing all you can to plant the seeds by proclaiming the full and true message of our precious Gospel.

- Remember the Danger! Does your feeling towards evangelism change when you understand that it is not the winning of souls?

- Defining evangelism as the winning of souls stops Christians from proclaiming the Gospel in five ways:

1. Failure

'Every time I proclaim the Gospel and the person listening is not saved I have failed!'

2. Bullying

'I must get this person to say the prayer when I've told them the message of the Gospel.'

3. Watering Down

'The full Gospel seems such a harsh message. Maybe I could just tell my friend how many good people she'll meet if she comes along to church, or focus on how her life will be better if she starts to pray . . .'

4. Fruitless Results

'One of my friends definitely made a Christian commitment. I know she did because I made her say the prayer and she started coming to church. Another of my friends started coming too, after I persuaded him his life would be happier if he started to pray. Neither of them have stuck around though. It's so discouraging!'

5. Red Card

'Our church tried evangelism last year, but it didn't work. We did a car wash in the village and handed out loads of tracts. Some of the braver ones even talked to people about the Gospel. It was great at the time but only a couple of people actually turned up to church the following Sunday. We've decided it's not worth the effort. We're going to do something else instead.'

17

A New Song

'So if the Son sets you free, you will be free indeed' (John 8:36).

If you've read or heard my testimony you'll recognise just how precious this Bible verse is to me. It was probably the lynch pin of my conversion to Christ. At the time I was a prisoner in the literal sense – incarcerated in jail in Cyprus – but the prison of my soul was far more binding than the thick walls of Nicosia Central. When Michael Wright, the missionary who had been visiting me, spoke that scripture, it threw me way off guard. First it gave voice to my rage. 'How could this idiot, this Bible-basher speak of freedom whilst I rotted behind bars?' I was a violent brute of a man at the time and barely needed an excuse to vent my anger, even though Michael had become a friend and something of a life-line. I still recall with horror how I battled the temptation to lash out with a quick and brutal punch:

> I could haul him over the table and floor him in a split second, before the guards could do a thing about it – that'd teach him to talk to me about freedom and this Jesus. That would shut him up![1]

But I know now that the Holy Spirit was at work and God, in His infinite love and compassion, was honouring Michael's prayers, and those of the faithful people at his church and the Logos School who had been praying for me – a man who deserved only their contempt – by name.

That precious scripture cut deep into my heart like the two-edged sword that it is. 3 May 1990 – freedom, pure, glorious liberty. That is what I tasted for the first time in my life. Those remarkable words – *'if the Son sets you free, you will be free indeed'* – became embedded deep in my soul and in the next few days I realised, with grateful certainty, that I would never go back to my life of bondage and self-serving.

All these years later I still get goose bumps every time I read or hear that Bible verse and I praise God that I still know the freedom of being a son, not a slave, of the Master. Yet I confess that, in a sense, I have taken new chains upon myself. In my passion for the lost, motivated by true gratitude for my own Salvation, I am aware of my tendency to take on a burden that is not rightly mine to carry. I perceive that this was a similar fate at one time suffered by the great missionary to China, Hudson Taylor. For years he strived, at great personal sacrifice, to introduce the Christian Gospel to the 'lost millions' of China. Though his efforts lost none of the zeal, there was a time when he recorded a quite desperate depression about his work. Biographer Roger Steer reports that Taylor prayed, agonised, fasted, tried to do better and made resolutions. He quotes Taylor:

> Every day, almost every hour the consciousness of sin oppressed me. I knew that if only I could abide in Christ all would be well, but I *could not*. I began the day with prayer, determined not to take my mind off Him for a moment; but pressure of duties, sometimes very trying, constant interruptions apt to be so wearing, often caused me to forget Him. Then one's nerves get so fretted in this climate that temptations to irritability, hard thoughts, and sometimes unkind words are all the more difficult to control. Each day

> brought its register of sin and failure, or lack of power. To will was indeed present with me, but how to perform I found not.[2]

Hudson Taylor battled and strived throughout the summer of 1869 but it is reported that when fresh revelation finally came it left him transformed and released new power to his ministry.

> As I thought of the vine and the branches, what light the blessed Spirit poured into my soul! How great seemed my mistake in having wished to get the sap, the fullness out of Him. I saw not only that Jesus would never leave me, but that I was a member of His body, of His flesh and of His bones. The vine now I see, is not the root merely, but all – root, stem, branches, twigs, leaves, flowers, fruit: and Jesus is not only that: He is soil and sunshine, air and showers, and ten thousand times more than we have ever dreamed, wished for or needed. Oh, the joy of seeing this truth! . . . The sweetest part . . . is the rest which full identification with Christ brings. I am no longer anxious about anything, as I realise this; for He, I know is able to carry out *His will*, and His will is mine.[3]

'I am no longer anxious about anything, as I realise this; for He, I know is able to carry out His will, and His will is mine.'
(Hudson Taylor)

I am sure many people in ministry can relate to the despair suffered by this great man of God. Despite all good and Godly intention, many of us fall into the trap of taking the burden upon ourselves and, before we know it, our special union with our Saviour is thwarted in urgency to get a job done. I know I am terribly guilty of this but, like Taylor, I also recall an enlightening and liberating point when I began to consider the truth of my motivation to be engaged in the battle of evangelism.

In the last chapter we talked of the folly of defining evangelism as the 'winning of souls'. I hope that you are already experiencing immense freedom as you begin to absorb the light of this revelation. But there is more, so much more. What *does* motivate us to evangelise? This is the discussion that weaves itself into the very fibres of this book and it is a question that I often find myself putting to delegates at evangelism training conferences. The answers, quite rightly and understandably, open discussions on Jesus' commandments, the Great Commission, our heart and love for the lost, our gratitude for our own Salvation, etc. These are all good, noble and seemingly biblical motivations, but in researching and meditating on this question I believe the Holy Spirit has granted me insight into a much higher, more pure and thoroughly 'true' motivation. I praise God for this revelation, because it is one that is completely liberating, refreshing and energising. Simply put – for it is the most *simple* and beautiful of things – our underlying motivation to share the Gospel comes most naturally and essentially out of a desire to glorify Christ.

Our underlying motivation to share the Gospel comes most naturally and essentially out of a desire to glorify Christ.

Martyn Lloyd Jones in his insightful book *The Presentation of the Gospel*[4] writes, 'The supreme object of the work of evangelism is to glorify God, not to save souls.' Indeed, it seems to me that with Christ at the centre, the focus is moved away from *us*, from our 'task' of evangelism. It also shifts our concentration from 'the lost' and our overwhelming mission to reach them. Instead it fixes our eyes firmly on Jesus, on all that He is and all that He has done for all eternity.

When our focus is on Christ and on glorifying Him we inevitably avoid the traps we have previously talked about. There is now no pressure to convert, no temptation to water down the Gospel, no feeling of failure or desperation that our evangelism efforts are thwarted or inadequate or useless. I admit, there was a time when each day I felt compelled to go out and make converts, completely misinterpreting the scripture that tells us to make 'disciples' (Matt. 28:19). I was determined to share the Gospel with as many people as I could so that they might give their lives to Christ there and then. But when I was liberated into the realisation that my motivation for evangelism should focus on nothing else other than bringing glory to Jesus, my whole approach altered. I am still determined on a daily basis to talk to as many people as possible about the Gospel, but these days I can almost feel Jesus whispering in my ear, 'Tony, relax, remember your main motivation is to exalt Me, to lift Me up.' And God the Father might chip in, 'Tony, I love you, I made you, I'm your Daddy in Heaven. Please, talk to this person, or that person. Tell My story, glorify Me to them, but please don't push them. Don't try to convert them, I will deal with that in My time. Listen to the Holy Spirit, He will guide you as to whether you should lead this person in a prayer of commitment. Please, don't do it in your own strength. Don't do it without Us – work with Us, so that My Son might be glorified. Please just do your part, speak the good news and trust in My perfect time.'

I will never forget my encounter with Charlie on the number 29 bus. I was working at an insurance company and every day I caught the same bus to work. In those days I made my own home-printed tracts to hand out to people. It was just a simple piece of paper with my brief testimony on one side and the Gospel message, a prayer and my contact details on the other. One day I watched an elderly gentleman getting onto the bus. I felt my hand reaching for the tracts in my pocket even before he had managed to sit down. As I prepared to get off at my stop I paused by the man and said, 'Excuse me, I'd really like to give you this.' He looked a little surprised but thanked me and smiled as he took it.

A week later I had a phone call. 'Are you the man on the bus? You gave me a piece of paper on the 29 bus last week. Was that you?'

I braced myself. I'd had similar such calls and expected some abuse. 'Yes, it was me,' I said.

'Why did you give it to me?'

I took a deep breath. Here we go, he's really going to go for me.

'Well, I know it might sound crazy, but I felt God asking me to give it to you.' There was a short pause and again I waited for the abuse.

'My name's Charlie,' he said. 'And I'm very glad you did.' I must admit I nearly dropped the phone in surprise. 'I was in the army as a young man,' Charlie continued. 'There was a time when we were in the trenches being shot at and I thought my time was up. My friend next to me was a praying man and he shared the Christian message with me. I really wasn't interested, so I just told him to go ahead and pray but leave me out of it.' Charlie's voice softened and almost choked as he continued. 'My friend gave me a challenge that day that I put off. You're the first person in forty years who has tried to give me that message again. This time I wasn't going to put it off. I said that prayer last night and I gave my life to God. I really want to change and go to church. Can you tell me what to do next?'

Charlie's story is never far from my mind and I often wonder about that faithful soldier who first shared the Gospel with him in the trenches. I pray that he never felt a failure, never felt discouraged. That day he glorified Jesus by telling his story to a friend and by sowing a first seed. All these years later I had the privilege of seeing the work of the Holy Spirit come to fruition and I'm sure the two men will enjoy a special embrace when they meet in glory. Dr John MacArthur writes:

> One of the greatest ways we can give glory to God is to declare the Gospel. Its message radiates the glory of God like nothing else in the universe. When we declare the Gospel we are declaring the clearest and most powerful aspect of God's glory. Thus declaration of the Gospel is one of the highest and purist forms of worship because it most clearly affirms the glory of God.[5]

What MacArthur and many other scholars and lay people alike recognise is that this is a heavenly strategy for evangelism that must be made known among the Church. Evangelism should be motivated by nothing more and nothing less than glorifying Jesus. Whilst the Church is ignorant to this fact and puts other motivations for evangelism as primary, it is open and exposed to attack from the evil one.

Of course there will be those who argue and contest this. On one of my missions in Australia a pastor took exception to this message. She pointed to their church's very successful feeding programme. Certainly they were to be admired. 'This is how we evangelise, by showing love to these people,' she told me. 'What is more important than showing them love?' I wouldn't deny there is a degree of truth in what she said. Of course we need to care for people but, as I've said before, good Muslims, good Hindus, good Buddhists and good atheists do that too. That's part of our human condition – praise God for it! OK, so perhaps many of the poor people being fed recognise that it is a Christian church doing the feeding, but even so, the best that can be said is they are seeing people doing good work because they love God. They are still not hearing about *God's love for them.* They are still ignorant of the fact that, because of this wonderful love of God, Jesus came to earth was put to brutal death but rose again *to save them.*

Showing love to others is a good motivation for any kind of action. But it is *not* the *primary* motivation for evangelism. Similarly, I became alarmed at the message one of our Avanti evangelists was giving as we ministered and encouraged a group of young missionaries in Finland. My friend is a fabulous evangelist, full of zeal and passion. I love travelling and working with him, but in his enthusiasm to inspire others to share the Gospel he began, on this occasion, to proselytise an idea that may sound biblically plausible but in fact it distracts from the real truth of what our motivation for evangelism should be.

'I hate the devil,' he said, to a hungry and excited audience. 'The devil put cancer in my body and I hate him for it; he's tried to take me down so many times,' he went on. 'But you know what I do? You know the best way to get back at the devil? Preach the Gospel. That's what you've got to do. If you want to get back at the devil, guys, just proclaim the Gospel!'

Later I had to gently challenge my friend on this idea. Should our motivation to do the work of evangelism be inspired by the devil and an attack on him? No. That is absolutely not the way of Christ. It is true that the devil uses all sorts of strategies to attack, but we must never stoop to his level. What did Jesus do? Did He come with legions of angels to slaughter the army of demons and attack the devil? No, He came in absolute humility and pure love, in meekness like a lamb to the slaughter. We should never preach the Gospel out of hatred, spite or anger towards the devil. When we preach the Gospel it should be motivated by and because of the pure love of Christ. It should be because He has asked us to do it and because our primary intention is to glorify Him.

What does it *mean* to glorify Jesus? According to the *Enhanced Strong's Lexicon* to 'glorify' means, 'To cause the dignity and worth of some person or thing to become manifest and acknowledged.'[6] Insert the name of Jesus then into 'some person or thing'. Then consider the word, 'worth'. This is defined as, 'A quality that commands esteem or respect or merit.' So to glorify Jesus is to cause Him to be dignified, esteemed and respected, to have His merits manifest and acknowledged. And when we define the word 'manifest' we find, 'to reveal or demonstrate plainly'.[7] The greatest motive for going to non-Christians with the Gospel then is to reveal the merits of Jesus, so that they see Him as He really is, the greatest of all heroes. How will Jesus be glorified to non-Christians? Only when you and I cause this to happen.

Looking at it this way, surely the obvious revelation is that evangelism is fundamentally nothing less than 'worship'. We could open up enough material for another entire book at this point, but I love to imagine your spirit is soaring as you contemplate for yourself the multifaceted gem that is 'worship' of our Creator and His precious Son, Jesus Christ.

When we go into the world and proclaim the Gospel we are worshipping God. There are many scriptures that make this clear. Psalm 96:1–4 is like a clarion call:

> *Sing to the* LORD *a new song;*
> *sing to the* LORD*, all the earth.*
> *Sing to the* LORD*, praise his name;*
> *proclaim his salvation day after day.*
> *Declare his glory among the nations,*
> *His marvellous deeds among all peoples.*
> *For great is the* LORD *and most worthy of praise . . .*

When we are giving the Gospel to non-Christians we are explaining how great Jesus is, we are proclaiming His worth. We are showing Him, and others, that He is 'worth it' to us that we should sacrifice ourselves in this way, dedicating our time, our money, our efforts to lift Him up, because He is so worthy. The apostle Paul stated in Galatians 6:14, *'May I never boast except in the cross of our Lord Jesus Christ.'* That was worship. When we put aside our pride and our fears, our inadequacies and our busy schedules to go to the world and evangelise, when we suffer persecution and rejection because of it, we are acknowledging that Jesus is worth it all and God surely sees this attitude as an act of worship.

This idea of sacrificial and joyful giving is easily recognisable in the human condition. What is it to be in love? When a man loves a woman he dedicates everything to her. He wants to be with her, he willingly sacrifices other things to see her, he spends money on her, listens to her problems, shares her worries and puts off other engagements in his natural desire to spend as much time as possible with her and for her benefit. No request is too big or problem too burdensome! A friend of mine tells the story of his wife who, in the early stages of pregnancy, had overwhelming cravings for oranges. They were enjoying a weekend break in London when, in the middle of the night, his wife woke him up, distressed by her longing and suffering through lack of fruit. What could he do? There was no room-service on duty so, without hesitation, he pulled his clothes on top of his pyjamas and set out into the night, looking for somewhere to buy oranges for his beloved who he so wanted to please. Why? Because she was so worth it.

When we come to that point with Jesus we will go to any length to tell others about Him, to proclaim His worth to the nations, no matter what the personal cost.

> *Then I saw another angel flying in mid-air, and he had the eternal gospel to proclaim to those who live on the earth – to every nation, tribe, language and people. He said in a loud voice, 'Fear God and give him glory, because the hour of his judgment has come. Worship him who made the heavens, the earth, the sea and the springs of water.'* (Rev. 14:6–7)

- What comes to mind when you think of worshipping and glorifying God?
- Had you considered that evangelism is one of the highest forms of worship?
- What does it mean to be *root* focused rather than *fruit* focused? How should this determine your church activity? How should it influence your broader life?
- Meditate on how being *root* focused helps turn the glory for the inevitable *fruit* back to God.

18

MUD

So how does the tea and coffee taste now? Is there still salt in that sugar bowl, now that we've exposed the devil and his lies, now that we've unearthed his sly manoeuvres to creep under the heresy radar of the Church and pollute the minds of the faithful? We saw back in Chapter 15 the damage of subscribing to the lie that defined evangelism as the winning of souls. Would you be surprised to find that our great adversary does not stop there? There is another 'wrong definition' of evangelism that must be exposed in the war over souls.

Evangelism is the proclamation of the Gospel. We now recognise that as a clear statement of truth. How about the assertion that:

> Evangelism is any activity that brings a non-Christian closer to the point of conversion?

Missiologist Dr James Engel developed a scale to explain how a person comes to faith. According to Engel's scale all people start at -8 with no knowledge of the Gospel. As their knowledge and understanding of the Gospel increases they move towards the point of conversion at zero. As they mature in their faith they move up the scale to the right of zero, to +5 and beyond.[1]

Unfortunately the excellent message of Engel's scale has been mistaken. Indeed, it appears it has been muddied by the devil in another of his devious schemes to spin the Church just one small – but very dangerous – degree off the truth. Engel was clear that although a person being drawn to faith is a 'process', only the act of preaching the Gospel is evangelism. Yet talk to many Christians and it's easy to see that a bogus idea prevails at the heart of the Church. The muddied message in the minds of many sincere believers is that any Christian activity that draws a non-Christian closer to the point of conversion *is* evangelism. A small error, perhaps, but this perfectly formed deception is assimilated with catastrophic consequences.

This might be better understood if we examine something more of the process of drawing a non-Christian to Christ. Let's break it down into six steps using an agricultural analogy:

1. Ploughing
2. Sowing
3. Watering
4. Growing
5. Harvesting
6. Threshing

'Ploughing' activities are those that prepare the hearts of non-Christians to receive the seed of the Gospel. They might include prayer and intercession, praise and worship, fasting, or things that are visible to a non-Christian such as good works, community projects, friendship, counselling, being a good example of a Godly life, exhibiting a miraculous answer to prayer, giving words of knowledge, etc. Such ploughing activities are vital. After all, unploughed, hardened ground will hardly yield a good harvest. Ploughing is an essential part of the process.

> *When the ploughman ploughs and the thresher threshes, they ought to do so in the hope of sharing in the harvest.* (1 Cor. 9:10)

Here the apostle Paul is using the natural world to illustrate a spiritual reality. The people of the New Testament knew the importance of preparing land before planting seeds. Ploughing activities by Christians make up this same crucial first step. Preparation is absolutely necessary if there is to be any harvest in the days to come.

But are these 'ploughing' activities evangelism? No, they are not! And the danger is that if we define them as evangelism it's likely that most people in the Church believe themselves to be *doing evangelism.* The natural conclusion? 'Yes, we're doing our bit for evangelism.' But hopefully you can spot the glaring error, the crucial missing element that is evangelism: there is *no proclamation of the Gospel.*

The second step in the process of drawing a non-Christian to Christ is *'sowing'*. Laurence Singlehurst offers a wonderful discussion on this in his highly acclaimed book *Sowing, Reaping, Keeping: People Sensitive Evangelism,*[2] where he explores what it means to sow the seed of faith, to reap the harvest when the seed of faith has taken root and to nurture the faith as it grows.

To sow *is* to proclaim the Gospel. To sow is to communicate the good news of Salvation through Jesus Christ. When we use our words this way we are engaging in cosmic power. We might think of ourselves as stuttering, stammering, faltering human beings but if we stand back and consider the gift of language and our ability to communicate, it is really quite mind blowing. Language is a prime factor that sets us above other species. Through our words and communications great wonders have been created, laws have been established, knowledge has been passed through generations, history has been documented, great people and events have been celebrated. Through the gift of language we give glory back to God, we sing or shout His praises, we worship Him, we petition Him in prayer and we are sometimes even given new heavenly language specifically for this

When we proclaim the Gospel we are joining with creation in declaring God's greatness.

purpose. God Himself created the universe by *speaking* it into being. With words Jesus defeated the temptation of the devil, calmed the storm, healed the centurion's servant. In Romans 1:16 Paul spells it out when he says the Gospel *'is the power of God for the salvation of everyone who believes: first for the Jew and then for the Gentile'.* This verse points forward to chapter 3 verse 2 when Paul speaks of the Jews being *'entrusted with the very words of God'.* When we proclaim the Gospel we are joining with creation in declaring God's greatness.

> *The heavens declare the glory of God;*
> *the skies proclaim the work of his hands.*
> *Day after day they pour forth speech;*
> *night after night they display knowledge.*
> *There is no speech or language where their voice is not heard.*
> *Their voice goes out into all the earth,*
> *their words to the ends of the world.* (Ps. 19:1–4)

We only have to look up at a star-filled night sky and it speaks to us of the omnipotence of God. Creation cries out in testament to His power and when we use language to share the Gospel we, too, join in this cosmic declaration of His glory. Gifted with the power of speech and writing, we have a supreme purpose to communicate the way of redemption and reunion with Almighty God.

When we proclaim the Gospel we are sowing the seed – an action that is dependent upon, but very distinct to the act of ploughing. Paul clearly recognised this in his dealings with the early believers. *'I planted the seed, Apollos watered it, but God made it grow,'* he says in 1 Corinthians 3:6.

'I planted the seed, Apollos watered it, but God made it grow.' (1 Cor. 3:6)

It's very important to make this distinction between ploughing and sowing but we should be sure not to esteem one more than the other. We must be careful to recognise them for what they are and to guard against labelling one as the other. In many cases churches have unwittingly drifted into focusing almost completely on ploughing without mobilising Christians to actually speak out the Gospel message. Acts of kindness are imperative, for into the warmth of an open heart a seed can be sown. Nevertheless, if a seed is never planted, even the most beautifully ploughed field will remain forever barren.

Naturally, when the farmer has ploughed and prepared his land and planted his seed the next important step is to '*water*'. Again, this provides an important parallel in the process of drawing someone to Christ. When the seed of the Gospel is sown it's then vital to provide good conditions for the seed to grow. Such activities might include prayer and intercession, praise and worship, fasting, good works . . . in fact many of the same activities that come under the 'ploughing' list. When a person begins to explore the Gospel and its implications for them, they undoubtedly look to the example of Christians. With this knowledge we should always be attentive and on guard, knowing that we, the body of Christ on earth, are the flesh of the watering and feeding process. I heard a story of one church that invited a young couple to take an Alpha course. 'Sorry, we won't be able to attend,' they said, 'we have young children and no babysitter.' Lovingly the church gathered together and sorted out a babysitting rota so that the couple could do the course. After a few weeks the couple started attending church and making friends as they continued with the course. One night they needed a babysitter so that they could go out socially. To their disappointment they found that the people on the babysitting rota were only willing to help out for the Alpha meetings. So we return again to Jesus and His story of the Good Samaritan, the man who went out of his way, who gave more than he needed to in an illustration of 'love your neighbour as yourself'. The point is that, for something to grow, we need to keep watering, keep tending to the young plant, keep providing good conditions to aid growth.

'This is why I told you that no-one can come to me unless the Father has enabled him.' (John 6:65)

'Growing' is the supernatural, saving work of the Father and the Holy Spirit. We can plough, we can sow, but we are kidding ourselves if we believe that someone becoming a Christian is entirely down to our efforts. Jesus was clear on this matter, as recorded in John 6:65: *'He went on to say, "This is why I told you that no-one can come to me unless the Father has enabled him."'* Later in the Gospel of John, Jesus also makes clear the Holy Spirit's part in bringing a person to the point of recognition. *'When he comes, he will convict the world of guilt in regard to sin and righteousness and judgment'* (John 16:8).

Many times Sara has planted beans with our boys. They always enjoy putting together little pots of compost, pushing in the beans and checking each day as they water and wait, hoping to see the first shoot appear. Usually within a few short weeks they are rewarded with a little plant ready to put out in the garden to flourish. Sometimes, however, as any gardener will testify, there is a pot that remains barren. The soil was the same, the beans came from the same batch, the pots were watered and cared for just the same, but for some unknown reason no shoot appeared. A mystery, a harsh reality and ultimately an illustration that all we can do is provide the right conditions. We can prepare the soil, we can sow the seed but the matter of growth is in the hands of a higher power.

We can prepare the soil, we can sow the seed but the matter of growth is in the hands of a higher power.

Our fifth step in the metaphorical process of drawing someone to Christ is '*harvesting*'. This is adding new Christians to the body of Christ. Harvesting, it seems, occurs in two ways. Firstly, God can harvest without us. It is quite within His power and His will to draw a person into the Church without any intervention from anyone else in the body. There are many documented stories of people experiencing the Word of God directly, usually through a dramatic dream or vision.

Khalil was a radical Egyptian terrorist, feared by many in his neighbourhood. A hater of both Christians and Jews he set out to discredit the Bible, but found nothing in the Scriptures that would suit his cause. Rather he began to question the basis of his own Islamic faith. In desperation he cried out for the true God to reveal Himself. That night he had a vivid dream. Jesus Christ came to him in peace and love. Khalil was instantly transformed and his neighbours witnessed a murderous 'Saul' become a forgiving 'Paul'.

In Indonesia Dini was a disruptive teenager who had been badly let down by family, friends and society. Trying to get her life in order she committed to a special night of prayer. Laying herself before Allah she was at first confused when in a vision she saw a man she recognised as Jesus. Yet as she reached out to

Him her heart was filled with peace. There were many tough days ahead as Dini declared her decision to follow Jesus but, even as persecution began and her family rejected her, Dini clung to Jesus and He protects and provides for her to this day.

The stories of Khalil, Dini and many others are verified and carefully documented. They can be seen through www.morethandreams.org, a mission that has discovered many stories of people who, without any contact with Christians, have become followers of Christ through a direct encounter with Him.

Such reports are marvellous, compelling testimonies to the fact that God can and does intervene directly with humankind, just as He did in Bible times. More often, however, God, in love with His children, chooses to use the body of Christ, that is us, in the harvesting process. When we invite non-Christians to become followers of Jesus we are again involved in this wonderful cosmic plan to draw mankind back to God. What an honour! Does God need us to do this? No. Sometimes when people ask us to do something it's because they really need our help. Not so with God. In fact sometimes I wonder what He's thinking of, asking me to help in the task of bringing people to Him. Surely He doesn't need me? Surely He can do a much better job without me? Yet he asks me to do it. It's as though He's saying, 'I love you and you're part of My family now, so get involved in the family business.' In God's divine wisdom and power He allows me to take part and, amazingly, seems to delight in my efforts.

My eldest son Ethan was only two years old when Sara suggested we build a playhouse in our garden. I don't get much time at home with the family and I could see this would be a big task. Sure enough, I realised Sara had marked out the entire weekend. It wasn't exactly my idea of a relaxing time, but I went out and bought the wood and other materials and became a man with a mission in the garden. I was focused and determined. It was going to be the best playhouse ever. As soon as I began to cut the wood Ethan bounced up dressed in his Bob the Builder outfit, complete with plastic hammer and various other tools. Soon he was tapping the wood, tipping out the box of nails, tapping my head, causing numerous hazards and generally getting in the way. I tried the usual distraction techniques but found myself getting more and more frustrated. 'Look, Ethan, just go away, go to your bedroom and play or something . . . can't you see I'm trying to do this for you,' I said in exasperation. Instantly the smile dropped from his little face and his lip began to quiver. He turned and walked sullenly back towards the house. I felt terrible. How could I be so mean to him? He just wanted to join in. 'Come on, Ethan, I'm sorry,' I called after him. 'Look, I really need your help now, I'm ready to hammer some nails in.' In a split second Ethan was back at my side, beaming as I held a nail for him to bash.

'It's not working, Daddy, it's not going in.'

'Well hit it harder then.' Ethan bashed and bashed. 'Come on, you can hit it harder than that,' I teased.

'No, Daddy, it won't do it,' he said as the plastic hammer began to puncture on the nail head. 'Daddy, I really need the big hammer, that will do it.'

'OK,' I relented, 'but be careful,' I said, passing him my hammer while still holding the nail in place. Before I could even think about it Ethan raised the hammer high above his head and brought it crashing down. Of course it missed the nail and hit my finger, very hard. 'Sorry, Daddy, sorry, sorry, sorry,' Ethan cried. It really hurt but I tried not to let Ethan see how much. 'Don't worry, let's carry on,' I said through gritted teeth. Ethan's smile returned and for a few more moments he busied himself trying to hammer in more nails and generally pass me tools I didn't need. Like all young children, he had a very short attention span so it wasn't long before he wandered off in the direction of the house, leaving me to complete the job and nurse my injuries.

Somc time later some friends came to visit and we went into the garden. 'That's the house I built with Daddy,' said Ethan proudly. I must admit, it pulled me up sharp. Part of me was thinking, 'No you didn't build the house, Ethan, you hurt my finger. *I* built the house!' But I realised that, for all my frustration, something very important had happened that day as we put that house together. We had made a memory. I realised that whenever Ethan looks at the ramshackle pinned together planks of wood he'll think, 'That's the house I built with my dad.' The truth is I didn't need him to help me. I'd have been better off without him around. I wouldn't have a sore finger. But Ethan and I working together is what makes us a family. It's the same thing when God turns to us and says, 'Here you are, have a go, pick up the hammer . . . go into the world and preach the Gospel . . .' the only difference is we didn't hit the nail on His finger, we hit it right through His hand.

Harvesting is a family thing. God doesn't need us to do it, but when we join in, we're being part of our Creator's business, building for our family's future. Isn't it disgraceful, then, the way we have almost turned 'evangelism' into a taboo word? Sometimes I perceive it's one of those ugly churchy words that we awkwardly dismiss and put to one side. Wouldn't it be amazing if we could just be like an energised and enthusiastic child, excitedly helping our Father God to build His house.

Harvesting is a family thing. God doesn't need us to do it, but when we join in, we're being part of our Creator's business, building for our family's future.

As any farmer will testify, the harvest is not the end of the process. Once the crop is gathered in, this is where the process of *'threshing'* starts. In drawing a person to Christ we can see this as the process of discipling, of bringing new believers to maturity so that they begin to flourish and in turn engage in the full six aspects of drawing others to Christ.

Consider each of the Ephesians 4:11–12 ministry gifts:

> *It was he who gave some to be apostles, some to be prophets, some to be evangelists, and some to be pastors and teachers, to prepare God's people for works of service, so that the body of Christ may be built up . . .*

Each of the 'gifts' (be careful here to think of 'gifts' not specific people) will mainly focus on one or more steps in the six-step process:

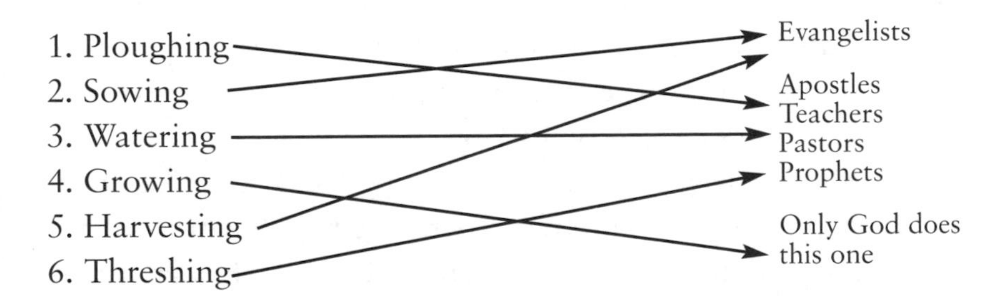

Apostles, teachers, pastors and prophets will primarily focus on ploughing, watering and threshing. Only God does the growing. Meanwhile, the evangelists (i.e. those with the 'gift' of evangelism, irrespective of what 'job' or 'position' they might hold in the church) will focus on sowing and harvesting. However, in our 'threshing' – our discipleship programmes – it is vital that Christians are trained in all areas. If pastors and church leaders do not include ongoing training in how to proclaim or spread the Gospel for everyone in their congregation, they are running glaringly deficient discipleship programmes. Imagine a farming academy specialising in training arable farmers. Imagine, then, if the academy fails to train them in how to sow wheat seed or fails to emphasise the importance of sowing. The curriculum is blatantly deficient and the academy a sham. So it is with our churches. After all, as disciples we are apprentices, or learners, aren't we? We are apprentices of the Lord Jesus and the apostles of the early church. What was one of the main priorities of their work? The proclamation of the Gospel, of course. So how can we say that our churches are 'making disciples' when so many fail in both teaching people how to spread the Gospel and in emphasising that this task is most integral in our walk with God.

How can we say that our churches are 'making disciples' when so many fail in both teaching people how to spread the Gospel and in emphasising that this task is most integral in our walk with God.

The point of using this farming analogy and breaking down the six steps is to illustrate that a person being drawn to Christ is a process with many varied contributing factors. Evangelism is an *event within this process.* All evangelism is mission, but not all mission is evangelism. All evangelism is outreach, but not all outreach is evangelism. Do you and your church have all six steps covered? Are you ploughing, sowing and watering? Do you see God 'growing' the individuals and are you working alongside Him in the harvest? Are you being trained and are you training others so the harvest

All evangelism is mission, but not all mission is evangelism. All evangelism is outreach, but not all outreach is evangelism.

will increase? Are you trying to emulate Jesus in your activities?

We can plough the soil and we can water it, but if we never sow anything, all we get is mud. What does MUD represent? Mighty Unbalanced Discipleship.

Evangelism is any Christian activity that brings a non-Christian closer to the point of conversion.

- How prevalent do you think this wrong definition is in the Church and among Christians?

- Which of the six steps below are you mainly focusing on?

  1. **Ploughing** *(Softening people's hearts to receive the seed of the Gospel)*
  2. **Sowing** *(Sowing the seed of the Gospel)*
  3. **Watering** *(Providing conditions favourable for the seed of the Gospel to grow)*
  4. **Growing** *(The supernatural work of the Father and the Holy Spirit to save souls)*
  5. **Harvesting** *(Inviting non-Christians to be followers of Christ)*
  6. **Threshing** *(Discipling)*

- Proclaiming the Gospel was a major part of the life of Jesus. Why do so many churches omit the spread and proclamation of the Gospel from discipleship training?

- Do you see all the six steps being covered in your church? If not, how could you help raise awareness and/or get involved in addressing those weak points?

19

A Nobody with Consequence

Edward Kimball was concerned about one of his young Sunday school students who worked at a shoe shop in downtown Chicago. One day he visited the shop where he found the young man in the back, stacking shoes. They talked for some time and Kimball led the student to Christ there and then. Dwight L. Moody eventually left the shoe store to become one of the greatest preachers and evangelists of all time.

Moody's international speaking brought him to Britain where he preached in a little chapel pastored by a young man by the name of Frederic Brotherton Meyer. In his sermon Moody told an emotionally charged story about the Sunday school teacher he had known in Chicago who personally went to every student in his class and led each one of them to Christ.

That message changed Meyer's entire ministry, inspiring him to become an evangelist like Moody. Over the years Meyer went to America several times to preach. Once, in Northfield, Massachusetts, a confused young preacher sitting in the back row heard Meyer say, 'If you are not willing to give up everything for Christ, are you willing to be made willing?' That remark led J. Wilbur Chapman to respond to the call of God on his life.

Chapman went on to become one of the most effective evangelists of his time. A volunteer by the name of Billy Sunday helped set up his crusades and learned how to preach by watching

Chapman. Sunday eventually took over Chapman's ministry, becoming one of the most dynamic evangelists of the twentieth century. In the great arenas of America, Billy Sunday's preaching turned thousands of people to Christ.

Inspired by a 1924 Billy Sunday crusade in Charlotte, North Carolina, a committee of Christians there dedicated themselves to reaching that city for Christ. The committee invited the evangelist Mordecai Ham to hold a series of evangelistic meetings in 1932. A lanky sixteen-year-old sat in the huge crowd one evening, spellbound by the message of the white-haired preacher, who seemed to be shouting and waving his finger at him. Night after night the teenager attended and finally went forward to give his life to Christ.

The teenager's name was Billy Graham, the man who has undoubtedly communicated the Gospel of Jesus Christ to more people than any other man in history.

The names Billy Graham, Billy Sunday, J. Wilbur Chapman, F.B. Meyer and Dwight L. Moody are celebrated in history. But where did this sequence of conversions start? A lone Sunday school teacher, a 'nobody' named Kimball who visited a student in a shoe shop. He was no stadium speaker, no great orator or celebrated theologian. He was just one man with a passion for the eternal future of another. Yet the consequences of that visit sing out in history. Millions of people have been affected by his decision to go to that shoe shop and share the gospel with one person. And millions more will continue to feel the impact of it.

This is the kind of story that sends shivers up my spine and I hope you feel the same. You don't have to be a 'called' evangelist to share the Gospel, you just need to be a follower of Christ, faithfully engaged in His Great Commission. Maybe you're reading this book and realising that you've never actually shared the Gospel with anyone. Imagine, then, that you put this book down and you do it now, maybe for the first time, today. Imagine that because of your action another person hears the Gospel and gives their life to Christ, not necessarily straight away, maybe even years later. You never know who that person might go on to influence. Maybe he or she might be the next Billy Graham, or maybe they'll just reach one more, who'll reach one more, who'll reach one more . . . Remember the boy saving the starfish on the beach? 'I can save this one, and this one, and this one.'

Perhaps up until now you haven't recognised the necessity, or perhaps you've always believed, quite genuinely, that you have a reasonable 'excuse' not to do it. The sad reality is that so many people in church make few attempts, or even no attempts at all, to reach out to people beyond church life. We allocate our time to good Christian fellowship and worship and meetings that build ourselves up in our faith whilst the challenge of the Great Commission is for the most part ignored. We've already talked about the many misunderstandings and excuses among Christians about sharing the Gospel: 'I can't do that, I feel inadequate, I don't know what to say, I'll leave it to those more qualified.' 'I don't even know how much I believe in the reality of the Gospel, in Heaven and Hell.' 'I think we need to earn the right to speak into someone's life before we try to share the Gospel with them.' 'Leading a good life and being a positive example is the way I evangelise.' 'My faith is a private thing, God hasn't told me to evangelise; until he tells me to I'm not going to do it.' 'Love is the most important thing and the most practical way to show love is to meet people's practical needs.' 'I can't share the Gospel because my lifestyle doesn't back it up, I'll look like a hypocrite.'

Each one of these excuses is like a fiery dart hurled by the enemy at our Lord. Each one, and many more like them, are evidence of the devil's stealth attack on the church. For as long as Christians hold onto such falsehood the devil need do little else in the battle for Lordship. He can concentrate on disrupting the lives of the wider population, with little fear that the people of God pose any threat to his schemes.

So let's engage in the battle right here and now. You believe yourself to be 'inadequate', 'unqualified', 'incapable' of sharing the Gospel? That's you and a big majority of other Christians. So let's expose this belief for what it really is – an attack by the devil that prevents Christians from doing what they've been asked to do by an ever gracious Master. Feeling inadequate and incapable is rooted in a lack of both skill and confidence. These might be very real, even crushing, obstacles but, in the light of the cosmic battle in which we are soldiers, neither of those factors constitute good excuses. Skills can be acquired. You can *learn* how to share the Gospel. Chapter 7 of this book gives you a good blueprint to help illustrate biblical reality and there are many analogies and explanations that give you the 'words' of the Gospel. You just need to explore them, learn them, use them.

When it comes to having 'confidence' this is, I believe, a bigger issue. It is very rare that I address a meeting feeling confident. More often I am terribly self-conscious and sick to the core with nerves. I doubt myself at every point, and it is only the power of the Gospel that drives me on to deliver its message. Whether addressing a large crowd or talking one-on-one I still struggle with embarrassment and insecurity about myself and I know I'm not alone. I will always remember a very self-assured, very capable businessman who attended one of our evangelism training courses in Scotland. At the end of the course he set himself a mission to approach a stranger and give the Gospel message. For five hours he wandered around a shopping centre trying to summon up the courage to talk to someone. Paralysed by lack of confidence, he returned home feeling ashamed and inadequate. He just couldn't do it.

Insecurity, fear of failure and embarrassment so often gets the better of us. Yet we must take encouragement, like soothing medicine, from the Word of God. Remember the long list of Bible heroes who felt inadequate in the task to which God called them. In Exodus 4:10 we see Moses crying out to God: *'O Lord, I have never been eloquent, neither in the past nor since you have spoken to your servant. I am slow of speech and tongue.'* Notice that Moses recognises that even after an encounter with the Living God his lack of eloquence is still an issue. Just because we have given our lives to Christ we are not suddenly super-skilled and super-confident. In fact in Moses' case he even goes on to argue with God despite clear reassurances. God reminds Moses of His omnipotence and reassures him, '*I will help you speak and will teach you what to say.*' But even then Moses retorts, *'O Lord, please send someone else to do it.*'

Another example is the prophet in Jeremiah 1:6–7:

> *'Ah, Sovereign LORD,' I said, 'I do not know how to speak; I am only a child.' But the LORD said to me, 'Do not say, "I am only a child." You must go to everyone I send you to and say whatever I command you.'*

So, too, we see this admission of almost crippling fear and reluctance from the apostle Paul. The early church revered him as a great leader and teacher yet he admits to the Corinthian believers, *'I came to you in weakness and fear, and with much trembling. My message and my preaching were not with wise and persuasive words, but with a demonstration of the Spirit's power, so that your faith might not rest on men's wisdom, but on God's power'* (1 Cor. 2:3–5). Paul preached the Gospel anyway because he put his confidence in the Holy Spirit. He recognised his inadequacy and weakness, but he pressed on, despite himself, so that ultimately his hearers would see and hear beyond him and experience the power of God. The crux of the matter lies in the fact that Paul had gone through a spiritual death experience, as he states in the letter to the Galatians, chapter 2:20 *'I have been crucified with Christ and I no longer live, but Christ lives in me.'* Many genuine Christians have this experience at the point of conversion. Others grow into it. Either way, as a soldier for Jesus Christ in the battle for souls we need to walk in Galatians 2:20 all the time. We need to recognise who we really are in Him, so that we can die to ourselves on a daily basis, putting aside embarrassment and insecurity, drawing instead on Christ living within.

'I have been crucified with Christ and I no longer live, but Christ lives in me.' (Gal. 2:20)

This in itself is a conscious decision. It can take grit and determination, but we should take heart in knowing that God knows how we are wired. He knows the inner battle we face. Our efforts do not come with ease, but never are they in vain and the reward is sweet. We are given the example in Psalm 126:5–6, *'Those who sow in tears will reap with songs of joy. He who goes out weeping, carrying seed to sow, will return with songs of joy, carrying sheaves with him.'* This is a stark illustration – a man weeping as he goes out sowing. I must admit this picture has become a personal affirmation to me. Though I consider myself a 'called' evangelist, I cannot say that 100 per cent of the time I feel tremendous joy at going out and sharing the Gospel. Rather I battle with the same feelings of inadequacy, fear and trembling as Moses, Jeremiah, Paul and many others. I also feel the weight of the sacrifice on my family and sometimes there are, indeed, very real tears at the task before me. But always I return with 'songs of joy', knowing in my spirit that what I have done is pleasing to God. At the end of the day do I have one single thing to complain about? How do I even dare mutter of my own suffering in the shadow of the cross and all that my Lord endured on my behalf!

Christians *do* struggle to share their faith. That's a sad fact but it is no reason to step away from the battlefield. We need to embrace it as a challenge, not an excuse. Samuel Shoemaker, co-founder of Alcoholics Anonymous, once said that the test of a man's conversion is whether he has enough Christianity to get it to other people. If he hasn't there is something wrong. This is our challenge and it is a challenge that should determine our days, a challenge that should see us equipping ourselves, acquiring skills, seeking out resources and putting on the armour so that we can overcome our feelings of inadequacy – or at least move ahead in the Spirit's power despite them – in full acknowledgment that 'God doesn't call the qualified, He qualifies the called.'

Feelings of inadequacy sometimes come as a direct result of perceived 'failure' in evangelism. Maybe you've shared the Gospel with someone on a number of occasions. Maybe you've been praying for them for years, witnessing to them whenever possible. But it's just not happening for them. No matter what you do and say they still don't seem to be anywhere near a point of conversion. We've discussed this already in Chapter 15 when we looked at the false definition of evangelism as the 'winning of souls'. If we measure our success in evangelism by the number of 'converts' we fall at the first hurdle. If we believe ourselves to be inadequate, not called and therefore unaccountable to the Great Commission, we fall at the next, and the next . . .

A key strategy in overcoming such hurdles is to work towards a clearer understanding of the sovereignty of God and the free will of people. We each have free will. It is a gift that God gives us. Yet when we choose to come under God's sovereignty our mindsets begin to change. Our natural reaction to free will is to offer up excuses: 'Great, so God's given you a call to evangelism, but until he makes it clear to me, I'm off the hook.' 'The Holy Spirit hasn't yet healed me of my fear, so I'll wait until He does.'

'I'm not a great advert for Christianity, so I'd better keep quiet.' But such mindsets are a mistake. As free beings we have a choice to decide to follow God's will, as it is revealed to us in His Word. Before I was a Christian I was a slave to sin and even if, in an attack of conscience and human decency, I decided for myself to be a 'better person', still I would have remained in bondage to sin. Even if I did not want to sin, I could not do otherwise. I was only freed from this bondage when I became a Christian. When God saved me He freed me from sin but, according to Scripture, I remain a slave. Now, rather than being bound to sin, I am bound to righteousness:

> *You have been set free from sin and have become slaves to righteousness.* (Rom. 6:18)

We can go round in circles discussing the apparent dichotomy of being freed into slavery to righteousness but, as the saints down the ages testify, when we commit ourselves to God's sovereign 'will' and follow His commands in obedience and worship, it is then that we further open up the gift of abundant life that is ours for the taking. It is then that He gives us the desire to *want* to do more. Free will is no longer an excuse. More, it is an act of decision, of surrender, of worship, of dedication to our Sovereign. Remember Steven Grellat in the empty logger's shack? To go ahead and preach his message when there appeared to be no-one to hear seemed quite absurd. Yet Grellat was acting in obedience and conviction, setting aside his own uncertainties, embarrassment and understanding and surrendering his own will to the will of God.

Free will is no longer an excuse. More, it is an act of decision, of surrender, of worship, of dedication to our Sovereign.

As we seek to mature in our Christian walk I believe it is imperative that we look to develop our understanding of this interplay between free will and the sovereignty of God. I have been immensely inspired and challenged by J.I. Packer's *Evangelism and the Sovereignty of God*[1] and Millard Erickson's *Christian Theology*.[2]

Secondly, let me reiterate once more this issue of 'sowing' as the act of evangelism. If we are to overcome our feelings of failure and inadequacy we must realise that our task is first and foremost to *proclaim* and not to convert. Understanding this brings immense relief and freedom. We are here to sow. It is up to God to grow. The Bible is clear that it is the Holy Spirit who convicts, so when we begin a conversation we should do so with our aim being nothing more than to give our message. Perhaps that message will lead to a person wanting to give their life to Christ there and then, but this is not always the case. In fact, more often it is not the case and this should by no means be seen as failure on our part. That doesn't mean we shouldn't invite people to accept Christ. Clearly we need to be looking to do this, but this new mindset takes the pressure off us trying to press and cajole someone into making a decision. It makes evangelism the loving and pleasant endeavour that it should be.

Yes, 'loving', 'pleasant', that's what I said. When we see the Gospel as the 'evangel', the message of victory and good news, and see ourselves as servants and deliverers of that message it figures that our attitude should be one of joy, excitement and urgency. It also reminds us that we are dealing with a specific message with specific content. We don't need to feel pressured to say something different each time. Naturally our approach might vary depending on who we are speaking with and the context of the conversation, but the good news is the good news, it never changes. We don't need to dress it up (indeed, we have already talked of the dangers of doing so!) we just need to know it and

Do you use Facebook, Myspace, Twitter, YouTube or any other web-based communication? Have you thought of posting up the Gospel message using these devices?

use it. There are many 'stress relieving' tools that can make delivering the message easier. It may be that you are confident in speaking and explaining the Gospel, but for many of us tracts, story illustrations, technology-based visual aids, books and the like give us something to 'talk around' or act as pieces of evangelism in themselves. Do you use Facebook, Myspace, Twitter, YouTube or any other web-based communication? Have you thought of posting up the Gospel message using these devices? Very recently a girl made contact with me who had read the Message on my Facebook space, said the prayer and given her life to God! I must admit, such impersonal communication is not my first choice of medium to deliver the Gospel, but the experience of this girl proves that the Gospel reigns in cyberspace and for Christians to dismiss its potential is grave error. After all, didn't the apostle Paul say, 'by all possible means'?

The way people use technology reflects something fundamental about human nature. In cyberspace you can cloak yourself from truth. You can be whoever and whatever you want to be. The real truth of 'you' can be hidden in a fabrication that you can manipulate and control. You can choose to dip in and out of relationships and conversations and the persona you project can be confident, bold and far more daring than you might be in true face-to-face conversation.

There is a story told of a young soldier and his commanding officer getting onto a train together. The only available seats were across from an attractive young lady who was travelling with her grandmother. As the four engaged in conversation it became obvious that there was mutual attraction between the young man and woman.

Suddenly the train went into a tunnel, plunging the carriage into darkness. Immediately two sounds were heard: the smack of a kiss followed by the whack of a slap across someone's face.

The grandmother thought, 'I can't believe he kissed my granddaughter, but I'm glad she gave him the slap he deserved.'

The commanding officer thought, 'I don't blame the boy for kissing the girl, but it's a shame that she missed him and hit me instead.'

The young girl thought, 'I'm glad he kissed me, but I wish my grandmother hadn't slapped him for doing it.'

As the train broke into the sunlight, the soldier couldn't help but smile. He had managed to kiss the girl and slap his commanding officer and get away with both!

It's hard to get away with anything in the light. Jesus was quick to point this out to Nicodemus. He knew why the faithful Pharisee had come to visit Him at night, under the cover of darkness. His words must have carried quite a sting:

> *Light has come into the world, but men loved darkness instead of light because their deeds were evil. Everyone who does evil hates the light, and will not come into the light for fear that his deeds will be exposed. But whoever lives by the truth comes into the light, so that it may be seen plainly that what he has done has been done through God.* (John 3:19–21)

Perhaps you see my parallel here? The anonymity of technology shrouds us from confrontation and allows us to explore in the shadows that which we hesitate to seek in the light of day. The sinister side of this is well acknowledged, but let us not be too damning here, for indeed, there is a very positive flip side. Jesus' exchange with Nicodemus is intriguing and has many facets.

'But whoever lives by the truth comes into the light, so that it may be seen plainly that what he has done has been done through God.' (John 3:21)

The religious leaders at the time were stuck in a bureaucratic religious system that made the system more important than the cause for which it was founded (not too unlike many religious denominations in our world today).

Nicodemus was one of these religious leaders; however, there is something going on in his heart and mind. Intrigued by the miracles Jesus has performed and His huge claims of being the Son of God, Nicodemus goes to Him in secret. He knows that fellow religious scholars believe Jesus' claims are a sham, that some believe Jesus is a threat to their religious institution. He also recognises the possible danger of the occupying Roman rulers viewing Him as a leader of a new revolution.

But Nicodemus is beginning to wonder. Perhaps this man is from God? After all, how else could they account for the miracles? How could they account for His staggering insight into the Scriptures and His understanding of the things of God? Nicodemus decides to find out more.

This whole story is about how a person becomes right with God. Nicodemus had his ideas, but they were only the traditions that had been handed down to him. In fact, he was fully indoctrinated in his thinking. To be found even exploring something different, something so radical as belief in the truth about Jesus, would cause uproar among his peers and drastically alter his way of life. Nicodemus comes in darkness but Jesus pours forth the full light of truth, leaving the Pharisee struggling and floundering with what he is told. Yet we hear of this man later on in John

7:5. It is Nicodemus who stands up for Jesus before the Sanhedrin and we are told that he went with another believing Pharisee, Joseph of Arimathea, to retrieve Jesus' body after the crucifixion (John 19:39). Nicodemus' approach to Jesus was in a private, personal, secret arena but it appears that the Lord brought his understanding to a whole new level. It appears that Nicodemus probably did take that step and become 'born again'.

The point I am making here is that people seek in darkness. Technology offers a deeper shroud of darkness still, but if we, as Christians, choose to fill it with the light of the Gospel, using our own testimonies and the many communication interfaces available to us, those who seek will, like Nicodemus, find. Dare I suggest that every church makes a video recording of the testimony of each member of their congregation and puts them all on YouTube?

So we return to another strategy that should help us overcome our excuses and this issue of 'failure' in evangelism. I sometimes cringe when I hear people speaking about 'spirit-led' evangelism. Now don't get me wrong here. I fully believe that the Holy Spirit clearly leads us to people with divine appointments with whom we should share the Gospel. Many times I have felt the strong conviction of the Spirit to engage with a particular person and often this has led to a very powerful time, sometimes with that person giving their life to God there and then. But this is not an everyday occurrence. What am I to do then? Am I to wait for the next 'warm glow', the next 'strong feeling', the next person who comes across my path asking me about Jesus? No. At the forefront of our understanding should be the recognition that we shouldn't wait around for people to come to us. God has given us brains, hands and feet and mouths to use. He has given us specific instruction to 'go' and this means being proactive, starting conversations and seeking out opportunities to share our message. Yes, we must always seek the prompting of the Spirit, for it is the Spirit of God who convicts a person of truth (1 Thess. 1:5) but we have also, already, been directly told by the Word of God to go out there and proclaim the Gospel.

Also at the front of our minds must be a decision to obey and to trust God no matter what. Time and again in this discussion we come back to our own personal relationship with God, don't we? And I urge you again and again to examine yourself and query whether this might be a reason that you lack the urgency, the vigour, the passion to share the Gospel with others. Roy Robertson believed himself to be a Christian, but he tells of the time when he realised the difference between religion and relationship. He writes:

> My ship, the West Virginia, docked at Pearl Harbour on the evening of December 6, 1941. A couple of the fellows and I left the ship that night and attended a Bible study. About fifteen sailors sat in a circle on the floor. The leader asked us each to recite our favourite Scripture verse. In turn each sailor shared a verse and briefly commented on it. I sat there in terror. I grew up in a Christian home, went to church three times a week, but I sat there terrified. I couldn't recall a single verse. Finally, I remembered one verse – John 3:16. I silently rehearsed it in my mind. The spotlight of attention grew closer as each sailor took his turn. It was up to the fellow next to me. He recited John 3:16. He took my verse! As he commented on it I sat there in stunned humiliation. In a few moments everyone would know that I could not recall from memory even a single verse. Later that night I went to bed thinking, 'Robertson, you're a fake.' At 7:55 the next morning I was awakened by the ship alarm ordering us to battle stations. Three hundred and sixty planes of the Japanese Imperial Fleet were attacking our ship and the other military installations. My crew and I raced to our machine gun emplacement, but all we had was practice ammunition. So for the first

> fifteen minutes of the two-hour battle, we only fired blanks hoping to scare the Japanese air planes. As I stood there firing fake ammunition I thought, 'Robertson, this is how your whole life has been – firing blanks for Christ.' I made up my mind as Japanese bullets slammed into our ship, 'If I escape with my life, I will get serious about following Jesus.'[3]

Roy Robertson went on to help Dawson Trotman found the Navigators, a Christian group that ministered to military personnel. God used his life in a powerful way when he moved from religion to relationship.

Not many days after I made a commitment to God in prison and prayed my prayer of conversion, I found myself with a blade to my throat. 'Alcaponey' was a beast of a man, an archrival who I had previously plotted revenge against for the brutalisation of my good friend, Shane. His sudden attack caught me off guard and put me in a life-compromising position. What should I do? I was a changed man now, but Alcaponey didn't know that, nor would he care. My instincts were to fight for my life, to hurt him, to teach him a lesson, as I knew I could. But I had Scripture in my head. Verses seemed to be speaking clearly to me as the threat of Alcaponey's blade demanded action. I had a decision to make . . .

Thankfully, that day I put my trust in God. I made a conscious decision to obey his commands, even if that meant laying down my life. As *Taming the Tiger*[4] recounts, I released my grip and laid myself open to Alcaponey's attack, calling on the name of Jesus as I did so. The effect was staggering. Against all earthly odds I escaped with my life, into fullness of life. I knew then that I had fully surrendered to Jesus, that He was my Saviour and my Lord and anything He asked of me I would be able to do in His strength.

It's vital that on a daily basis we decide to put our trust in Jesus, no matter what. We need to make that decision to obey

'Fear of man will prove to be a snare, but whoever trusts in the L*ORD is kept safe.' (Prov. 29:25)*

Him and then live our lives in the light of that decision. Every day we should remind ourselves that we are dying to self, that we must decrease as He increases in us (John 3:30). That is the only way we will get over fear of public exposure. We have not joined some sort of club. We have joined an army, God's army. When Jesus says what He does in Mark 16:15 we cannot back down from this command. Failure? Yes, it will come. Ridicule? Probably. But following Christ's command is what brings us closer to Him and His purposes. Surely then we should embrace the blows to pride – the disappointment of friends labelling us religious nutcases, the fear of approaching a stranger, the anxiety in public exposure – as we put ourselves on the line to tell His story. What is pride? And what worth is human approval? Proverbs 29:25 reminds us, *'Fear of man will prove to be a snare, but whoever trusts in the* L*ORD is kept safe.'* So then let us grasp hold of the simplicity of the message, train ourselves in the art of its telling and live every day to obey Jesus' command. For there is no greater reward this side of eternity.

- It is a huge relief when we understand that our job is only to 'sow seeds', since it is only God who does the 'growing'. However, we still get disappointed when people reject our message and it's easy to see that as rejection of us personally. What measures can we put in place to handle such feelings? Read 1 John 4:20.

- Do we look more at God's hands than His face? Consider how we should focus more on *who God is*, rather than on *what He can do* for us.

- Reflect on Roy Robertson's realisation that his life had been 'firing blanks for Christ'. Are there areas in your life where you feel you do the same?

20

A Run on the Roman Road

It is as we obey Christ's commands to evangelise that urgency and compassion come. (Dr Leighton Ford)[1]

Leighton Ford is Vice President of the Billy Graham Evangelistic Association and Honorary Life Chairman of the Lausanne Committee for World Evangelisation. He has addressed millions of people on every continent and received high recognition as a teacher, evangelist and author. He is a man who knows first-hand that the drive to spread the Gospel of Jesus Christ increases as we obey Christ's commands. His assertion concerning urgency and compassion is one that I recognise in myself and I challenge anyone to put it to the test.

How often have I had people say to me something like: 'But, Tony, I just don't feel the same passion for the lost as you. I can't help it. I just don't have the same drive to speak to others. It's obviously not my gifting.'

A friend of mine recently started running. Being rather unfit and a little overweight she tentatively began a gentle training schedule, along with a friend in similar condition. Both women were reluctant athletes to say the least, but they committed to each other to get out three times a week for a twenty-minute fast walk. It was tough at first and my friend reports that it was only the commitment to one another that got them off the sofa some evenings. It wasn't long, however, before the fast walk was interspersed with periods of slow jogging. Soon after that the women found they could do a whole circuit of slow jogging, which then progressed into periods of faster running. What's more they found they were enjoying the time together and seeing remarkable benefit when it came to energy levels, fitness and weight loss. The reluctant twenty minutes had now become something they looked forward to and they began setting challenges to run further, faster and longer. After a month or so of training they entered their first 5-kilometre race and completed it in respectable time. 'I never thought I'd be able to call myself a proper runner,' my friend reported, 'but as I crossed the finishing line, with many other runners behind, I knew I really was one of them. The amazing thing now is I have a real *need* to run. It has really changed my life. I have much more energy and I look forward to getting out there and doing it. I'm thinking of working towards the Marathon!'

Any athlete or musician or artist will testify that to get better you have to practise, and the more you do something, the more you love it. This is my experience of evangelism. When I first became a Christian I was so radically changed and so overflowing with joy that I couldn't help but share the good news of Jesus Christ. Yet as the years went by, and especially as I was faced with life outside prison, my zeal and excitement began to wane. Thankfully it was replaced with deeper passion as I began to study the Scriptures and learn more of what it truly means to be a follower of Christ. To that end I made the conscious decision and commitment I talked about in the previous chapter: to obey Christ's commands no matter what and to equip myself with skill and resource to share the Gospel with anyone whenever and wherever I possibly can. Having taken those steps I can wholeheartedly testify that my passion for the lost grows on a daily basis. The more I practise sharing the Gospel, the more I love the

Gospel. You don't *learn to draw* and then start *drawing*. You don't learn to play the piano and then, when you've done that, start *playing* the piano. No, the activity is perpetual. From the moment you put pencil to paper or fingers on keys you are *drawing* or *playing*. And, usually, the more accomplished you become at the art, the more you love it and the more you do it. Similarly, the only way you will start to operate as an evangelist is to start evangelising. And when you start evangelising I'm fairly certain you'll find you get more of a heart for the lost.

Experience teaches me that the more I love the Gospel the more I share the Gospel, and the more I love Christ and what He has done to save me. The closer I come to Christ, the more abundant joy I receive . . . and the more I want to practise evangelism . . . So, when people ask, 'Why don't I share the same passion for the lost as you?' my reply is simple: 'Try following Christ's commands in Mark 16:15. Try *practising* the Great Commission.

The closer I come to Christ, the more abundant joy I receive . . . and the more I want to practise evangelism . . .

Is the war over for people who struggle in this way?

Is the war over for you?

No. We have exposed some of the devil's schemes – the lies that hide the necessity for *all* Christians to participate in the Great Commission; the lie that tells us we are not 'evangelists' therefore someone else will do the job; the lie that tells us befriending non-Christians, setting up feeding programmes, holding 'outreach' events that don't feature the giving of the Gospel message are evangelism; the idea that evangelism is the winning of souls and our efforts always fail because we don't see 'converts' when we do share the Gospel; the crushing belief that we are incapable, inadequate, unqualified . . .

No, I will not accept that the war is over for anyone who professes to love the Lord Jesus Christ. With the lies exposed we are ready to rise again. We can take steps to get back into the fight, to rediscover – or discover for the first time – a passion for the lost, a zeal to share the Gospel, an urgency to engage in Jesus' commands, because we want to lift Him up, because we want to glorify Him and because the consequences for those who we fail are too terrible to contemplate.

In the previous chapter we looked at this issue of feeling inadequate and I say again that with millions of encounters under my belt I still feel these same crushing doubts every time I go out to evangelise. Every time I take to the stage or the pulpit or even approach an individual with the intent to share the Gospel I am still taunted with the little voice, 'Why are you doing this? Why you? Surely there's someone else who can do a better job? What's the point in all this anyway? Why do you need to put yourself up for rejection and ridicule? When this happens it's important to understand that feeling inadequate is a normal experience for people who are advancing spiritually. Remember, if we are in a war, our enemy is not going to let us win easily. He knows this, we know it, God knows it and He calls us to obey Him, to trust Him, to ground ourselves in His Word and His commands so that we might be strong and overcome the attack of the enemy. When Joshua faced the huge and daunting task of leading the people into the Promised Land he had every reason to feel anxious and inadequate. He was, after all, taking on the mantle from God's great servant Moses. Much was at stake. The people of Israel had wandered for years, lost in the desert. They, too, were fearful and doubting. They had a migrant legacy and the promise of their own land must have seemed a dim reality, especially in view of Moses' death. Yet God knew their hearts. He recognised their anxiety and fear of the unknown and told Joshua and His fearful people not to be discouraged:

> *No-one will be able to stand up against you all the days of your life. As I was with Moses, so I will be with you; I will never leave you nor forsake you. Be strong and courageous, because you will lead these people to inherit the land I swore to their forefathers to give them. Be strong and very courageous. Be careful to obey all the law my servant Moses gave you; do not turn from it to the right or to the left, that you may be successful wherever you go. Do not let this Book of the Law depart from your mouth; meditate on it day and night, so that you may be careful to do everything written in it. Then you will be prosperous and successful. Have I not commanded you? Be strong and courageous. Do not be terrified; do not be discouraged, for the LORD your God will be with you wherever you go.* (Josh. 1:5–9)

The *NIV Study Bible* makes insightful comments in its introduction to the book of Joshua. It draws the parallel between Joshua and Jesus and highlights that the purpose of this account is to prophetically illuminate the destiny of all people in light of God's supreme purpose:

> War is a terrible curse that the human race brings on itself as it seeks to possess the earth by its own unrighteous ways. But it pales before the curse that awaits all those who do not heed God's testimony to Himself or His warnings – those who oppose the rule of God and reject His offer of grace. The God of the second Joshua (Jesus) is the God of the first Joshua also. Although now for a time He reaches out to the whole world with the Gospel (and commissions His people urgently to carry His offer of peace to all nations), the sword of His judgment awaits in the wings – and his second Joshua will wield it. (Rev. 19:11–16)[2]

So here we are again back at the uncomfortable crux and reality of the Gospel message – a reality that should spur us on in urgency to inform others of this 'sword of judgment'. As we have already discussed, there is a natural yet very worrying tendency among Christians to deliver the 'niceties' of the Christian experience without speaking of the whole truth of sin and judgment. Such 'watering down' has catastrophic consequences for the unsaved, so part of our 'training' in how to deliver the full Gospel message must include an understanding of Scripture that speaks clearly of the path to Salvation. Chapter 7 offered a blueprint for the 'words of the Gospel' but now let's look in detail at the Scripture from which this, and similar concepts were devised. In doing so we will hopefully also address another 'excuse' sometimes offered by Christians not to speak of the Gospel, which is concerning personal doubt as to the reality of Heaven, Hell, judgment and redemption.

There are many areas of Scripture to draw on here, but one of the most inclusive passages where the words of the Gospel can be readily identified is in John's gospel where Jesus is teaching about the work of the coming Holy Spirit:

> *When he comes, he will convict the world of guilt in regard to sin and righteousness and judgment: in regard to sin, because men do not believe in me; in regard to righteousness, because I am going to the Father, where you can see me no longer.* (John 16:8–10)

When you ingest these words you'll find there is great release and freedom in this passage. It is the Holy Spirit that does the convicting. That is, you don't have to. In fact, you cannot. Only the Holy Spirit can convict a person, so really we must not worry about whether a person is believing or doubting. Our job is simply to deliver the message. The truth is that many people will doubt. Many will reject, just as they did in New Testament times and down the ages ever since. The Apostles suffered terrible rejection and persecution but their sights remained set on preaching the message clearly and lovingly in the best way it could be understood by their hearers. Remember Paul's declaration to the church in Corinth?

> *I make myself a slave to everyone, to win as many as possible. To the Jews I became like a Jew, to win the Jews. To those under the law I became like one under the law (though I myself am not under the law), so as to win those under the law. To those not having the law I became like one not having the law (though I am not free from God's law but am under Christ's law), so as to win those not having the law. To the weak I became weak, to win the weak. I have become all things to all men so that by all possible means I might save some.* (1 Cor. 9:19–22)

It's never easy to talk to someone about sin, though, is it? It seems such an old-fashioned concept. As we've already discussed, there's good reason for this. The devil does everything he can to shut our mouths and stop us mentioning sin. His first device is to eliminate sin as a topic of discussion in proclamation of the Gospel. When this happens we present a watered-down version of the Gospel and jeopardise the Salvation of those we are trying to reach. F.B. Meyer hammers home this point with his emphasis on the interlink between the convicting work of the Holy Spirit and our commission to tell the whole truth about men and women in relation to God:

> The weapon here is the Holy Spirit. He convicts men of the sin of refusing to believe in Jesus Christ. So we must tell the unchurched world about sin. It is a great mistake to entice sinners by describing the moral grandeur of Christ's character and teaching. We should at once seek to arouse them to a sense of their great sinfulness. When a man realises that his life is being eaten

> out by some insidious disease he will need no further urging to go to a physician. This is the weakness of the modern preaching, that we expound on the value of the remedy to men who have never realised their dire necessity.[3]

Non-Christians must be convicted that they are lost before they can be found. If they're not aware they are lost, they will never see a need for a Saviour. How does the Holy Spirit do this? Whilst the New Testament speaks of redemption for those under the law (as though the law is an oppressively strict schoolmaster – Gal. 4:1–7 for example), Scripture also extols the *worth* of the law as a utility by which the Holy Spirit convicts of sin. *'Therefore no-one will be declared righteous in his sight by observing the law; rather, through the law we become conscious of sin'* (Rom. 3:20). God has given the law to us for this reason. Its function was never to bestow Salvation, but to convince people of their need for it. As we know, nobody has ever been able to keep the law, God's perfect standard. Instead, we sinners break it every day, no matter who we are, where we come from, how 'good' a person we seem to be. '*There is no difference, for all have sinned and fall short of the glory of God*' (Rom. 3:22–23). John Stott, in his book *Our Guilty Silence: Church, the Gospel and the World*, highlights Martin Luther's statement that 'It is the work of the law to terrify and the work of the Gospel to justify.'[4] Such recognition led the great preacher John Wesley to assert, 'Before I preach love, mercy and grace, I must preach sin, law and judgment.'[5]

Non-Christians must be convicted that they are lost before they can be found. If they're not aware they are lost, they will never see a need for a Saviour.

When I present the Gospel, particularly in a public meeting, I often start by getting the congregation to do a short test. It's little more than a fun ice-breaker, but it also helps highlight an important point. I ask people to give themselves a score, between 0 and 10, for each statement:

I give to charities
I pray
I help strangers in need
I read the Bible
I forgive people when they hurt me
I love and help family members
I am loyal with my friendships
I put other people first when they need me
I am totally honest in the things I say and do
I see the best in people

Those who record a cumulative score between 68 and 70 are then labelled 'angelic'. An achievement of between 64 and 67 makes you 'saintly', 35–63 good, 25–34 struggling and those who manage under a meagre 25 are told 'seek help'!

I emphasise again that this is all just a bit of fun, but I then go on to say, 'Now let me show you what Jesus would say to a "good" person like you.' The message then follows the blueprint illustrated in Chapter 7 that gets a person to understand that all have broken God's laws – all have lied, cheated, not forgiven, held onto pride, greed and jealously. (Using visuals and through the tone with which I deliver this message I usually receive a light-hearted humorous response.) I go on to highlight the fact that even though we humans are very quick to differentiate between 'good' and 'bad' people, in God's eyes there really is no difference *'for all have sinned and fall short of the glory of God'* (Rom. 3:23). We might consider ourselves fine upstanding citizens, but by asking a series of questions (again in a light-hearted manner), I easily get people to understand that according to the biblical remit they are really no better than liars, thieves and murderers (to which there is usually a sobering chuckle or a laugh out loud).

> The utility of the law is that it convinces man of his weakness and compels him to apply for the medicine of grace which is in Christ. The law was given that it might make you guilty. Been made guilty might fear. Fearing might ask indulgence and not presume on your own strength. The law was given to turn a great man into a little man. (St Augustine)[6]

So you see this modern tendency not to speak of the law is serious folly. It is well worth an extended study of Paul's teaching in Romans to understand the relationship of the law to grace and righteousness. He extols the law and stresses what we need to hear today: that really there is no excuse not to use the law or not to speak about sin and Hell. 'What shall we say, then? Is the law sin? Certainly not! Indeed I would not have known what sin was except through the law' (Rom. 7:7); *'So the law was put in charge to lead us to Christ that we might be justified by faith'* (Gal. 3:24).

John Stott has much to say on the matter, emphasising the necessity of a person coming face to face with his or her own inherent and very real sinfulness:

> The first is through Christ Himself, confronted by Him and the perfection of His self mastery and self sacrifice we cannot help falling down at Jesus' knees with Simon Peter and crying out, *'Depart from me I am a sinful man O Lord* (Luke 5:8).'[7]

Stott goes on to remind us that another way Christ convicts sinners of their sin is through Christians. The light of God's law that shines brightest through Jesus shines through His disciples too and this light exposes the shame in the darkness.

> *This is the verdict: Light has come into the world, but men loved darkness instead of light because their deeds were evil. Everyone who does evil hates the light, and will not come into the light for fear that his deeds will be exposed. But whoever lives by the truth comes into the light, so that it may be seen plainly that what he has done has been done through God.* (John 3:19–21)

After sin has been awakened either through the Holy Spirit and the law or through Christ directly or through Christian witness, the second element of the Gospel to be presented is *righteousness.*

Righteousness is the central theme of Paul's teaching in the book of Romans. In chapter 3:21–26 he highlights that all are unrighteous but that God has *provided* righteousness for mankind in justification by grace. God declares a person to be guilty, but in Jesus He cancels the guilt of the person's sin and credits righteousness to him. Even though all are sinners God declares that everyone who puts their trust in Jesus is no longer guilty, but righteous. The *NIV Study Bible* notes that 'This legal declaration is valid because Christ died to pay the penalty for our sin and lived a life of perfect righteousness that can in turn be imputed to us . . . Christ's righteousness (His obedience to God's law and His sacrificial death) will be credited to believers as their own.'[8]

In our presentation of the Gospel I use the idea of the 'perfect record' to illustrate this point. (The idea of the 'record' is taken from the picture in Revelation in which everyone has a book recording his or her deeds – Rev. 20:12). Though our record – the long list of violations of God's law – renders us badly short of God's standard and fit only for eternity apart from Him, we have the possibility of replacing our imperfect record with a new, perfect one – that which Jesus freely offers us because He has already paid the price and taken the punishment for all sin.

So first we are wounded by realisation of our sin. We stand condemned and incapable of making ourselves right before God. But the sheer beauty of the Gospel is that it quickly comforts with the knowledge that this unrighteousness can be exchanged for Jesus' righteousness. We can claim this righteousness as our own, even though it is undeserved. The terror and anxiety of knowing that we are not right with God can be exchanged for peace and tranquillity. Righteousness is the balm that the Holy Spirit uses to soothe the wounds inflicted by the awakening to sin. This is, indeed, the Good News.

Righteousness is the balm that the Holy Spirit uses to soothe the wounds inflicted by the awakening to sin.

But there is more to understand, more to grasp and more to communicate when we share the full Gospel in the hope of a person's Salvation. Just as our natural tendency is to shy away from the subject of sin, so we struggle to speak of the biblical truth of 'judgment'. Yet the fact of judgment is sure:

> *Just as man is destined to die once, and after that to face judgment, so Christ was sacrificed once, to take away the sins of many people.* (Heb. 9:27–28)

> *For we must all appear before the judgment seat of Christ, that each one may receive what is due to him for the things done while in the body, whether good or bad.* (2 Cor. 5:10)

There are many more verses we can draw on. Jesus referred to the 'Day of Judgment' on several occasions. In our Gospel presentation we use the analogy of the court judge with the guilty man before him. He is bound by his position to make a decision for the sake of justice and, as we all so readily seem to agree, they who are found guilty are to be punished. And what is this punishment? Scholars tell us that there are three words in Scripture that are translated in our modern Bibles as 'Hell': 'Gehenna' is found in Matthew 5:22 and 29, 10:28 and James 3:6 and means place of punishment; 'Hades', also a Greek word meaning 'abode of the dead, is found in Matthew 11:23, 16:18, Luke 16:23 and Acts 2:27. 'Sheol' is a Hebrew word meaning 'the grave' which appears in Psalm 9:17, 86:13 and 18:5–7.

Can we conclude, then, that 'Hell', or whatever we choose to call it, is a biblical reality? I ask this question in the context that a staggering number of Christians seem to take issue with the certainty of Hell and punishment. Some believe that Hell is to be annihilated, to cease conscious existence, to have eternal sleep. Yet Scripture paints a different picture. In Luke 16:19–31 we are given the chilling account of the rich man and Lazarus. The point to note here is the conscious state of the rich man in Hell. He speaks of his torment and the agony of intense thirst. Similarly Mark's Gospel records Jesus' graphic reference to the horror of being thrown into Hell in Mark 9:42–49.

In many places the Bible describes the fate of the unsaved in terrible, fearful terms, yet again, when we speak to others about what it means to be a Christian, our tendency is to shy away from mentioning what the Gospel compels us to accept as truth. Once again it seems that the devil's devices are at work. 'Don't talk about it, don't make people feel bad. Isn't this all too scary and far-fetched? Surely there isn't really a place of such intense suffering after death? It's much more likely that we just fall asleep and know nothing, just like before we were born.'

It might not be popular to proclaim Hell when we're talking about good news but, as we've already seen, it is vital that we do proclaim the *whole truth*, rather than a watered-down version of the Gospel. Heaven, Hell and the final judgment are vital elements of the Gospel and the consequence of ignorance can be devastating. C.S Lewis in his work *The Great Divorce* famously asserts, 'There are only two kinds of people in the end: those who say to God, "Thy will be done," and those to whom God says, in the end, "Thy will be done." All that are in Hell, choose it.'[9]

'There are only two kinds of people in the end: those who say to God, "Thy will be done," and those to whom God says, in the end, "Thy will be done." All that are in Hell, choose it.' (C.S. Lewis)

When we are clear on the three elements of 'sin', 'righteousness' and 'judgment' we can more easily begin to explain the truth about Jesus as 'Saviour'. I recommend you revisit Chapter 7 to see again how we can use the analogy of the imperfect record being exchanged for Jesus' perfect record. You will notice, too, the emphasis this presentation makes on how we can be forgiven, addressing the all too prevalent belief that behaviours such as going to church, trying to be good, believing that God exists, being christened, baptised or confirmed make us right with God. There's no doubt these are all positive things, but do they give us forgiveness? Do they reconcile us to God? Do they assure our place in eternity with Him? No. When we use the illustration of swapping Jesus' perfect record for our own we can clearly impress on the non-Christian *why* we must be saved and the truth about Jesus as our Saviour.

Jesus as Saviour is the fundamental heart of the Gospel and I encourage every Christian to carry in their heart some of our most beloved pieces of scripture that enforce and celebrate this fact:

> *But God demonstrates his own love for us in this: While we were still sinners, Christ died for us.* (Rom. 5:8)

> *So if the Son sets you free, you will be free indeed.* (John 8:36)

> *For God so loved the world that he gave his one and only Son, that whoever believes in him shall not perish but have eternal life.* (John 3:16)

As we know, however, there is more to the Christian life than simply believing and accepting Jesus' gift of grace. Again, I believe, this is something often missing in our communications of the Gospel message. And again I can see the hand of the deceiver at work here, wheedling away, moving Christians just a small degree off the truth, so that if a non-Christian should respond to their 'gospel' they later find it lacking in truth and substance and turn away. We are very quick to enthuse to a non-Christian that all they have to do is say 'yes' to Jesus, that Jesus will be the answer to all their problems, but is this really fair? Is it the truth? Many people will openly admit that their life is lacking in some way, that they are perhaps unfulfilled or suffering with addiction or with a problem that controls and manipulates their life. Such people are often willing to 'try' something that might be offered as a 'cure'. But we are desperately at fault if we lull them into the belief that all will be well once they have said a prayer of commitment. As Laurence Singlehurst in his insightful book *Sowing, Reaping, Keeping: People Sensitive Evangelism* writes:

> Conversion to Christianity is not some first aid plaster, not some magical cure, rather it requires understanding, not only of the wonderful benefits of forgiveness and the healing but also of the need for repentance and surrender of the giving up of our own self-centredness.[10]

We have already discussed this issue back in Chapter 6, but I perceive there is so much confusion about repentance and accepting Jesus not only as Saviour, but also as Lord. It's a huge mistake to teach – or imply – that nothing less than genuine heart-wrenching, gut-level repentance is an absolute prerequisite to conversion. John Stott writes:

> The Gospel offer is not unconditional. It is clear that every sinner cannot be forgiven if they persist in clinging to their sins. If they desire God to turn from their sins in remission they must themselves turn from them in repentance. We are charged therefore to proclaim the condition as well as the promise of forgiveness. Remission is the Gospel offer, repentance is the Gospel demand.[11]

I must admit, this has never been too much of a stumbling block for me. When I became a Christian it was not the awe and wonder of an eternity in a fine mansion in Heaven that drew me to Christ. Nor was it even the idea that my sins could be forgiven. Of course these are overwhelmingly great things, but the realisation that really caused me to prostrate myself at the feet of Jesus was that *He died for me.* Now I know I'm talking from a very personal testimony here and different aspects of the Gospel are more powerful to different people, but all these years later, it is this recognition that Jesus died for me that keeps me on my knees before Him. His crucifixion seems so wrong. His body should never have been touched. He was a perfect and innocent man – God with skin on – who should never have gone through one shred of torture and torment. Yet He did it. This is what happened. It was unbelievably horrific and it was because of, and for, *me.* What amazing love, what amazing grace! If I serve the Lord Jesus, then, it's not because of what is now available to me. Nor is it because it's the least I can do to say thank you. Rather it is because He made me, He knows me, He deserves *everything* of me.

William Barclay cautions against the trend to 'lure people to the altar with the promise of blessing as we hide the cost of becoming a Christian'.[12] Even when Jesus walked the earth there was that kind of temptation. Jesus could have given the people what they wanted. He could have bribed them with material things, with almighty shows of power and strength, but what did He give them? Humiliation, torture, degradation, injustice, incomprehensible suffering: the cross.

So when I present the Gospel message I always make a point of emphasising the need to turn and surrender to Jesus. I refer to the fact that God made us in the womb and that He made the entire universe that surrounds us. I then ask the question, 'Don't you think He deserves to be the central person in your life?' To make Jesus Lord is to put Him at the centre of all our decisions. Once we have turned to him in this way we call on Jesus to determine how we use our time, our money, who we have as friends, what we watch on television, who and how we love. Every thought, attitude and action is now filtered through Jesus and our learning and understanding is drawn from our instruction manual, the Bible.

Every thought, attitude and action is now filtered through Jesus and our learning and understanding is drawn from our instruction manual, the Bible.

This crucial reality of acceptance of *Jesus as Lord* must never be neglected in our explanations of the Gospel message to others. Having said that, I believe that it is only as we begin our walk with Jesus that we begin to realise what this really means. For me it began with the hard-hitting episode with Alcaponey in the prison. In truly putting my trust in Jesus I had to be willing in those pressurised moments, with a blade at my throat, to literally offer up my life. For others, surrender to Jesus is realised in a much more gentle process as we progress through our days with Him at the helm. The point I'm making here is that this part of the Gospel message is perhaps the one that matters most in that it requires an *ongoing decision.* It requires a continual nurturing of an inner relationship with God in Jesus Christ.

Let's look again at the gospel reports of Nicodemus. Here was a very religious man. He knew the Scriptures, kept the law and was dedicated to the 'church' in a big way. As a Pharisee he was a spiritual descendant of the Hasidean movement – the group whose name came from the Old Testament concept of the Hasidim, which means 'the faithful' or 'the saints'. You couldn't get a much more 'righteous' and respected man than Nicodemus. God was on his mind a lot. But the writer of John's gospel uses the story of Nicodemus to tell us that a right standing with God does not come through correct beliefs. Nicodemus even believed in Jesus, in that he believed He was sent from God: *'We know you are a teacher who has come from God. For no-one could perform the miraculous signs you are doing if God were not with him'* (John 3:2).

But in spite of Nicodemus' belief in God, his belief in Jesus, and the Scriptures, Jesus recognised what was wrong inside Nicodemus. Jesus seemed to bluntly change the subject on Nicodemus when He said, *'I tell you the truth, no-one can see the kingdom of God unless he is born again'* (John 3:3). At this the Pharisee must have been quite taken aback. Was Jesus implying that he, a respected, God-fearing servant of the Temple, might not see the Kingdom of God? What more could be required of him? Didn't Jesus recognise his life of faithfulness?

Jesus went on to speak about what it means to be 'born again' and about the difference between physical and spiritual re-birth. There is so much to explore in this wonderful exchange, but the point I want to draw out from the Nicodemus experience is that a right standing with God comes only through an ongoing

God is not looking for your faith or your obedience as much as your heart. He wants to have this relationship with you, and if you have missed having this relationship you have missed everything.

relationship with Him. It does not come through having the right beliefs or the right behaviour. It is not the result of scholarly or moral commitment. A right standing with God comes only when we realise that we don't know it all and are willing to see our great need for Him. When Jesus said, 'You must be born again,' He was saying that the Christian life is not a set of beliefs or a moral code; it is an experience. That experience consists of confessing my sin and need of God, feeling God cleansing and filling me with His love and His Spirit. God is not looking for your faith or your obedience as much as your heart. He wants to have this relationship with you, and if you have missed having this relationship you have missed everything.

John 3:16 and 18 talk of 'belief': *'Whoever believes in him shall not perish but have eternal life'*; *'Whoever believes in him is not condemned, but whoever does not believe stands condemned already because he has not believed in the name of God's one and only Son.'* When we read these verses as they are set, in the light of the Nicodemus conversation, we understand that the kind of belief that Jesus was after was not a belief that accepts a set of facts, but the kind of belief that places your whole trust in Christ. That means you believe he is *'the way and the truth and the life'* (John 14:6), your whole life is centred in that reality, your complete trust is in Christ and you live in an ongoing relationship with Him.

This is the message we must preach, but to do that it is the message we must understand, accept and embrace with our whole heart. Then, urgency and compassion for the lost will come.

- Consider doing a Bible study on some of the 'heroes' of the Bible. Make note of their weaknesses and the way God dealt with them and worked with them to reveal His glory.

> *'When he comes, he will convict the world of guilt in regard to sin and righteousness and judgment: in regard to sin, because men do not believe in me; in regard to righteousness, because I am going to the Father, where you can see me no longer.'* (John 16:8–10)

- What effect does this particular scripture have on you when you consider your own efforts in evangelism?

21

The Fifth Column

Ghengis Khan (1167–1227), established the Mongol nation, conquered most of the known world and earned a reputation as one of the great military leaders of all time. Although he is often thought of as a 'barbarian' leader of the Mongol 'hordes', history shows us that behind the renowned terror tactics and barbaric slaughter he achieved his victories through brilliant organisation and stealth strategy. The Great Wall of China was one of his most notorious challenges. Twenty-five feet high, thirty feet wide and 1,500 miles long, it was considered impenetrable. Kahn employed his most powerful weapon. Whilst his military forces bombarded the wall, his army of spies, scouts and reconnaissance infiltrated the Chinese ranks and Kahn was able to enter in through the 'front door'. When he took power it was not because of weakness in the wall, but because of weakness on the inside. Poor government, poverty and rebellion opened the way for Kahn's stealth warriors to infiltrate and attack using the device of the fifth column.

Kahn's tactics have influenced military strategies throughout history. A uniformed army marches in four columns, but the unrecognised 'fifth column' is made up of civilian-clothed sympathisers who spread defeatism amongst the enemy. Satan tried to employ the same strategy with Jesus, using one of His own to undermine the work of the Master. Working through Judas, the devil tried to destroy the purposes of God. Jesus was only able to defeat him by keeping completely within the will of the Father. We dare not ignore this lesson. If this book does nothing else, I hope it highlights the fact that we have drifted out of the will of Jesus with respect to the Great Commission. We have succumbed to the devil's fifth column. Both Jesus and the apostle Paul experienced the devil's hindering influence. One of my main goals in my teaching on evangelism is to remind Christians that we, too, are targets.

Targets we may be, but with the devil's devices exposed, and the Godly provision of heavenly armour (Eph. 6), we are ready to start a new day in personal and corporate evangelism. Dr James Kennedy, founder of Evangelism Explosion, made the point that if an outstanding international evangelist were to lead 1,000 people a night to the Lord it would take 16,348 years to reach the whole world of 6 billion people. However, if we were proclaiming the Gospel the 'Jesus' way and were able to lead even just one person a year to the Lord and could train that person to do the same – win one person each year, and so on – it would take just 33 years to win the entire planet for Jesus.[1] It is entirely feasible to evangelise the earth in a very short space of time. I find this completely staggering and totally challenging. Why hasn't this happened yet? Is it because our efforts in evangelism have been hindered by the devil's devices, by people working with a false view of what evangelism is and what it should be? It appears, more than ever, that the biblical definition of evangelism is the key.

So how do we move forward? The answer is to make a new wineskin.

> *No-one sews a patch of unshrunk cloth on an old garment, for the patch will pull away from the garment, making the tear worse. Neither do men pour new wine into old wineskins. If they do, the skins will burst, the wine will run out and the wineskins*

> *will be ruined. No, they pour new wine into new wineskins, and both are preserved.* (Matt. 9:16–17)

First of all we need to clear the ground. We need to treat the diseased soil with a strong solution of 'Round-Up' to decimate the weeds. That means teaching fellow Christians about the devices of the devil. As church leaders we must clear away the theological weeds and misunderstandings about evangelism from the minds of our church members. This means teaching everyone the difference between the 'wide' and the 'general' use of *the Gospel* and its sharply defined New Testament use. It means teaching all Christians the difference between the 'words', 'works' and 'effects' of the Gospel. It means carefully defining key words like 'evangelism', 'evangelist' and 'evangel'.

It is also critically important that all Christians know the content of the words of the Gospel and grow confident in communicating them effectively and graciously. This requires training, and it is up to the Church at grass-roots level to provide this training. The goal should be that everyone in a church is able to view his or her actions through the lens of the six-step model of drawing a non-Christian to Christ:

1. Ploughing
2. Sowing
3. Watering
4. Growing
5. Harvesting
6. Threshing

When everyone in a congregation views themselves and others through this model it will help them to clearly see where everything fits and how all can work together for the great goal of seeking and saving the lost for the glory of God.

Remember the story I shared in the opening of this book about our group activity painting Van Gogh's *The Sower*? Each team of people was set the task to recreate just one disparate square of canvas. We didn't know where we were heading when we began and, for most of us, our plan appeared to require little more than abstract splashes of colour and irregular shape. Only when all the individual canvases were complete and placed together in order by our 'master artist' did the big picture emerge. This activity was a superb illustration in faithfulness, teamwork and the importance of following a given plan even when it doesn't seem to make sense. In many ways it was a perfect model of the Christian life and one that can easily be applied to our efforts in evangelism. The extension of the image, of course, is that God has revealed the bigger picture to us already. It may be dimly lit and hard to fathom, but it is there as a promise. As a church, then, it is surely our task to ensure that all pieces of the canvas are being covered. A church may be renowned for great worship, or for its services to the community, or for its dedication to Bible teaching, or its emphasis on prayer, but if it fails to train and mobilise its people in evangelism then it is critically lacking. It is disobeying the Master Artist, failing to follow His blueprint. It will always be missing that one vital canvas and will never make up the whole glorious picture that it should be.

When we exhort others to evangelise, we will only be effective if they have clear and full understanding of what that means.

When we understand our gifts and recognise the mandate of biblically defined evangelism in our church life and its critical importance in our personal life, then we begin to operate in the big picture. Only when we are awakened to the devil's devices can we begin to erase the black ink of deception that he tries to introduce to our efforts. When we exhort others to evangelise, we will only be effective if they have clear and full understanding of what that means. Remember our 'one degree off the truth' theory that finds many well-meaning people honestly believing they are engaged in evangelism, only to find the key thing that defines evangelism – the proclamation of the Gospel – is nowhere to be found?

As we have begun to see, the devil's strategies are so clever and so subtle that they operate at a sub-conscious level. This is what makes them so very effective and so deadly. The only way to bring them from the sub-conscious to the conscious level is to teach about them, to expose them as we are commanded to do.

> *Have nothing to do with the fruitless deeds of darkness, but rather expose them.* (Eph. 5:11)

> *Do your best to present yourself to God as one approved, a workman who does not need to be ashamed and who correctly handles the word of truth.* (2 Tim. 2:15)

> *Rather, we have renounced secret and shameful ways; we do not use deception, nor do we distort the word of God.* (2 Cor. 4:2)

The second way to defeat these devices of the devil is to pray into them. '*We demolish arguments and every pretension that sets itself up against the knowledge of God, and we take captive every thought to make it obedient to Christ*' (2 Cor. 10:5). This means petitioning God in prayer that our pastors and leaders will teach about the devil's strategies and the truth concerning the collapse of the Great Commission. We should pray that our media will communicate these matters, that there will be books written, that teaching conferences and camps will highlight the issue to Christians. We should pray that proclamation of the

Gospel for believers returns as top priority in all churches, that denominational leaders will take decisive action and unite as they lead with authority on these issues. We should pray that this subject matter will be the key agenda in our Bible colleges and seminaries and cry out to our Lord in expectation that every Christian, everywhere will be mobilised to regularly go into the world and proclaim the Gospel.

The council of God is unmistakably clear. Blessing, spiritual prosperity and multiplication are all inextricably connected to walking in the Truth and to obedience.

> *Walk in all the way that the LORD your God has commanded you, so that you may live and prosper and prolong your days in the land that you will possess.* (Deut. 5:33)

If we think and act biblically with respect to evangelism, we will multiply. To make our new wineskin we must deal with the root of the problem. The fruit is that most Christians don't regularly engage themselves in the spreading of the Gospel. The root is the devil and his devices.

If we think and act biblically with respect to evangelism, we will multiply.

When we have made our new wineskin we must fill it up with fresh wine. We must make ongoing evangelism training a priority and equip ourselves with a range of tools and resources to help us effectively communicate a clear Gospel message. In my experience we make two great mistakes with evangelism. First, we overestimate how much non-Christians know. Secondly, we underestimate how much they want to know. Remember the Gospel is a specific message. We can vary how we portray that message, but there are clear facts that must be communicated. We can consider the *words* of the Gospel like a twenty-five-piece jigsaw puzzle. The content must be spoken in sequence in order for it to make complete sense. Consider some of the things a non-Christian might hear when we try to communicate the message:

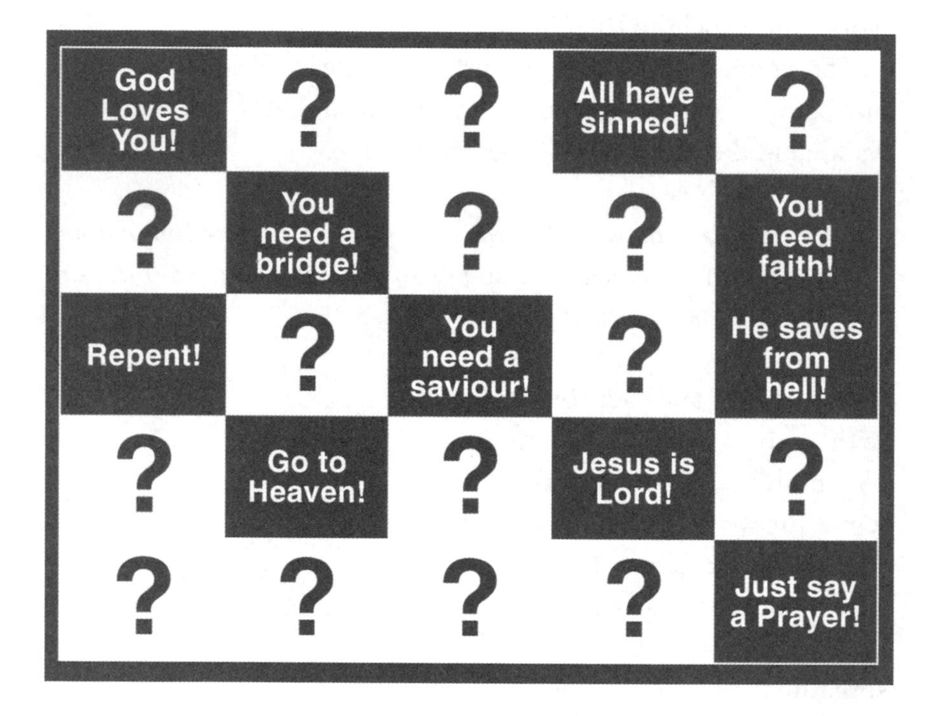

These are just ten pieces of the puzzle, out of our twenty-five pieces of information, our non-Christian has heard. They are 'Gospel bites'. They probably make perfect sense to us. We can fill in the gaps and put them in sequence. But for millions of non-Christians this message is completely confusing. It is like a shot-gun approach to evangelism. We fire off these ever-so-churchy phrases but they mean nothing of any constructive use to anyone hearing.

Our message makes no sense whatsoever! Content, clarity, sequence and simplicity are critical issues in our Gospel presentations.

As long as the Bible is the Bible, evangelism will always be the 'in' thing with God.

Only when we can master this can we evangelise effectively. It's imperative, then, that we are equipped with good resources to help us communicate properly. We can write and make our own tracts and technology-based presentations, but there are also many organisations that provide quality material for us to use.

With fresh wine in our new wineskin our next challenge is to stay focused. We must keep evangelism as the bullseye of church life. Over and over again we must define evangelism, preach the Gospel, teach our congregations to present the Gospel message and never shy away from exposing the devil's lies that can so easily infiltrate our activity. So often our church programmes and visions become sidetracked as new ideas come along. There will always be a temptation to ditch evangelism in favour of 'the latest thing'. But the Bible clearly tells us that evangelism *is* the main thing and we must keep it that way. As long as the Bible is the Bible, evangelism will always be the 'in' thing with God. He doesn't have 'seasons' with evangelism or 'years' of evangelism. His heart for the lost of the world is constant, relentless, tireless and passionate. It led Him to the cross. Little frustrates me more than churches who plan activities: 'Next year we will be focusing on prayer and in two

Evangelism begins right here, right now with every one of us who claims to be a follower of Jesus Christ.

years' time we will be focusing on evangelism.' What rubbish! Evangelism begins right here, right now with every one of us who claims to be a follower of Jesus Christ. It is vital that as a Church we focus on evangelism *now* and don't take our eyes off the ball until the day when the Lord returns.

Part of our commitment to staying focused is to invest in the 'Ephesians 4:11–12' evangelists. Those who are especially called and gifted need support from the wider church. They need regular ongoing training, opportunity and profile in the church so that they motivate and equip the wider Body for evangelism.

Furthermore, we should consider how we might set up systems that allow believers to be accountable to one another for the spread and proclamation of the Gospel: *'As iron sharpens iron, so one man sharpens another'* (Prov. 27:17). Being held accountable means that we can honestly assess whether or not evangelism is taking place. If we don't have any accountability in this area of our Christian lives, how will we ever know if anyone is proclaiming or spreading the Gospel? Our unaccountability is one of the main reasons the devil's devices have been able to propagate unchecked and unnoticed for so very long. Very few churches in the world have any accountability whatsoever with respect to evangelism. Remember an idea I put forward back in Chapter 9 for a 'Great Commission Offering'? If there was such a thing in our church every Sunday it would soon challenge every member of the congregation to take part in some way.

Our unaccountability is one of the main reasons the devil's devices have been able to propagate unchecked and unnoticed for so very long.

Accountability helps us do the will of the Lord. It is our way of saying we want to take the Great Commission seriously and we want to encourage others to do the same. If we monitored evangelism as seriously as we monitor church income, we would evangelise the earth in no time. The topic of tithing only takes up one per cent of the teaching of the New Testament. In contrast, the subject of the Great Commission is ten times more prominent, yet we dedicate almost no time and effort to making sure it is happening! Where is its prominence in our Sunday services? If we make ourselves accountable in this area we will set goals for spreading and proclaiming the Gospel and establish systems in our churches that accurately monitor our progress.

New life in evangelism for your church will come through you.

If you have any position of leadership in your church, model yourself as an evangelist. New life in evangelism for your church will come through *you*. Paul, an evangelist, encouraged Timothy, a pastor, to *'do the work of an evangelist'* (2 Tim. 4:5). Let your congregation see you handing out tracts and proclaiming the Gospel. Speak about your experiences. Write about them. Do bulletins to your congregation. Ask specifically for prayer in this matter. No matter what your position in the church, you can encourage others by incorporating evangelism into your everyday activity and by talking about it.

This chapter has been a call to action, a call to war. It requires the people of God to get up and begin the fight. It requires us to change our ways. It asks leaders to consider the priority of evangelism in their teaching and motivation. It asks every member of the church to make themselves accountable to the Great Commission and to take responsibility in personal evangelism. It requires change at both personal and corporate church level. Change can be hard and painful. It will be met with resistance, especially if this teaching only remains in small pockets of the congregation. But, as we have hopefully clearly demonstrated, this is biblical truth and we are men and women called and commissioned by God Himself. If we think and act biblically with respect to evangelism we will multiply. History bears witness to this truth. This is your moment in history. Pray for the courage to embrace this new way. Get on board with evangelism, not just for a few days of a campaign or a summer camp or a 'year of evangelism', but for the rest of your life. What will your legacy be?

- What will your legacy be?
- Now you've had time to reflect on some of the solutions to defeat Satan and fire up the Great Commission, how are you personally inspired and challenged? What are you deciding to do about it?
- Consider writing some action points for yourself that you can check back on, or share these ideas and make a commitment to a church leader or Christian friend who can help hold you accountable to them.

22

The Story of Frank Jenner

In Crystal Palace, London, a Baptist church service was drawing to a close. As the pastor gathered his notes and prepared to offer a final blessing, a man at the back of the church caught his eye. 'Excuse me,' offered the man, raising his hand, 'I wonder if you might allow me to share a brief testimony with you?' This was quite unusual. This pastor looked at his watch. 'OK, you have three minutes,' he said a little tentatively. The man stood up, smiling gratefully. 'I have just moved here from another part of London,' he began, 'but before that I was staying in Sydney, Australia. One day I was walking down George Street, the bustling main road that runs the length of the city from the Harbour Bridge out to the suburbs. Suddenly an elderly gentleman stepped out from a shop doorway, put a pamphlet in my hand and said, "Excuse me, sir, are you saved? If you die tonight are you going to Heaven?" I was astounded by these words,' he said. 'No-one had ever asked me that. I thanked him and hurried on but all the way home to London this incident puzzled me. As soon as I could, I got in touch with a friend who I knew was a Christian. Thank God he led me to Christ and here I am today,' the man finished, beaming all over his face.

The pastor and the congregation applauded and welcomed him into their fellowship.

A week later the pastor flew to Adelaide, Australia. He was taking part in a three-day teaching series at an Adelaide church when a woman came up to him for some counselling. He wanted to establish where she stood with Christ and asked her about her conversion. 'I used to live in Sydney,' she offered, 'and just a couple of months back I was doing some last minute shopping down George Street. A strange little man stepped out of a shop doorway and offered me a pamphlet. "Excuse me, madam," he said courteously, "are you saved? If you die tonight are you going to Heaven?" I was disturbed by those words,' she said. 'When I got home to Adelaide I knew this Baptist church was on the next block from me. I sought out the pastor and he led me to Christ. So I am telling you that I am a Christian, it's just that I am struggling with my faith.'

The London pastor was now quite puzzled. Twice in two weeks he had heard the same testimony. He then flew to preach in Mount Pleasant Church in Perth. When his teaching series was over the senior elder of that church took him out for a meal and he asked the elder how he was saved. 'I grew up in this church from the age of fifteen. I never made a commitment to Jesus, just hopped on the bandwagon like everyone else. Because of my business ability I grew up to a place of influence,' he said. 'I was on a business trip to Sydney just three years ago. An obnoxious, spiteful little man stepped out of a shop doorway, offered me a religious pamphlet – cheap junk – and accosted me with a question, "Excuse me, sir, are you saved? If you die tonight are you going to Heaven?" I tried to tell him I was a Baptist elder. He wouldn't listen to me. I was seething with anger all the way home from Sydney to Perth. I told my pastor, thinking that he would sympathize, but he agreed. He had been disturbed for years knowing that I didn't have a relationship with Jesus, and he was right. My pastor led me to Jesus just three years ago.'

The London preacher flew home and was soon speaking at the Keswick Convention in the Lake District and he threw in these three testimonies. At the close of this teaching series, four elderly pastors came up and explained that they, too, had been saved between twenty-five and thirty years earlier through that same man on George Street, offering them a pamphlet and asking that same question. The following week he flew to a similar convention in the Caribbean to missionaries. He shared the same testimonies. At the close of his teaching three missionaries came forward and said that they had also been saved between fifteen and twenty-five years earlier by that same man's testimony and the same question on George Street in Sydney. Next the pastor stopped in Atlanta, Georgia, USA to speak at a Naval chaplain's convention. Here, for three days, he spoke to over a thousand Naval chaplains. Afterwards the Chaplain General took him out for a meal and he asked the chaplain how he became a Christian. 'It was miraculous. I was a rating on a Naval battleship and I lived a reprobate life. We were doing exercises in the South Pacific and we docked at Sydney harbour for replenishments. We hit Kings Cross with a vengeance. I was blind drunk, got on the wrong bus and got off in George Street. As I clamoured off the bus, I thought I was seeing a ghost as this man jumped out in front of me, pushed a pamphlet in my hand and said, "Sailor, are you saved? If you died in the next twenty-four hours where would you be in eternity: Heaven or Hell?" The fear of God hit me immediately. I was shocked sober, ran back to the ship and sought out the chaplain. He led me to Christ. I soon began to prepare for the ministry under his guidance. I am now in charge of a thousand chaplains who are bent on soul-winning today.'

Six months later that London pastor flew to a conference for five thousand Indian missionaries in a remote part of North East India. At the end the head missionary took him to his humble little home for a simple meal. The pastor asked how he, as a Hindu, had come to Christ. 'I grew up in a very privileged position,' he said. 'I worked for the Indian Diplomatic Mission and I travelled the world. I am so glad for the forgiveness of Christ and

His blood covering my sin. I would be very embarrassed if people found out what I got into. One period of diplomatic service took me to Sydney. I was doing some last minute shopping, laden with toys and clothes for my children. I was walking down George Street when a courteous gentleman stepped out in front of me and offered me a pamphlet. He said, "Excuse me, sir, but can I ask you, if you died in the next twenty-four hours where would you be in eternity: Heaven or Hell?" I took the pamphlet, thanked him and hurried away, but his question was disturbing me. I got back to my town and sought out our Hindu priest. He couldn't help me, but he advised me that to satisfy my curious mind I should go and talk to the missionary in the Christian mission home at the end of road. That was fatal advice because that day the missionary led me to Christ. I quit Hinduism immediately and began to prepare for Christian ministry. I left the Diplomatic Service and here I am today, by God's grace, in charge of all these missionaries who have together led more than one hundred thousand people to Christ.'

Eight months later that London pastor was preaching in Sydney. He asked the local Baptist minister if he knew of a man who handed out tracts on George Street. He replied, 'Yes I do. His name is Frank Jenner, although I don't think he does it any more because he is quite elderly.' Two nights later they went to seek out Mr Jenner in his little apartment. They knocked on the door and a white-haired man greeted them. He sat them down and made them tea as the London preacher told him of all these accounts from the previous three years. Tears began running down his cheeks. He told them his story. 'I was a rating on an Australian warship. I was living a reprobate life. In a crisis I really hit the wall. One of my colleagues, to whom I gave hell, was there to help me. He led me to Jesus and the change in my life was like night to day in twenty-four hours. I was so grateful to God. I promised God that I would share Jesus in a simple witness with at least ten people a day. As God gave me strength I did just that. Sometimes I was ill and couldn't do it, but I made up for the days I missed at other times. I wasn't paranoid about it,' he smiled, 'I have done this for over forty years. In my retirement years, the best place was on George Street where I saw hundreds of people a day. I got lots of rejections, but a lot of people courteously took the tract. In forty years of doing this, I have never heard of one single person coming to Jesus until today.'

Someone did a rough calculation and worked out that Frank Jenner had led over 146,100 people to Christ. During the Second World War, Sydney was the port of call for thousands of service men and women from different parts of the world. Jenner picked George Street as his regular beat, meeting these people as they came off battleships, all very aware of their own mortality and the possibility that their next mission might be their last. His heart was for the souls of those sailors. On Sundays he would stand on Gowlbourn Street and work the parks of the city offering his pamphlets to families and people from all walks of life. If anyone showed interest in his message he would guide them to a local church where they could learn more of the precious Gospel that had so transformed him.

What a testimony – to show such gratitude and love for Jesus to do that for forty years without hearing of any result! It seemed that through the London pastor God was able to show Mr Jenner just the tip of the iceberg. How many more people had come to Christ because of this one man's testimony and commitment? Mr Jenner died two weeks later. Can you imagine the reward he went home to in Heaven?

Frank Jenner shared his faith not for results, not out of duty, but out of sheer gratitude for his Salvation. Those who knew Jenner testify to his generous, warm nature. It is said that he quickly inspired trust in others and that his life was marked by persistence in prayer. What we know now is that he was a man with an overflowing heart, a man who, in gratitude to God, sought to pay back something of the debt of love he recognised that he owed.

How grateful am I? How grateful are you?

Mr Jenner was a remarkable man and it's only right that his story be told. But he was qualified by nothing more than the call that we too share. He was anyone and everyone – just one human being grateful for his Salvation and lovingly obedient to his Master, even though he saw nothing for his efforts. Is that you? I pray that through this book your eyes and heart might have been opened to many new things. It began with a story of a retreat picture-painting experience. At the time I never imagined that a simple team-building exercise might be the springboard for this book, but I don't think it's any coincidence that our host happened to have chosen Van Gogh's *The Sower* for us to copy. The picture and its creation so appropriately underpins the teaching of this book and of Release (the international evangelism training conference that I teach in the hope of 'releasing the handbrake on the Great Commission'): everyone doing their little bit, despite their doubts, until a joyful unveiling of the complete picture: a simple man sowing seed in hope of a good harvest.

Since that time I have discovered an artistic theme is also used for an analogy of the Gospel message called *The Good Artist*, produced by CWR. This is a particularly good illustration to use with children. I cannot emphasise enough how important it is to be confident in knowing the 'words' of the Gospel. It's my hope that illustrations such as this, or the outline in Chapter 7 of this book, or one of the other Gospel presentations at the end, will be a great resource for you to confidently spread the Good News about Jesus Christ.

If this book does anything, I pray that it encourages you to pick up the paintbrushes and start making your mark on this glorious creation. Follow the Master Artist's blueprint and you won't go far wrong. Be bold, be confident, be colourful and paint with joy and expectancy, not caring what others think but seeking only to please He who is the Author and Finisher of all things. When the pieces come together and the picture is complete, I pray that you'll recognise the face of the sower as your own and know that the fruits of your labour are harvested and firmly rooted in our Saviour Jesus Christ.

Afterword

He who saves the life of one man . . .

Schindler's List is one of the most powerful movies of all time.[1] It tells the compelling story of the German businessman Oskar Schindler who comes to Nazi-occupied Poland looking for economic prosperity and leaves as a saviour of more than 1,100 Jews.

A charming and sly entrepreneur, Schindler bribes and befriends the Nazi authorities to gain control of a factory in Krakow, which he staffs with Jewish slave labourers. Very soon he is making a fortune. Among the Jews who work for him is Itzhak Stern, the plant manager who, in his benevolence, sees to it that Schindler's workforce includes the most vulnerable and cherished members of Krakow's Jewish community.

Schindler is just like many men. He has a love for good wine and beautiful women, and pursues happiness through the success of his business. Whilst his empire is being built, however, the film portrays the murderous fate of millions of innocent Jews – a time now labelled as one of the darkest periods of human history.

As Schindler comes to realisation of this fact he begins to change. To the joy of Itzhak Stern and his workforce, the self-centred money-hungry entrepreneur gives up his worldly goals and turns his efforts to save the lives of many Jews.

The story reaches a dramatic crescendo with Schindler preparing to flee. As a Nazi Party member and a self-described 'profiteer of slave labour', he must escape the advancing Soviet Army. Although SS guards have been ordered to 'liquidate' the Jews in Brinnlitz, Schindler persuades them to return to their families as men, not murderers. In the aftermath, he packs his car in the night, and bids farewell to his workers. They give him a letter signed by every worker in case he is captured explaining that he is not a criminal to them. He is also presented with a ring secretly made from a worker's gold dental bridge and engraved with the Talmudic quotation, *'He who saves the life of one man, saves the world entire.'* At this point Schindler breaks down in deep shame and tears.

'I could have got more . . . I could have got more,' he says clinging to Stern. 'Why did we keep the car? We could have got more people. We could have got ten more people. Look at this pen, it's gold, it could have given me two more people, even one more person.' Schindler realises that he threw away so much money. Stern tells him in those solemn moments, 'There will be generations because of what you did. You did so much.'

The film ends by showing a procession of now-elderly Jews who worked in Schindler's factory, each of whom reverently sets a stone on his grave. The actors walk hand-in-hand with the people they portrayed, and also place a stone on Schindler's grave. The audience learns that at the time of the film's release, there are fewer than 4,000 Jews left alive in Poland, while there are more than 6,000 descendants of the Schindler Jews. Today there are more than 7,500 descendants of his Jews living in the United States, Europe and Israel.

Oskar Schindler died in Hildesheim in Germany, 9 October 1974. He wanted to be buried in Jerusalem. As he said: 'My children are here . . .' Schindler died penniless, but he earned the everlasting gratitude of his Jews. He was mourned on four continents and generations will remember him for what he did.

What will our legacy be? How do we use our time, our money? Do we measure success by the profitability of our business, our wage packet, the state-of-the-art home cinema system, the holiday, the latest computer gadget, the new car, the clothes, the company we keep . . . How might our world change if Christians begin to measure every resource at our fingertips in terms of souls? Some say 'time is money', but no, time is souls. How about making that next extravagant gift a gift for the Lord's work? A new computer game, or one hundred Gospel tracts delivered to a spiritually isolated place somewhere in the world? A new handbag, or a dozen Bibles to the Middle East? A trip to the cinema, or an evening handing out tracts outside? If our hearts could only be drawn to the value of the eternal, this globe could be reached and we will not be disappointed. We will become rich in the things of Christ. And treasure in Heaven can never be taken away.

> *Do not store up for yourselves treasures on earth, where moth and rust destroy, and where thieves break in and steal. But store up for yourselves treasures in Heaven, where moth and rust do not destroy, and where thieves do not break in and steal. For where your treasure is, there your heart will be also.* (Matt. 6:19–21)

This is your time.

Who Else Believes This?

In my studies regarding Jesus' mandate and priority for the Church, I have discovered a broad range of scholars and theologians, clergy and lay people who share common belief and resolve. Here are just a few quotes to assure and inspire:

Dr John Stott

The Church's mission of sacrificial service includes both evangelistic and social action, so that normally the Church does not have to choose between the two. But if the choice has to be made, then evangelism is primary. Our first duty is to communicate this Gospel.

(John Stott, Making Christ Known, *Historic Mission Documents from the Lausanne Movement, 1974–1989, Paternoster Press, 1996)*

Millard Erickson

The one topic emphasised in both accounts of Jesus' last words to His disciples is evangelism. In Matthew 28:19 He instructs them, 'Go therefore and make disciples of all nations . . . *'In Acts 1:8 He says, 'But you shall receive power when the Holy Spirit has come upon you; and you shall be my witnesses in Jerusalem and in all Judea and Samaria and to the ends of the earth'* . . . this was the final point Jesus made to His disciples. It appears that He regarded evangelism as the very reason for their being.

(Millard J. Erickson, Christian Theology, *Revell, a division of Baker Publishing Group, 1998)*

Dr Derek Prince

The supreme purpose of every true Christian Church, the chief duty of every Christian minister, the main responsibility of every Christian layman is to present to all who may be reached in the clearest and most forceful way, the basic facts of the Gospel of Christ, and to urge all who hear to make the definite personal response to these facts which God requires. To this, the supreme task, every other duty and activity of the Church, must be secondary and subsidiary.

(Derek Prince, Foundation series, Volume 1, *Sovereign World Books, 1986)*

Dr William Lane

The proclamation of the Gospel to all men is an absolute priority.

(William L. Lane, The Gospel of Mark, *Eerdmans, 1995)*

Dr Michael Green

Dr Michael Green called proclaiming the Gospel 'The Church's first priority.'

(Michael Green, Evangelism in the Early Church, *Highland Books, 1970)*

Dr Peter Wagner

I would love to see membership declines in the mainline denominations bottom out and begin to soar upward. But I am afraid that they will not unless and until the evangelist mandate is restored to its biblical position as the top priority.

(Peter Wagner, Leading Your Church To Growth, *Regal Books, 1984)*

Oswald J. Smith

Commenting on Mark 13:10, And the Gospel must first be preached in all the nations. Why did Jesus use the word 'first'? He stated that the Gospel must first be proclaimed among the nations. He wanted to say that before we did anything else, we were to evangelise the world.

(Oswald J. Smith, The Passion for Souls, *Marshall, Morgan and Scott, 1978)*

Dr Lewis Drummond

There is no excuse for anyone for not giving evangelism first place in individual covenant church life.

(Lewis A. Drummond, Reaching Generation Next, *Baker, 2002)*

1988 Anglican Conference in Lambeth

Resolution 43 referred to evangelism as . . . the primary task given to the Church.

(*Cited in:* J.John. Natural Evangelism: How to share the good news with friends with no artificial ingredients, *Lynx Press, 1996)*

Dr Morna D. Hooker

Commenting on Mark 13:10 ('*The Gospel must first be preached in all the nations*') . . . This saying (of Jesus) becomes a reminder to the disciples that their primary task is that of evangelising.

(*Morna D. Hooker,* The Gospel According to Mark, *Hendrickson, 2009)*

Charles Spurgeon

Paul's great object was not merely to instruct and to improve, but to save. To compass their salvation, he gave himself up with untiring zeal to telling abroad the Gospel, to warning and beseeching men to be reconciled to God . . . He became a servant to all men, toiling for his race, feeling a woe within him if he preached not the Gospel . . . the Gospel was the one all important business with him.

(*C.H. Spurgeon,* Morning and Evening Devotionals, *December 7, Evening Reading)*

Ray Comfort

Right from the beginning of His ministry, Jesus made it clear that His supreme mandate was to reach lost humanity with the Gospel.

(Ray Comfort and Kirk Cameron, The Way of the Master, *Bridge-Logos Publishing, 2006)*

The Sower by Vincent Van Gogh

Gospel Presentations

Chapter 7 gives a clear presentation of the Gospel that I have found works very well both in group and in personal settings. It can be viewed as a high definition presentation at www.avantiministries.com/think.php. A high quality multimedia presentation is available at the back of the book.

There are many more excellent ways of explaining the basics of the Gospel message. Here are just a few ideas:

The Good Artist

In the beginning there was a blank page.
It belonged to the Good Artist who was well known for making perfect pictures.
He never made mistakes.
One day the Artist began to draw on the page.
He drew the sun and sky.
He drew the land and the sea.
He drew the animals, fish, birds and insects.
Then He drew Man.
When He finished, everything was perfect.
The Good Artist told Man, 'All this belongs to you.'
Man was happy in his new picture, but he was happiest when he spent time with the Good Artist. The Artist shared everything He had with Man, but there was just one thing he wasn't allowed to touch ...
... THE FORBIDDEN PAINT POT.
DO NOT TOUCH
The Good Artist made Man a friend, someone to help him.
She was called Woman.
One day Man and Woman broke the Artist's rule. They picked up brushes from the Forbidden Paint Pot. As soon as they disobeyed the Artist ...
... SPLAT!!!

The whole picture
was now a mess.
It was ruined!
Now Man and Woman were stained.
They had broken their friendship with
the Artist and there was
no way they could get
rid of the stains!

As time went on, many people
tried to draw like the
Good Artist. At first
they drew good things like
clothes and shelter.

However, without the Artist's help and
instructions, people also drew bad things like ...
... weapons.

It was not a pretty picture.
People began to argue and fight with each other,
instead of asking the Good Artist what to do.

This caused a lot of hurt and pain.

Some people read the instructions and tried to follow them. They found it hard because they were used to drawing and doing what they wanted.

Some people didn't even believe there was an Artist! Although many read the book, only a few would follow the instructions.

This was a problem. No matter how hard people tried, they could not draw as well as the Artist and they certainly couldn't rub out the mistakes they made.

The Artist had the answer and He performed a great miracle. He sent His only spotless Son into the picture to show people how to live and draw as the Artist wanted them to.

Many people followed Him. He taught them how to live and draw like the Artist.

He began to rub out the mistakes people had made ...
... and because He was the Artist's Son, He drew perfectly like His Dad. He didn't make any mistakes.
The Artist's Son told many people all about the Good Artist and how much He loved them.
The Son told off the leaders of the people for using the instruction book to boss people around.
This made them angry.
The leaders called Him a liar. They didn't believe He was really the Artist's Son, so they stained Him to death because they wanted to live their own way.
But because they weren't His stains, the Artist drew His Son again.

The Artist's Son told His followers that anyone who believed in Him must be drawn again as children of the Artist.
Then the Son returned to His Father.
When anyone believed in the Artist and the Son, they were drawn again. Now people could once again be friends with the Artist.
Those who had been drawn again told others about the Good Artist.
Many other people came back to the Artist and were drawn again.
At the very end of the Artist's picture, those who believed in His Son were taken out to live with the Artist and His family forever.

not The End.

The Bridge

The Bridge is a presentation that uses six pictures to look at various stages of development as you illustrate the concept of Christ bridging the gap between human beings and God. It can be viewed on line at www.discipleshipint.org/the_bridge.

- God's Love
- Man's Problem
- Man's Remedy
- God's Remedy
- Man's Response
- Summary

God's Love

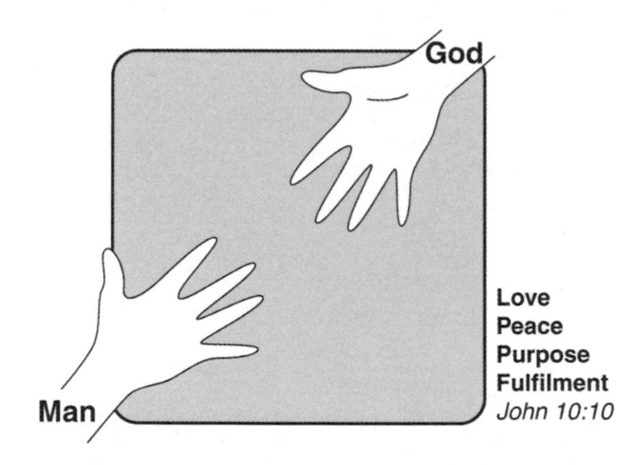

The Bible teaches us that God is love and that He loves us. He desires that we experience an abundant life. This would include such things as love, peace, purpose, and fulfilment. Jesus, speaking about His purpose for coming to earth, said, *'I have come that they may have life, and have it to the full'* (John 10:10b). In the beginning, when God put man on earth, God and man had a relationship which produced an abundant life.

Man's Problem

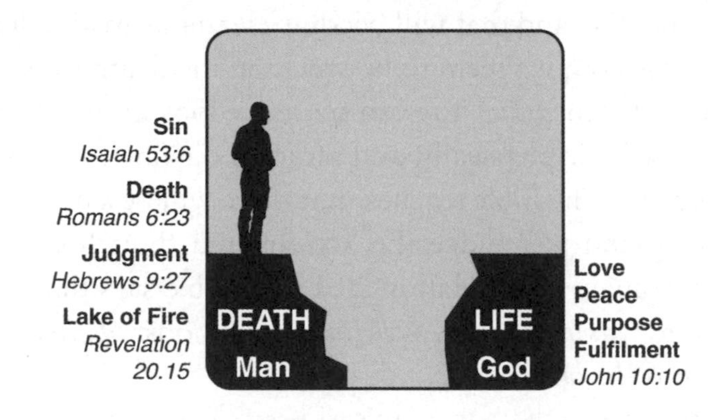

But God did not create man like a robot who would automatically love and have fellowship with Him in return. He gave man a will and the freedom of choice.

Man could keep God's commandments or he could live his life apart from God. Man chose to go his own way. This resulted in a separation between God and man. God is completely holy and perfect, while man is sinful and imperfect. The Bible says, *'We all, like sheep, have gone astray, each of us has turned to his own way'* (Isa. 53:6). People continue to go their own way today. And this applies to all men. Each one of us is guilty. All of us have made decisions and done actions and had thoughts that were contrary to what God desires. We have been like wandering sheep.

The result of turning away from God and doing things that are displeasing to God is spiritual death – eternal death. The Bible also says, *'For the wages of sin is death, but the gift of God is eternal life in Christ Jesus our Lord'* (Rom. 6:23). For now we will just look at the first half of this verse.

Paul states here that the consequences or payment we receive in return for our sins is eternal death. So you can see that on man's side we have eternal death, and on God's side there is eternal life. The last part of this verse talks about the free gift of God being eternal life, and that will become clearer as we develop this diagram. For now, we seem to be stuck on the death side.

(Next read Heb. 9:27.) You can see as we look at this verse that each of us will die physically, and after we die physically we will face judgment. The Bible teaches that there will be a day of judgment when God will judge the actions and thoughts of every man and woman. In Revelation 20:15 the Bible says that *'If anyone's name was not found written in the book of life, he was thrown into the lake of fire.'*

So you can see that on man's side we have sinned, and the penalty of those sins is eternal death. Also we see that the consequences of our sins is for us to face the judgment of God. This gives a pretty dismal picture of our situation on this side of the chasm that separates us from God.

Man's Remedy

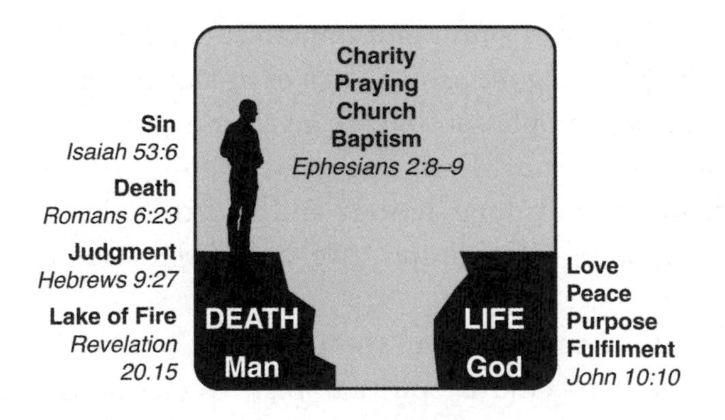

Human beings think they can devise their own way to obtain God's favour and blessing. They usually devise codes of conduct and requirements that need to be performed in order to please God. These include giving to charity, helping others, praying, attending church, or being baptised. However, God's Word states that all these efforts are useless in the sight of a holy God to obtain God's Salvation. (Next read Eph. 2:89) From this verse we understand that good works will never suffice to meet God's requirements but that God's Salvation is a gift that is obtained by grace alone through faith alone.

God's Remedy

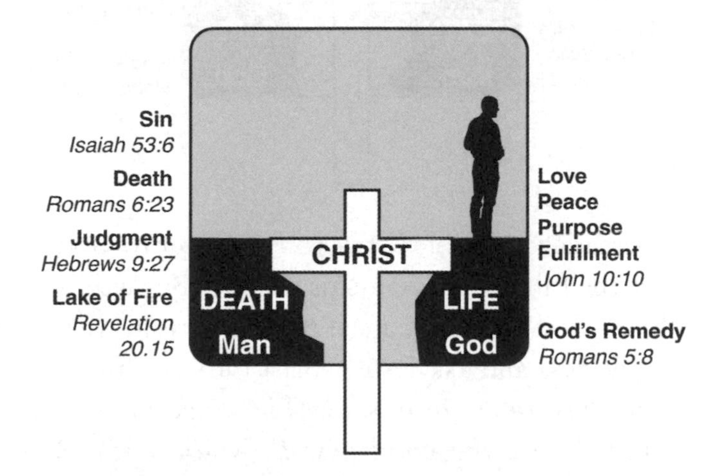

In spite of the fact that we have turned our backs on God and have disobeyed Him, God still loves us and desires that we know Him personally so that He can bless us.

Only one adequate bridge can cross the gulf that exists between man and God, and that bridge is through Jesus Christ and His death on the cross.

The Bible also says, *'But God demonstrates his own love for us in this: While we were still sinners, Christ died for us'* (Rom. 5:8).

The Bible teaches that when He died on the cross, He died in our place. He paid the penalty and took the judgment for our sins so we could be forgiven for all our wrongdoings. The slate could be wiped clean.

Man's Response

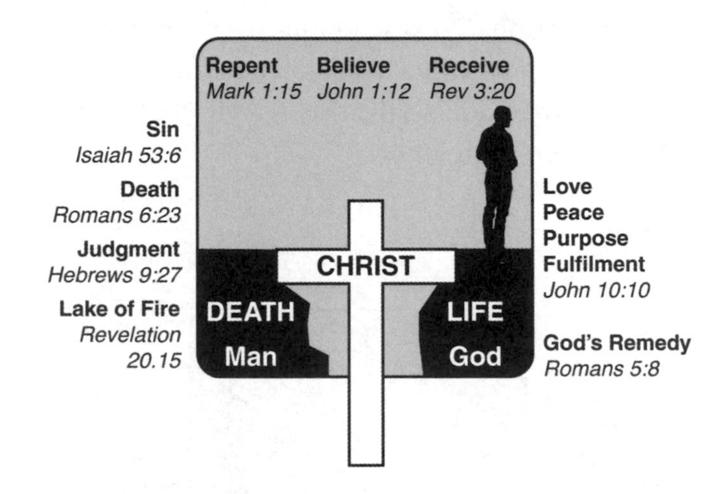

Christ has made it possible for us to cross over to God's side and experience the full life He wants us to have. But we are not automatically on God's side. We need to take action; we need to ask God's forgiveness and ask Jesus Christ into our lives.

'The time has come,' Jesus said. 'The kingdom of God is near. Repent and believe the good news!' (Mark 1:15). Repentance means to reverse direction. We must give up our efforts to reach God by man's remedies and accept God's remedy for our sins.

The Bible also says, 'Yet to all who received him, to those who believed in his name, he gave the right to become children of God' (John 1:12). We 'reach out' to God through prayer and receive the gift of eternal life.

Now let's add another verse here (Rev. 3:20) that goes right along with John 1:12. This is Jesus Christ talking. (After the verse is read, you would continue.) So the door on which Jesus is knocking is the very centre of our lives – the heart, the core, the innermost part of our lives. He is knocking and would like to come into our lives. So He wants us to open the door and invite Him in.

Summary

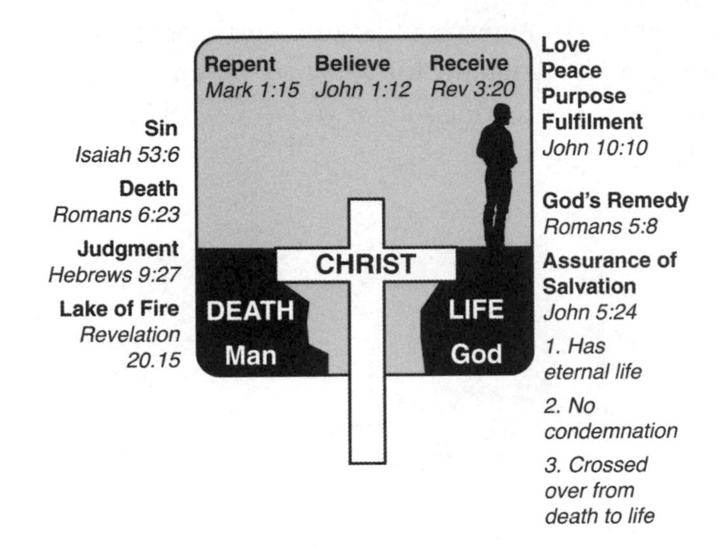

Let's take a look at John 5:24. This statement of Jesus summarises all we have talked about: *'I tell you the truth, whoever hears my word* [the things we have been discussing here] *and believes him who sent me* [believe means to receive, that is, to invite Christ into our lives] *has eternal life* [a present possession] *and will not be condemned* [judgment]; *he has crossed over from death to life.'*

The Paper Tear

This is a great visual piece and, with a little practicse, it is easy to present and intriguing for anyone, of any age, watching. Rehearse the paper tearing so that you can 'work' the illustration as you speak.

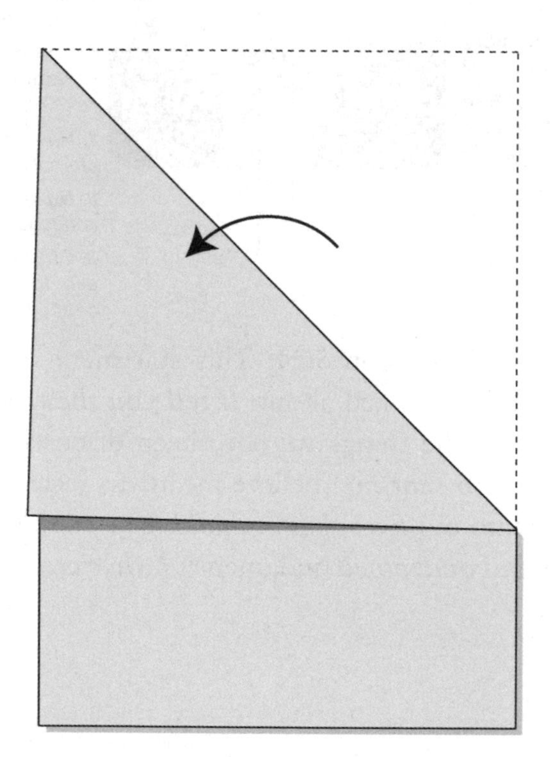

Imagine this piece of paper is like a person's life. This person wants to enjoy his life. He enjoys nice things, nice clothes and nice gadgets, and he needs a nice home to put them in.
(Take the top right-hand corner of the page and fold it across to the left side of the paper to make a semi-detached house.)

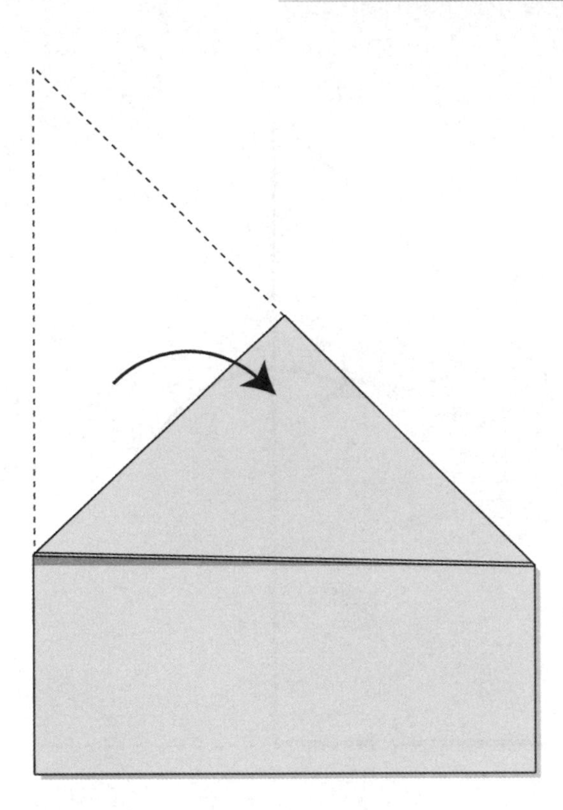

The man sees that other people have nicer and bigger houses. He aspires to have what they have and works even harder to get a better house, maybe with a nicer garden and even a lovely swimming pool.

(Take the top left-hand corner of the page and fold it across to the right side of the paper. You should now have something that looks like a detached house with a pointed roof.)

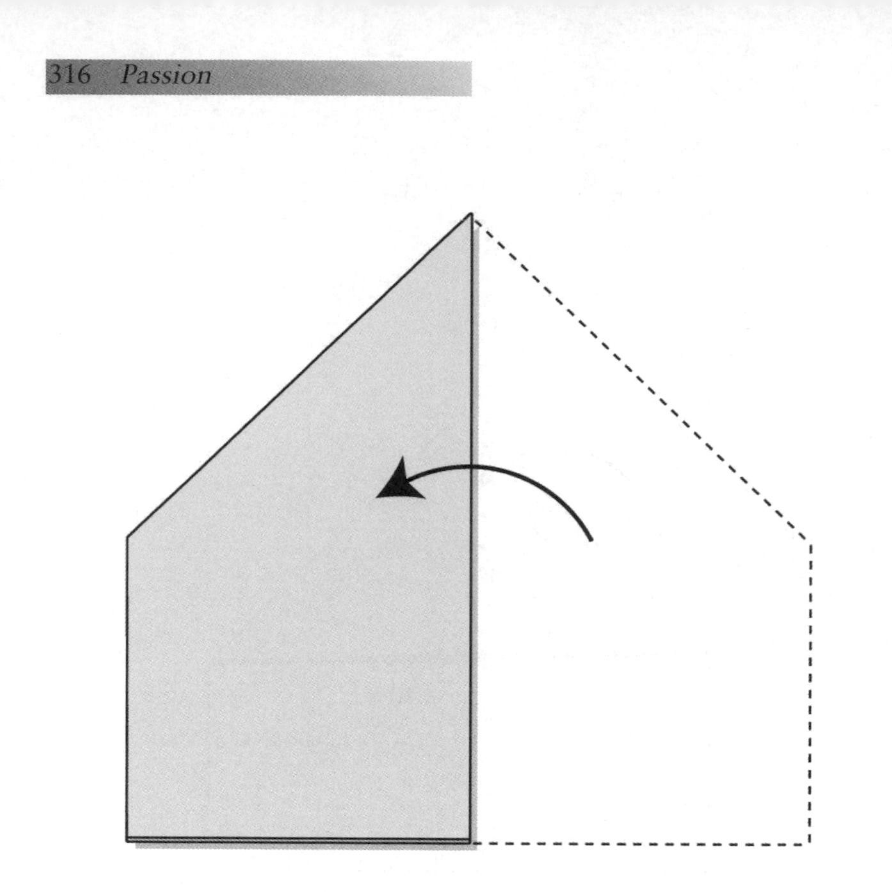

But the man is still not happy and really wants to enjoy his short life. So he decides he needs a holiday. He gets on a plane and flies to Hawaii. Now Hawaii is so beautiful, but after two weeks, he's got to come home to work again to pay for his next holiday. *(Continue making a plane by folding the house shape in half. Crease it down the centre. You should now have something that looks like a paper plane. Fold the wings down to have a quick play.)*

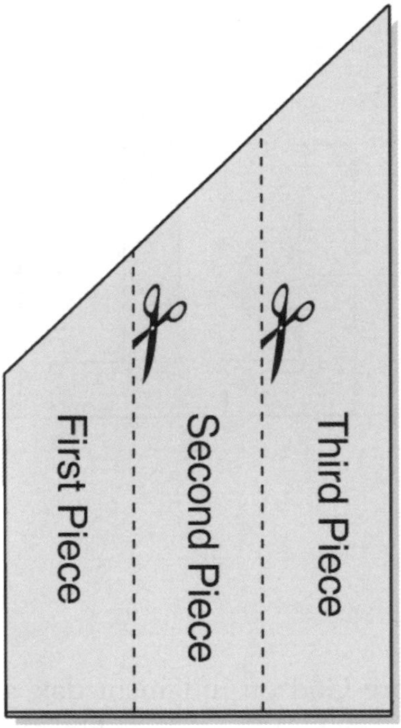

But the man is *still* not happy and as he gets older, he takes different things from life to try to be happy. He goes to parties and soon he meets a lovely lady. He gets married to her and has four lovely children. As he gets older, he gives money to charities, and he even goes to church sometimes. But one day, the man finally dies.
(Turn the point of the plane towards the sky, with the shorter edge to your left. Start at the top left side, place your thumbs and fore-fingers a little more than a third across to the right, and carefully tear downwards in a straight line, until you have torn the first piece off . Place the torn piece on a table where it won't blow away. Then rip off another (little more than a third), vertically (rip it as straight as you can). Place this second piece with the other, then put the remaining (long) third piece on the table, away from the other two strips.)

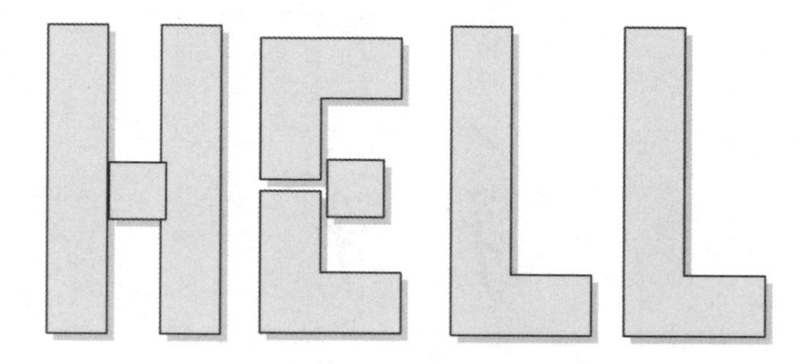

The man went before God on judgment day, and God said to him, 'I love you so much and I have kept Heaven perfect for you, because I do not want to give you anything that is less than perfect. What have you done in your life that is so good that I can let you into Heaven?'

The man said to God, 'Well, I went to church, I gave to charity, I got married, had lovely children, had a nice job . . .'

But God said to the man, 'Many of these things were good, but they were not good enough to allow you access into a perfect Heaven. All of these things were short lived and of no real eternal value. I'm afraid that all the things you devoted your life to can only send you to . . .

(Now open the two pieces, and carefully make them into letters. You will find two 'L's and the other pieces of paper will form the letters 'E' and 'H'. When you put them all together, you will have the word 'HELL'.)

God said to the man, 'This is so sad, because I tried to prevent this from happening. That is why I sent My own Son, Jesus Christ.' *(The remaining long piece, when opened, will form a perfect cross. You may wish to give this cross to the person you have shown the Paper Tear Gospel.)*

You may wish to end the presentation here, but if possible go on with a brief explanation such as this:
Isn't that clever! Now let me leave you with this thought. The Bible says that God is 'Holy', which simply means perfect. God cannot allow anything imperfect in to Heaven, otherwise it would not be Heaven any more. All of us have a body and a soul, and when we die, our soul lives on forever, either in Heaven or Hell. If we've broken just one of God's laws, for example if we've ever lied once, cheated once or hated once, then our soul becomes imperfect and we cannot enter Heaven.

The Good News is that God wants to forgive us! Jesus Christ came to our world and lived a perfect life. He died a cruel, painful death on a cross to take the punishment that we all deserve for breaking God's laws. If we put our trust in the sufficiency of what Jesus did for us and do two things we can be forgiven and one day enter Heaven.

First . . . be willing to turn away from anything that we know is wrong in our life and say sorry to Jesus. God promises to help us with the things that we are powerless to give up, if we allow Him.

Second . . . we must surrender our life to Jesus Christ, acknowledging Him as God, and then humble our lives to Him in service.

If we do these two things, one day when we die we will go before God on judgment day, and God will say to you, 'My beautiful son (or daughter), you have accepted my free gift of forgiveness through the death of My only perfect Son, Jesus Christ. So, welcome to heaven!'

Further Recommendations

Two Ways to Live

Two Ways to Live is a way of sharing the Gospel using six simple pictures. The jargon-free presentation is theologically profound, so the explanation can be used both apologetically and in teaching and follow-up. This explanation of the Gospel, devised by Philip Jensen, has been used widely in the UK for many years in evangelistic events, youth and children's camps and for student work.
Visit this link to view the presentation:
http://www.matthiasmedia.com.au/2wtl/

Four Spiritual Laws

Bill Bright, founder of Campus Crusade for Christ, wrote the *Four Spiritual Laws* in order to provide believers with an excellent way to introduce people to Jesus Christ and God's plan of salvation. Just as there are physical laws that govern the physical universe, so are there spiritual laws which govern your relationship with God. This illustration presents the Gospel in a thorough way.
Visit this link to view the presentation:
http://4laws.com/laws/english/flash/

The4Points Gospel

The4Points communicates the Gospel in a clear and memorable way using four images that look like an equation. Because the equation ends with a question mark, people will often want to know what it means. This simple concept, developed by Dave Sharples, can be adapted to work in pretty much any situation, anywhere in the world. From schools to prisons, city-wide campaigns to personal evangelism, *The4Points* effectively breaks down language and literary barriers and creates opportunities for people to share their faith.
Visit this link to view the presentation:
http://www.the4points.com/

Steps to Peace with God

Steps to Peace with God is used by the Billy Graham Evangelistic Association. It is a very clear presentation, drawing from Scripture to illustrate four simple steps necessary to establish a relationship with God.
Visit this link to view the presentation:
http://www.billygraham.org/SH_StepsToPeace.asp

Christianity Explored

Developed by Rico Tice, this is a course, rather than a concise illustration, but it is an excellent exploration of the Gospel through studying the life of Christ.
Visit this link to find out more:
http://www.christianityexplored.org/

Endnotes

Chapter 1 – Passion

[1] William Booth quote from http://www.brandonacox.com/2009/16/inspiring-quotes-about-missions.
[2] Charles G. Finney, Robert A. Engelhardt, *Power, Passion and Prayer*, Bridge-Logos Foundation, 2004.

Chapter 2 – War and Romance

[1] Jenty Fairbank, *William and Catherine Booth: God's Soldiers*, Hodder Headline Educational, 1974.
[2] See 'Who Else Believes This?' section on page 296.
[3] Charles G. Finney, *Crystal Christianity*, Whitaker, 1986.
[4] C.S. Lewis, *Mere Christianity*, HarperCollins, 1997.
[5] C.T. Studd, *Fool and Fanatic*, WEC, 1980.

Chapter 3 – All in the Balance

[1] See 'Who Else Believes This?' section on page 296.
[2] John Stott, *The Message of 2 Timothy: Guard the Gospel*, IVP, 1973.
[3] John Stott, *Making Christ Known: Historic Mission Documents from the Lausanne Movement, 1974–1989*, Paternoster Press, 1996.
[4] Millard J. Erickson, *Christian Theology*, Revell, a division of Baker Publishing Group, 1998.
[5] See 'Who Else Believes This?' section on page 296.

[6] Millard J. Erickson, *Christian Theology*, Revell, a division of Baker Publishing Group, 1998.
[7] Derek Prince, *Foundation Series, Volume 1*, Sovereign World Books, 1986.
[8] Oswald J. Smith, *The Passion for Souls*, Marshall, Morgan and Scott, 1978.
[9] K.P. Yohannan, *Revolution in World Missions, Revolution in World Missions,* Gospel For Asia books, 2009. Used by permission.
[10] K.P. Yohannan, *Revolution in World Missions.* Used by permission.
[11] K.P. Yohannan, *Revolution in World Missions.* Used by permission.
[12] Text of Billy Graham's 'Why the Berlin Congress?' in 1966. © Wheaton College 2006. www.wheaton.edu/bgc/archives/berlinaddress.htm.

Chapter 4 – Words, Works and Effects

[1] Lewis A. Drummond, *The Word of the Cross: A Contemporary Theology of Evangelism*, Broadman Press, 2000.

Chapter 5 – The Whole Truth

[1] Used by permission of Ray Comfort and Bridge-Logos Foundation.

Chapter 6 – The Price of Freedom

[1] Cited in Greg Laurie, *How to Share Your Faith*, Tyndale Books, 1999, p.43.
[2] J.I. Packer, *Evangelism and the Sovereignty of God*, IVP, 1999, p.47.
[3] Oswald Chambers, *My Utmost for His Highest*, Barbour & Co. Inc., 2009.

Chapter 7 – The Words of the Gospel

[1] Tony Anthony with Angela Little, *Taming the Tiger*, Authentic, 2004.
[2] Angela Little, *Cry of the Tiger*, Authentic, 2006.

Chapter 8 – The State of the World

[1] Not the person's real name.
[2] Cited in *Fifty Great Soul-winning Sermons*, compiled by Jack R. Smith, Home Mission Board of the Southern Baptist Convention, Atlanta, Georgia, 1994.

[3] George Barna, *Evangelism That Works: How to Reach Changing Generations With the Unchanging Gospel*, Regal Books, 1995.

[4] Office for National Statistics 2001 April Census summary of religion in Britain released 13 February 2003. Cited in *Religion in the United Kingdom: Diversity, Trends and Decline*, by Vexen Crabtree, 5 July 2007 www.vexen.co.uk/UK/religion.html#BI_001.

[5] The Christian Research English Church Census 2005 www.christian-research.org.uk/ecc05/precc05.htm.

[6] Jonathan Petre in the *Daily Telegraph*, 18 September, 2006.

[7] Tearfund research, *Churchgoing in the UK*, 3 April 2007. The survey involved 7,000 UK adults aged 16 or over, interviewed between 8 February and 5 March 2006.

[8] www.creativebiblestudy.com/Blondin-story.html.

Chapter 9 – Itchy Ears

[1] www.holyobserver.com/detail.php?isu=v02i04&art=madonna.

Chapter 10 – The Man in the Mirror

[1] Tony Anthony with Angela Little, *Taming the Tiger*, Authentic, 2004.

[2] MORI report, cited at http://www.guardian.co.uk/politics/2009/sep/27/trust-politicians-all-time-low.

[3] Cited in David C. Egner, *Our Daily Bread* daily devotional, 17 January 2002, RBC Ministries.

[4] Robert Fulghum, as cited in Wayne Rice, *Hot Illustrations for Youth Talks*, Zondervan, 1994.

Chapter 11 – Leaning Towers

[1] John Stott, *Christian Mission in the Modern World*, IVP, 1975, p.39.

[2] Lausanne Committee for World Evangelism (LCWE). Used by permission.

[3] Lausanne Commitee for World Evangelism (LCWE). Used by permission.

Chapter 12 – Called and Qualified

[1] Dr Bill Bright, cited in Ray Comfort (ed.), *The Evidence Bible*, Bridge-Logos Foundation, 2003. Used by permission.

Chapter 13 – The Ends of the Earth

[1] Lausanne Committee for World Evangelism (LCWE). Used by permission.

Chapter 14 – Call Me Crazy!

[1] Charles H. Spurgon, *The Soul Winner*, BiblioBazaar, 2008.
[2] *Gladiator*, DreamWorks, 2000.
[3] Angus Buchan, *Faith Like Potatoes*, Monarch, 2006 (book), Global Creative Studios, 2006 (film).

Chapter 15 – Salty Tea

[1] Michael Green, *I Believe in Satan's Downfall*, Hodder & Stoughton, 2nd revised edition, 1995.
[2] Story told by Ravi Zacharias in his message 'The Lostness of Man', given at Amsterdam '86 Conference and rebroadcast on *Let My People Think*, a radio programme of Ravi Zacharias International Ministries (www.rzim.org). Adapted and excerpted by permission of RZIM.
[3] Charles H. Spurgeon, *The Soul Winner*, BiblioBazaar, 2008.

Chapter 16 – One Degree Off

[1] *Good Will Hunting*, Miramax Films, 1997.
[2] J. Oswald Sanders, *Satan Is No Myth*, Moody Press, 1995.
[3] Darius Salter, *American Evangelism: Its Theology and Practice*, Victor Books, 1996.
[4] J.I. Packer, *Evangelism and the Sovereignty of God*, IVP, 1991.

Chapter 17 – A New Song

[1] Tony Anthony with Angela Little, *Taming the Tiger*, Authentic, 2004.
[2] Roger Steer, *J. Hudson Taylor: A Man in Christ*, Authentic, 2005.
[3] Roger Steer, *J. Hudson Taylor: A Man in Christ*, Authentic, 2005.
[4] Dr Martyn Lloyd Jones, *The Presentation of the Gospel*, Inter-Varsity Fellowship, 1949.
[5] Dr John MacArthur, *The Legacy of Jesus*, Moody Press, 1986. Used by permission.
[6] *Enhanced Strong's Lexicon*, Logos Reserch Systems, Inc., 1995.
[7] *The American Heritage Dictionary of the English Language*, Houghton Mifflin Company, Delta, 2001.

Chapter 18 – MUD

[1] The Engel Scale recorded in Mark McCloskey, *Tell It Often – Tell It Well*, Thomas Nelson, 1986.
[2] Laurence Singlehurst, *Sowing, Reaping, Keeping: People Sensitive Evangelism*, IVP, 2006.

Chapter 19 – A Nobody With Consequence

[1] J.I. Packer, *Evangelism and the Sovereignty of God*, IVP, 2009.
[2] Millard J. Erickson, *Christian Theology*, Revell, a division of Baker Publishing Group, 1998.
[3] Peter Kennedy, devotional E-Mail *Devotions in 1 Corinthians*, copyright 2003.
[4] Tony Anthony with Angela Little, *Taming the Tiger*, Authentic, 2004.

Chapter 20 – A Run on the Roman Road

[1] Dr Leighton Ford, *The Christian Persuader: A New Look at Evangelism Today*, Harper & Row, 1974, p.44.
[2] *NIV Study Bible*, 2nd revised ed., Hodder & Stoughton, 1998.
[3] F.B. Meyer, *The Gospel of John*, Christian Literature Crusade, 1992.
[4] John Stott, *Our Guilty Silence: Church, the Gospel and the World*, IVP, 1997.

[5] Cited in Ray Comfort, *Hell's Best Kept Secret*, Whitaker House, 1989, p.23.
[6] R.C. Sproul, *The Soul's Quest for God*, P&R Publishing, 2003.
[7] John Stott, *Romans: Encountering the Gospel's Power* (John Stott Bible Studies), IVP Connect, 2008.
[8] *NIV Study Bible*, 2nd revised ed., Hodder & Stoughton, 1998.
[9] C.S. Lewis, *The Great Divorce*, Harper Collins, 2002.
[10] Laurence Singlehurst, *Sowing, Reaping, Keeping: People Sensitive Evangelism*, IVP, 2006. Used by permission.
[11] John Stott, *One Race, One Gospel, One Task*, World Wide Publications, 1976.
[12] William Barclay, *The Gospel of Matthew*, Edinburgh Press, 1965, pp.60–61.

Chapter 21 – The Fifth Column

[1] Dr James Kennedy, *Evangelism Explosion*, Tyndale House, 2002.

Afterword

[1] *Schindler's List*, Universal Films, 1993.